Psychology of Language Development
A Primer

Psychology of
Language Development

A Primer

Larry R. Riley

Northwest Missouri State University

C.J. Hogrefe, Inc.
Toronto · Lewiston, NY · Göttingen · Zürich

Library of Congress Cataloging-in-Publication Data

Riley, Larry R.
    The psychology of language development.

    Bibliography: p.
    Includes index.
    1. Language acquisition. I. Title.
    P118.R54   1986   401'.9   86-14916
    ISBN 0-88937-017-6

Canadian Cataloguing in Publication Data

Riley, Larry R.
    The psychology of language development

    Bibliography: p.
    Includes index.
    ISBN 0-88937-017-6

    1. Psycholinguistics. 2. Language acquisition.
    I. Title.
    P37.R54 1986   401'.9   C86-094196-5

C.J. Hogrefe, Inc.
P.O. Box 51
Lewiston, NY 14092

Canadian edition published by
C.J. Hogrefe, Inc.
12 Bruce Park Ave.
Toronto, Ontario M4P 2S3

Printed in Germany

ISBN 0-88937-017-6 Hogrefe Toronto · Lewiston, NY · Göttingen · Zürich
ISBN 3-8017-0272-3 Hogrefe Göttingen · Zürich · Toronto · Lewiston, NY

PREFACE

The field generally titled "The Psychology of Language Development" dates its current history from ca. 1954 and then proceeds to explode upon us in the form of a hydraheaded creation filled with diffuse philosophies, theories, and discussions of application potential. Most readers are initially confused by the subject matter since few books concern themselves with the basics. Indeed, most assume the reader already knows those basics and is eagerly awaiting presentation of the most subtle, advanced material available to date. Fifteen years of teaching subject matter in this field has convinced the author of this book that it is time to readdress the core issues so that (1) those of us who seek a comfortable starting point may now have one in the form of this book, and (2) those of us who are occasionally now "rediscovering the wheel" may better place the latest research into its proper historical perspective. In addressing the core issues, great care has been taken to present a thorough, yet easily readable treatment of concepts and events. The implications are rich for all readers no matter what their interests in language might specifically be. In pursuing the second goal above, this book attempts to challenge the advanced reader by continually asking the reader to assess his/her recall of the events that resulted in the current trends clearly outlined throughout the book. In that sense, the book truly serves as "a Primer" for all. By its very nature, a primer cannot become dated. Without one, we can do little but confound our already-existing misunderstandings and even further alienate those among us who seek to join in a search for the explanation of how human language develops and functions. Our goal to achieve such understanding will be difficult at best. Without a primer, it becomes nearly impossible as this author perceives it.

Larry R. Riley

v

ACKNOWLEDGEMENTS

The writing of this book would have been virtually impossible if it had not been for the support and professionally constructive comments provided by my wife, Nancy, and my brother, Douglas. Their belief in the project's value served as an inspiration.

Suzanne Schmaljohn and Marty Marsh must be publicly thanked for their many hours of editing and proofreading. Mary Lyons proofread the final draft and made many helpful suggestions regarding its style and content. Her work is sincerely appreciated.

Karen Ehlert deserves my lasting gratitude for having typed the first draft from my hand-written copy. Her continued belief in the value of this book is also deeply appreciated. Sandy Knisley typed the final draft of this book and, therefore, deserves my enduring gratitude for carefully seeing that the book became a concrete reality. Her efforts will never be forgotten.

I would also like to thank those of my colleagues who continued to support my efforts throughout the years of this project. Anthony J. Buhl read and critiqued the early chapters. Audrey Buhl's encouragement was much appreciated. Morton and Jean Kenner showed continuous interest in the project and reinforced my efforts to complete it.

I wish to thank my parents, Betty and Charles Riley, for their continued support of the writing of this book. Their belief in its potential contribution was an excellent source of encouragement toward the book's completion.

Larry R. Riley

CONTENTS

– 1 –

ORIGINS – HISTORICAL AND PHILOSOPHICAL

As long as humans have had the cerebral capacity to produce language in any form, surely some interest has existed regarding that language's origins and functions. Paradoxically, the research/theoretical interest in language development and its functions seems remarkably sparse until the 18th and 19th centuries in Europe. Work prior to this period qualified not so much as research as it does speculation of a more or less rigorous nature.

Preliminaries

According to Dale (1976, pp. 1 and 6), the Egyptian Pharoah Psammetichus I conducted a variety of crude investigations prior to 610 B.C. He commanded that two infants be placed in the care of a shepherd and be observed by that shepherd so as to determine what "word" would be the first spoken. His assumption was simple and, unfortunately, quite naive; he assumed that specific words were the natural outcome of mere developmental age increases. As the story goes, the actual "first word" was the Phrygian word "becos" which means "bread." Supposedly, the shepherd had heard the word several times from both children before reporting it to the Pharoah who, upon hearing it himself, declared an end to the time-worn Egyptian concern over what the oldest language in the world happened to be. The matter was ended; Phrygian had come first, and Egyptian was, naturally enough, second. The origins of the word "becos" in the vocabulary of two infants who had no vocabulary at all when the investigation began is indeed something of a mystery since the infants were isolated from all humans, save for the shepherd, who was under the strictest instructions by Psammetichus himself to avoid any possible reinforcement of any sounds produced by the children. Issuing and following such instructions are different issues; it is most likely that the shepherd did inadvertently reinforce the pair through perhaps his nonverbal behavior, if indeed he managed to avoid all verbal cuing and reinforcement. In any case, there is no evidence that Psammetichus nor any other ancient Egyptian pursued the issue further. It is somewhat ironic and noteworthy that this study used only two children, as many of the most recent 20th century studies still persist in using very small numbers of "subjects" for reasons presented later in this book.

A second crude investigation is also reported by Dale (1976, p. 1) regarding St. Augustine. Supposedly, St. Augustine believed he could trace his own language/cognitive development. His account of this is reported in Book I of *The Confessions* for those interested in a somewhat insightful, albeit poetic, discussion of a single child's language evolution. It is rather curious to see reference to Aristotle missing in Augustine's work at this point since Aristotle did, generally speaking, profoundly affect Augustin's writings. Perhaps this can be explained when one considers the fact that Aristotle, as well as Socrates and Plato, was more concerned with the uses of language in cognition rather than in the actual origins or evolution of language within humans individually or in a group.

Scholarship on language during the European Renaissance indicates increased concern over the role language played in sensation, perception, and cognition, e.g., the debates over the use of language in determining the superiority of "rationalism (mentalism)" over "empiricism." The terms "rationalism" and "mentalism" are essentially the same in meaning and refer to the "arm-chair" approach to reasoning one's way through a problem to its successful conclusion. "Empiricism," which received its notoriety through the writings of the British scholars John Locke, James Mill, John Stuart Mill, George Berkeley, David Hume, and Jeremy Bentham, stressed the input of the senses (vision, hearing, touch, smell, and kinesthesis) in determining truth. For one interested in empiricism, the only truth is that which can be sensorially verified; all arm-chair reasoning must be subject ultimately to empirical verification no matter how interesting or plausible the product of the reasoning process may seem from one's arm-chair perch. The debate over rationalism/mentalism versus empiricism returns to us in the 20th century in a slightly different form. The question in the 20th century will be one of which technique is better to use in the study of language, rather than where language fits into the use of either of the two investigatory techniques.

During the mid 1800s, the French Academy of Science in Paris experienced a sudden and unexplained increase in scholarly papers dealing with the origins of natural language and how these origins affected cognition. Interest held sway for approximately 30 years and then died as suddenly as it had appeared. Part of the Academy's reluctance to continue pursuing the area may very well have stemmed from the many and vastly differing opinions produced during the 30-year debate. Solutions to the discovery of the origins/functions of the languages of the world were complicated by the issues of rationalism/mentalism's superiority or inferiority to empiricistic approaches, which were admittedly few in number. This 30-year period in the French Academy was paralleled nowhere else in the Western hemisphere during this same time period. This seeming indifference in the rest of the Western hemisphere remains unexplained, but perhaps it is reasonable to speculate that the French Academy served more as a geographic focal point than intellectual focal point—insofar as those scholars in the remainder of the Western hemisphere were concerned.

Psychology, per se, seems to have entered the picture in the late 1800s for a variety of reasons based fundamentally upon coincidence, concern over philosophically related language issues, and observations of mental patient's behaviors which would not yield to simple analyses. In some cases, the entry into the field was dramatic; in other cases, entry was so quietly done that it is still somewhat conjecturable as to whether it was actually an entry. Three apparent entries were made; all occurred at approximately the same time, and all had different assumptions and methods of study to offer those interested. Admittedly, the number "interested" at the very first were few, perhaps because psychology as a field was new, and the fact that "language existed" had been known as long ago as humans first had the cerebral development to perceive their own use of that tool in cognition. For the convenience of the reader, and perhaps for the need to most clearly compare and contrast the three entries, they will be labeled as (1) the Human Verbal Learning Camp, (2) the Innateness Camp, and (3) the Learning Theory/Conditioning Camp. Although each camp begins at approximately the same time period and persists today despite numerous "ups and downs" regarding scholarly research interest, each camp except for the Human Verbal Learning Camp appears to suddenly start, run a short pace, grow dormant, and then reappear. Only the Human Verbal Learning Camp can boast of a history filled with relatively few interruptions; and yet, ironically, it may be the most viable of the three camps if the issue of natural language learning is our primary interest.

The Human Verbal Learning Camp

Ernest Hilgard made it clear in his introduction to the Dover edition (Ruger, Russenius & Hilgard [Eds.], 1964) of Hermann Ebbinghaus' *Memory* (1885), that Ebbinghaus was not himself caught up in the dealings of the French Academy of Science regarding language origins/ functions. Rather, Ebbinhaus' interest appears to come more from his efforts to solve philosophic questions regarding word association processes. Hilgard notes that the interest was spurred by the writings of the philosopher, Herbart, who frankly seems to have strongly disagreed with the entire approach used by Ebbinghaus. What Herbart would have to agree to though, were the rather spectacular reviews other philosophers could give *Memory*. Ebbinghaus crossed the line from Herbart's mentalism to the use of empiricism and actually included what Hilgard has considered an excellent section in the book which deals solely with the statistical (empirical) analysis of such issues involved in analyzing word associations between single and multiple words. As Hilgard points out, we are stretching the meaning of the term "word" if we look at Ebbinghaus' materials since he invented something called the "nonsense syllable" or consonant-vowel-consonant: (CVC) to use in his language analysis. The influence of 17th- through 19th-century British Empiricists such as Locke, Hume, and Berkeley are seen in Ebbinghaus' work and possibly was reinforced in his thinking because he acted as a postdoctoral tutor in England. Hilgard indicates that the methods and conclusions of Ebbinghaus' *Memory* are clear enough, but we would be quite hard pressed to assume that a CVC was in any fashion an attempt on Ebbinghaus' part to construct a language filled with "natural words" as vague and meaningless as the actual natural language words a child receives in daily practice. Ebbinghaus was apparently not interested in children's acquisition of language, per se, as much as he was in the development of word associations by people at any age level. This is more clearly illustrated by looking at his actual work as seen below. If the reader is somewhat surprised that Ebbinghaus could apparently so coolly dismiss the issue of children's language being different from that of adults, it would be best to recall the time frame in which *Memory* was written. Even late 19th-century Germany, which was Wundt's academic, philosophical, and actual home, generally believed children were miniature adults in all issues of cognitive, emotional, and physical growth (Mussen, Conger & Kagan, 1974, pp. 2–10). If children had been viewed differently, perhaps Ebbinghaus would have defended the use of CVCs solely on the grounds they were just as ambiguously meaningless for adults as natural language words were for children; he makes no such implication in his work. Hilgard leaves us with the speculation that CVCs were chosen because they are free of the numerous inconveniences of words in a natural language, e.g., natural language words not only have multiple meanings, but also act metaphorically at times. Although Ebbinghaus used CVCs, he did not limit himself solely to their use as is seen in his partially completed work with lines from *Don Juan*. The number of CVCs used in a chain, the possible connections between individual and groups of CVCs in that chain, and various methods of rehearsing/recalling the chains were all issues of interest to him and his readers.

Let us assume you wish to see firsthand how his experimental approach worked (and still works today with some slight variations in approach due to advances in technology). As a general rule, Ebbinghaus used only himself as a subject (he was approximately 35 years old when his book was published), but he claimed that it really mattered very little what number of subjects he used. Basic principles appear in one subject as well as in a group, and vice versa as long as the principle being demonstrated is a "basic" one. He engages your attention as follows:

1. You are shown a card upon which 10 CVCs are typed in a row with a space or two between each CVC e.g., XER CEF DAX, etc. to a total of 10. (This is his method of "complete presentation," which is quite useful in many situations today where strict laboratory control is not required, i.e., classroom demonstrations. It has been generally replaced by the use of a method known as "serial anticipation" where a machine known as a memory drum presents the CVCs one at a time with each presentation of a CVC in the window of the memory drum being preceded by an opportunity to "guess" which CVC is about to appear in the window at the next rotation of the clock/cylinder inside the machine.)

2. You are asked to spend some constant time period, i.e., two seconds, looking at each CVC and then are asked to recall the CVCs you have seen either (a) in order from first to last (this is known as "serial order") or (b) in any order you so desire (this is known as "free recall").

3. The results of your recall attempts are tabulated with each attempt at memorizing the entire list to be labeled as a "trial" and your successful achievement of a "criterion" of learning coming when you have completed two perfect trials in a row. The word "perfect" refers to no errors of recall on any CVC item, which you are usually required to spell out orally rather than pronounce or write.

As you might very reasonably guess, some CVCs are harder to recall than are others, and this is most true if you used CVCs which have been "quantified" for level of difficulty. Glaze (1928) and Archer (1960) were among the first to attempt to see if certain CVCs are as "nonsensical" as are others. For example, NOT qualifies as both a CVC and a real English word, whereas QEL qualifies only as a CVC. Both Glaze and Archer's lists indicate that CVCs which are both CVCs and real words have a higher associative value and are generally easier to learn and retain than are CVCs which cannot qualify as words. But assuming that the person preparing the list to begin with controlled for the difficulty of the list by choosing CVCs of similar or identical difficulty, the results of the memorization of the CVC list should reflect not so much CVC association strength for each item as it will the position of the CVC in the list itself. In other words, if the CVC in position seven in the list is checked for ease of learning, we would not be too surprised to see that it is harder to learn than is, say, the third CVC in that list since, after all, there were six CVCs to be learned prior to the seventh and only two prior to the third. Hypothetically, it should work this way, but we must recall that it was mentioned above that Ebbinghaus discussed both serial and free recall as two differing methods of learning a list. When the typical serial and typical free recall results are graphed using 10 CVCs of equal difficulty with adult subjects, the results appear as follows:

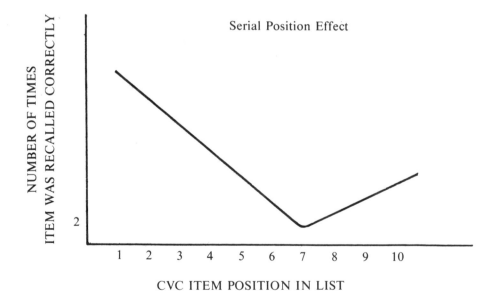

FIGURE 1.1: Curve depicting recall in serial order of 10 CVCs of equal strength by an adult subject learning the list to a criterion of two perfect repetitions in a row.

The free recall curve appears as follows:

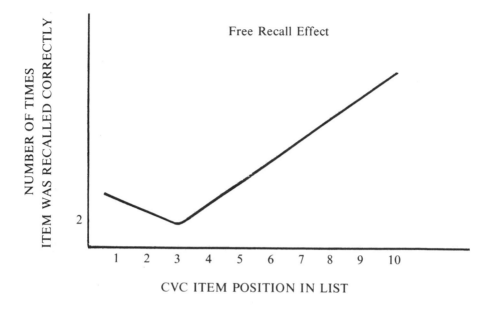

FIGURE 1.2: Curve depicting recall in free order of 10 CVCs of equal strength by an adult subject learning the list to a criterion of two perfect repetitions in a row.

It can easily be seen that our assumption that CVC number seven must be harder to learn than CVC number three depends upon how the lists were approached by the learner. Admittedly, it is curious that inspection of the curves actually shows them to be reverse copies of each other. For example, turning the free recall curve around produces the serial position effect curve. The reasons for the curve shapes are complex, but they can essentially be summarized as follows with the first three reasons being shared by both serial and free recall:

1. The memory span of adults is limited to approximately seven plus or minus two units of information (Miller, 1956). For all practical purposes here, a single CVC serves as a single unit for most adults.

2. Within each list, there are proactive facilitation/inhibition and retroactive facilitation/inhibition effects of extraordinary complexity. "Proactive" effects occur when the learning of a previous item either assists (facilitates) or interferes with (inhibits) items following it. Retroactive effects occur when a recently learned item facilitates or inhibits

7

the recall of an item previously learned. Proactive and retroactive effects do not simply affect just those items closest to the item doing the facilitating or inhibiting. For example, the seventh item in a list could easily affect, say, the third item in the list more than the sixth or the eighth if the seventh and the third items shared more common elements (letters or sounds) than the seventh did with the sixth or eight. The actual calculation of how much facilitation or inhibition takes place between any two single items or any two groups of items is beyond our needs here. It almost goes without saying that such a task is a challenge and is rather time-consuming but quite useful if the person preparing lists is interested in facilitating (or inhibiting) learning. It should also be noted here that there are cases in which an item may have no facilitating or inhibiting effects whatsoever if indeed that item is distinctly different from all items surrounding it. This would be very rare, but it is hypothetically possible.

3. There are "anchor" points in any list. These are usually the first and the last items in each list. These "anchors" are generally less affected by the complex facilitations/inhibitions which occur among the items between these anchor points. These anchors "stand out" as if they had purposefully been treated as being different from other items. Highlighting or separating any item in a list from its associate items has long been known to produce more frequent recall of that item, albeit there are no guarantees the item will be recalled at the correct position it occurs in the actual list (vonRestorff, 1933).

Reasons (4) and (5) tend to separate serial from free recall; it is interesting that only these two seem to clearly cause the separation. There are surely better reasons, or at least more reasons, but at this time they seem lacking definition.

4. In serial recall, but not free recall, there is a clear trend for the learner to recall item 10 before it is time to recall it. Thus, item 10 usually begins to be recalled in the position held by item 7 as if item 7 actually were the end of the list. This is probably due to the 7 plus or minus 2 memory span issues discussed above. Recalling item 10 in item 7's position obviously produces serious problems; perhaps the best way to see how serious the problem becomes is to look back at the worst point in the serial recall, e.g., at or closely around item 7 itself. This faulty anticipation of the list's end is not a problem in free recall since free recall is just that—free. There is no "end" except as the learner cares to perceive one—if the learner indeed cares to do so.

5. This reason is perhaps the weaker of the two that separate serial and free recall. It says simply that in serial recall there is actually a gap between the end of the list and the beginning (restart) of that list. Practi-

cally speaking, no such gap exists in free recall, since, again, the order of recall is entirely of the learner's choosing. This reason tells us less than the fourth one but is still useful.

By this point, the reader should see that Ebbinghaus' ideas are straight-forward enough and experimentally "clean" to the point that researchers of his day through the present could devise endless variations upon his basic studies, e.g., increasing or decreasing the list length, changing associative values of CVCs from list to list, determining if various styles of practice assisted or hurt the recall of items, etc. In fact, there are presently so many studies dealing with serial and free recall, that it is tempting to discover a variation no one has found and spend one's life researching it to its last gasp. Some researchers seem perfectly content today with such a line of study. Ironically, Ebbinghaus himself was not: He did very little research on this topic after *Memory* was written. There is no documented reason for his seeming lack of interest in continuing in hot pursuit after his own dynamic breakthroughs. It is however, a very tempting speculation that perhaps he saw something in the work of his colleague, Wundt, that may have dampened his spirits. He could not predict, Wundt to the side for the moment, what would occur in his own camp in the 1950s that would radically alter the perception of the importance of serial/free recall research. From 1885 until the 1950s, the Ebbinghaus approach to human verbal learning had remained generally uncriticized, although some authors had already speculated that perhaps there was more to language learning than serial/free recall. There seemed no doubt, however, that serial/free recall existed and that most probably serial recall was the major source of how humans created sentences by stringing words together one word at a time in a left to right direction with the strength of the associations between the individual words and phrases being based upon our ability to recall accurately what we had heard other people say in the past.

G. A. Miller and J. A. Selfridge (1950) were apparently aware of the complexities of Ebbinghaus' work and all the research that had followed. All readers of Ebbinghaus' Memory knew that he had actually experimented with "real" words and had found both the serial and free recall effects, but everyone knew he had been far less prone to use real words than CVCs because of the complexity of meaning and degree of emotion the former produced. There seemed little doubt that understanding serial recall was beneficial in learning any verbal task that allowed itself to be highly structured and orderly and required sequential recall, e.g., memorizing lines and paragraphs in a play, or learning the exact procedures needed to dial a long distance phone number.

Miller and Selfridge asked a question which had not been addressed until 1950. It was simply the question of what would actually happen if adults, using their native language, were given the chance to memorize sentences in any order they wished. Miller and Selfridge reasoned that adults would choose a serial recall approach to memorizing almost anything that had a language base to it if Ebbinghaus' assumption was correct that the language used by humans was a product of serial chaining. Miller and Selfridge reasoned that a serial recall approach would be used by adults regardless of the nature of the material's organization since, after all, adults had been using serial recall learning strategies for far too many years to abandon them in the face of such a small nuisance as disorganized verbal material. How better could one impose structure upon material than by using the most powerful strategy one had always used to learn the language?

The materials chosen were not CVCs since CVCs defy becoming "disorganized" if the CVCs are other than real words while at the same time being CVCs. The materials were defined as "approximations to English" and were operationally defined as follows:

(1) *Zero-order approximation to English*: The words are randomly selected from the dictionary and placed one by one in the order in which they were selected into a sentence which exceeds the normal adult memory span of seven words.

(2) *First-order approximation to English*: An already existing sentence longer than the normal adult memory span of seven words is randomized internally to produce a "scrambled" sentence.

(3) *Second-order approximation to English*: In essence, a sentence longer than the normal adult memory span is created by pairing two words at a time so that the two words match each other but have no connection to any of the other pairs in the created sentence. The entire sentence consists of matched word pairs in which the pairs stand alone.

(4) *Third-order approximation to English*: The words in the sentence seem to follow a normal syntactical order for the first three words only. The fourth word usually fits in sequence after the second and third words, but does not easily fit into the sequence if the first, second, and third words are seen before the fourth one. The fifth seems to fit in sequence with the third and fourth but it definitely seems out of place if the first and/or second words are shown in sequence with the third and the fourth words. By analogy, the seventh word fits well with the fifth and sixth, but it appears progressively to become a poorer fit in that position as the fourth, third, second, and finally the first words are revealed following the observation of the fit of the seventh word with

the original fifth and sixth. Ultimately, the created "approximation to English" will be longer than the adult memory span.

(5) *Fourth-order approximation to English*: This order is the same as the preceding order with the exception that the first three words in the sentence easily fit into sequence with the fourth. By analogy to the previous approximation, the fifth word fits nicely into sequence with the three preceding words but looks out of place when the first word is included in the sequence. This sentence, like all the preceding and like all the remaining approximations, will exceed the adult memory span when the sentence is completed. If the reader sees the general pattern developing from the second through the fourth approximations, the seventh-order approximation should be easily understood to be one where the first seven words in the sentence fit into a perfectly grammatical sequence. If the eighth word were added, it would fit in sequence with the second through the seventh but would seem an unusual fit if the first word were included. If a ninth word were added, it would fit nicely with the third through the eighth words, but it would seem marginally out of place if the second word were added and much more out of place if the first word were added.

Miller and Selfridge's findings are quite clear. The zero- and first-order approximations to English are learned and recalled by English-speaking adults as if those adults were using free recall, not serial recall. Not until the seventh-order approximation did the adult subjects in this study freely produce a clear serial position effect in the way the words in the sentence were recalled. The transition through approximations from the second-order through the sixth order shows what could be interpreted as a shifting from the free to the serial position effect. If Ebbinghaus had assumed that language was learned in a serial position manner, why did not well-practiced adults speaking their native language show this approach until at least seven words in a row were in perfectly grammatical order? What was even more disturbing was the fact that Miller and Selfridge agreed that most adults in normal conversation rarely use anything more sophisticated than a fith-order approximation to the ideal form of the sentence in their native language. An even greater challenge to Ebbinghaus' work comes when we realize that to some extent children do model the language system they believe they hear adults using. If the children are modeling adults who are not usually using even seven words in a row perfectly grammatically correctly, how then do these children grow to become adults who apparently first show the serial position effect when at least seven words in a row are in perfect order? Miller nor Selfridge nor anyone else interested in human verbal learning seemed capable of answering the question, and it is interesting that Miller himself left the pursuit of human verbal learning to look at the field of language study essentially begun by one of Ebbinghaus' own colleagues, Wundt. If, at this point, the reader were to draw the conclusion that the field of human verbal learning had died or had at least been dealt a severe blow, the reader would be wrong at least in the sense that the pursuit of serial/free studies persisted in abundance through the present day. Miller and Selfridge did draw many away from the field, but they did not stop the field. Nor should they have, for that matter, since serial/free recall is quite important in many forms of language learning as long as we are careful to avoid using serial or free recall as explanations for natural language learning. Sequential verbal instructions/commands must still be memorized, lines in plays must still be learned, lectures and speeches still exist in abundance.

A second approach to human verbal learning existed in the shadow of Ebbinghaus' work until the early 1900s. It was known as "paired-associate acquisition" or simply as PA learning, and it addressed the question of specifically how single pairs of words are associated free of the constrictions of a sentence's form. Perhaps the most famous of all researchers in this area were Underwood, Runquist, and Schulz, whose work spans the 1940s through the 1960s.

PA learning looks quite different from serial/free recall studies and, unlike the latter, resists graphing. In a PA study, the subject is given a stimulus word or CVC and is expected to associate a word or CVC to that stimulus. In some cases, pictures are used as either stimuli and/or responses; the type of material used is irrelevant to the method. The general procedure is that the learner is presented a stimulus on a card or via the memory drum and is asked if any response seems appropriate. Even though the person has probably already previewed the list of stimuli and responses, recall of "the" appropriate response is very difficult until some practice has occurred; this is the generally accepted statement today since Underwood essentially destroyed Rock's (1957) contention that the pairs were learned in an "all-or-none" fashion; either you completely learned a pair when you saw it, or you completely missed it. Since most PA studies force the learner to recall the responses, the inability to recall a stimulus does not necessarily mean the learner could not recognize the stimulus. Recognition is widely accepted as a far more sensitive measure of learning than is recall. Multiple presentations of the list of PAs gradually shows that the learner (1) first learns a response and then (2) "hooks" that response to its stimulus (Underwood, Runquist, & Schulz, 1959). If the learner has 10 PAs to acquire, analysis will show that the learning of various responses and the hook-ing of various responses to their appropriate stimuli are occurring continuously in a relatively orderly fashion. This form of learning in no possible sense explains or even describes the way we develop word order in a sentence (syntactic development), but it does do a good job in setting the basis for the learning of semantics, as we shall see later in this book.

A good example of the use of PA learning would possibly appear in an elementary school student's learning synonyms in a spelling lesson. Let us assume the stimuli are "cow" and "dog" respectively. Let us further assume the responses are "bovine" and "canine," respectively. The procedure used would be as follows:

(1) Show the child the stimuli and responses in the proper sequence, e.g., "cow-bovine" and "dog-canine." This is referred to as the "predifferentiation" stage and lasts only long enough for the child to see the pairs once.

(2) The child is given the stimulus and is asked to recall the response.

(3) Within some time period previously determined, the entire stimulus-response pair is shown so the child's "guess" is either confirmed or denied.

(4) Steps (2) and (3) are continued with the two pairs being selected for random presentation so the child does not simply begin to memorize only responses and, thus, turn the entire learning process into little more than a serial recall study where the list to be learned is always "bovine" and "canine" in that order.

Data by Brown and Berko (1960), Ervin-Tripp (1961), Anderson and Beh (1968), and Riley and Fite (1974) strongly indicate that even PA learning is not a simple form of human verbal behavior; this research will be pursued in the chapter on semantic development. This form of human verbal learning has kept many of its followers for the simple reason that PA learning has adjusted to the times by researching the effects of cognition upon the very process of PA learning itself. Any student interested in the currently popular field of "split-brain" research will find ample new ground to cover with PA learning. For example, attempts to understand how a "left-brain" stimulus word can elicit a "right-brain" response picture.

The Innateness Camp

A colleague of Ebbinghaus richly deserves the credit for having started a line of thought in language development which really would not become popularized until the late 1950s in the United States. He was Wilhelm Wundt, the person generally conceded to have been the "Father of Experimental Psychology." Wundt's writings on the topic are not complete and, frankly, were not his real interest area in psychology. His major interest was in experimental psychology, per se, and especially in the development of the technique of reporting experience via introspection. Introspection fought valiantly to avoid the use of commonplace, multidefinitional terms, which made understanding one's experience most difficult. Introspection attempted to replace these problem areas by asking trained human experimental subjects to use words which were "less ambiguous" or simply less open to multiple interpretation by a listener. In that sense, introspection was most interested in the use of language rather than the development of language itself. So, the question may be rightfully asked as to why Wundt is credited with being the founder of a major language camp when apparently his major interest was in avoiding the complexities of that very language. The answer lies in his secondary interests—if indeed the area even qualified as a secondary interest rather than some interest far lower on the scale. He was interested in his own children's speech and kept diaries concerning the development of various parts of speech. The diaries were informative in nature, and there is no way to determine how accurately records were kept or, for that matter, how frequently Wundt "sampled" the children's language. There really is no evidence to show that Wundt was the only record keeper. However, there seems little doubt that what he was seeing was dramatically opposed to anything that Ebbinghaus was seeing in his serial/free recall data. Wundt was aware that children seem to develop language in an orderly fashion, which seemed remarkably consistent from his first through his last child. Nouns usually came first in the natural order of things; verbs followed closely behind. Despite his observations of these natural patterns, he seemed generally more concerned about language's use in introspective issues and remained content to let the diaries develop more or less as they might on their own. Although his method of introspection was studies by and brought back to the United States by Titchener, the diaries stayed at home with Wundt *while he wrote from 1880 until his death.* Titchener seemed to have little or no interest in natural language learning but was highly interested in introspection. When Titchener's use of introspection was attacked by the early Behaviorists in the United States (Watson, 1913 and 1924), the hopes of any discussion from Titchener regarding Wundt's position on natural language development seemed doomed. The predictions held; Titchener did not discuss natural language development, and his "Structuralist" psychology he had so painstakingly borrowed from Wundt died an easy death under the apparent pragmatism purposed in Watson's *Behaviorism* (1924). Wundt's diaries, and more importantly, the ideas he had formed while making the diaries were of no interest temporarily to anyone in psychology.

Wundt was looking at an approach to language development that Ebbinghaus was not in the remotest contact with. Nowhere in Wundt's work is there the mention of the importance of studying serial or free recall. Nor is there any mention of Ebbinghaus' contributions to the understanding of word associations in chains or as single item associations. Likewise, Ebbinghaus does not cite Wundt's diaries nor his work in introspection. Both men stood as colleagues in the same country, Germany, and virtually ignored each other's contribution regarding language since both apparently saw its utility as being more important than its development, and each had defined utility in different terms. Ebbinghaus looked for utility in the analysis of word associations, and Wundt looked for utility in terms of how the language was used to describe experiences primarily of a sensory nature—e.g., accurately reporting what one had seen or had heard without actually labeling the thing seen or heard in some trite, confusable, commonplace verbal-labeling manner. Unlike Ebbinghaus' camp which flourished in scholarship and research from the publishing of Ebbinghaus' *Memory*, the Innateness Camp would grow dormant and lie peacefully until the late 1950s. In 1957, with his publication *Syntactic Structures*, Noam Chomsky would specifically state what Wundt had broadly implied: Children have the innate capacity to create sentences, and are indeed going to do just that, if the environment at least provides some kind of adult "model" of what that language should be when the child's learning task is fundamentally completed. In one sense, Wundt was at least half a century ahead of his times and is, therefore, rarely recalled for his contributions.

The Learning Theory/Conditioning Camp

The founder of this camp might have been somewhat surprised to find himself labeled as such because he, as Wundt, was interested in language only as a by-product of another area of study, classical conditioning. Ivan Pavlov lived in the latter part of the 19th and the early portion of the 20th centuries. He was a contemporary of Ebbinghaus and Wundt and was to stand chronologically alongside such greats as Sigmund Freud, William James, and E. L. Thorndike just to name a few. He had worked with Bekterev in their homeland, Russia, and was very well known before the end of the 19th century for his work in infrahuman physiology. His work regarding classically conditioning dogs to salivate to the sound of a bell is known by virtually every beginning psychology undergraduate.

What is far less familiar to most readers is his work on the nature of the "second signal system." This system dealt solely with language production and was essentially constructed to explain those aspects of language that "first signal system" conditioning could not. The first signal system covered all aspects of his rigorous system of classical conditioning, which included five varieties of learning paradigms and several models for "forgetting," or, more properly, "extinction," which is the term used to define an absence of performance when reinforcement has been withdrawn. A more lengthy discussion of Pavlov's first signal system occurs in the chapter devoted to the writings of the Behaviorists—e.g., O. H. Mowrer's work.

Pavlov supposedly developed the second signal system quite late in his professional career and far later than the first signal system. The first signal system was straight forward; it was capable of producing easily graphable and interpretable data defining the contiguous arrangements that pair, say, a bell and meat powder together and then plot the number of drops of saliva on each trial as the laboratory animal learns the association. Second signal system processing was different. Language was, according to Pavlov, something that failed to lend itself to easy analysis. On the contrary, Pavlov contended that first and second signal system conditioning were not even directly related. First signal system conditioning was not the prerequisite nor the foundation for second signal system processing, but he did admit that the two forms of "signaling" could possibly affect each other's performance if one was trying to occur in the presence of the other. For example, if one is talking or listening (second signal system processing), the possibility of being classically conditioned simultaneously to the sound of a buzzer if, say, that buzzer is followed by harsh electrical shock is directly dependent upon how much facilitation or inhibition is being produced by the second signal system. Of course, the reader could easily turn the analogy around and see the buzzer/electric shock have just as strong an effect upon one's attempt to have a conversation (Hilgard & Bower, 1975, pp. 72, 79–86). Even at that, the two systems were still distinctly separate. Ironically, the reader will see in the chapter dealing with the S-R Behaviorists that O. E. Mowrer in the 1950s apparently either chose to ignore Pavlov's comments regarding the separateness of the first and second signal systems or simply did not really understand Pavlov's distinction. It is interesting to note that an attempt was made to create an adequate description of language using the very one system rejected by its inventor as being a logical tool for building a language model. Ironically, Mowrer (1954) does not do an altogether poor job of using Pavlov's first signal system, but it is also true that he and Pavlov may have been looking at language from different perspectives—e.g., Pavlov looking at syntax (as is seen in his work regarding the "word salad" language of schizophrenics) and Mowrer dealing with semantics.

Pavlov's writings on the second signal system seem yet today mostly ignored. Perhaps this is due to two factors: first, his work on the first signal system was virtually revolutionary and received instant acclaim and no serious criticisms. It was popularized in this country to some extent by E. L. Thorndike but most especially by the "Father of S-R Behaviorism," J. B. Watson, in 1913 with "Psychology as the Behaviorist Views It" and again, and most emphatically, in 1924 in his *Behaviorism*. Watson's book emphasized the utility of classical conditioning in actual problem solving and removed psychology instantly from the tenuous grip of Titchener's structuralism (see above). Second, Watson's popularizing of the first signal system did little, if anything, for the second signal system. In Watson's day, a system that would produce did not need to be slowed by the notes of the system's creator regarding the possible serious restrictions the to-be-popularized system might actually have. The second signal system had died a quiet death after an exceedingly short life of rather timid, nonexperimental observation/speculation on Pavlov's part.

O. H. Mowrer (1954), as the reader will see later in this book, is the person who is most usually heralded as the founder of the Learning Theory/Conditioning Camp despite the fact such a claim is in error. His article, "The Psychologist Looks at Language," is a masterpiece of application of first signal system functioning in a realm in which such workings should never fit. "Tom is a thief." is the simple, present-tense declarative sentence that occupies Mowrer's time and ours at a later date as Mowrer attempts to awaken psychology as a science to the "new field" of language development.

It was a mere three years after Mowrer's article that B. F. Skinner, a strict S-R Behaviorist, and Noam Chomsky, a follower and then leader of Wundt's approach, simultaneously shook psychology and linguistics not to mention philosophy to their cores with *Verbal Behavior* (1957) and *Syntactic Structures* (1957). Each book, as the reader will later see, had an approach all its own but still clearly connected to its respective roots (to Wundt, in the case of Chomsky; and to Pavlov in a far less than obvious manner, by Skinner). Mowrer's impact upon Skinner is strictly philosophical; both were strict S-R Behaviorists. Skinner's impact upon C. E. Osgood and M. D. S. Braine was profound; Mowrer's impact was almost non-existent with these S-O-R Behaviorists.

To this point, we have seen that human verbal learning as a camp survived admirably from its starting point in 1885 with *Memory* and continues to flourish today. Wundt's Innateness approach first appeared around the same date as *Memory* but was perhaps too loose or too subtle a position to live long; it was, however, awakened from its slumbers by Noam Chomsky's *Syntactic Structures*—and grew. Ivan Pavlov, like Wundt, inherits a title as a position leader more because of what he did not say rather than what he did say. The first person in camp to bring his system to life again, albeit may have been the wrong "system," was O. H. Mowrer in 1954; the approach grew. The human verbal learning approach does not easily interact with either the Wundtian or Pavlovian approaches. The human verbal learning approach seems essentially to ignore the other two approaches and sits apart far enough to miss the criticisms each has for the other and, parenthetically, for the human verbal learning camp if that camp should come near. If we set human verbal learning aside for all but a few purposes at this point (trusting it will take care of its own as it has easily done in the past), we are left with the Learning Theory/Conditioning Camp and the Innateness Camp to act as the focal points toward which one must gravitate whether one calls oneself a theorist or even pretends an interest in anything resembling theory. In the most simplistic way, the two camps separate on the grounds of how much, if any, contribution the child makes to the development of his or her own language development. It is the philosophical debate of Kant on the innateness side (Durant, 1926, pp. 277–282). Some things in the universe have innate structure or at least the tendency to yield rapidly into a structured form. The position of the philosophical empiricists is that all is known through the senses. But there are other differences as well which are not perhaps as critical as the philosophical differences but which are nevertheless just as real and potentially as confusing to the beginning student as any other set of issues. The differences are defined as limits of each other's discipline, e.g., the Innateness Camp's knowledge of linguistics versus the Learning Theory/Conditioning Camp's knowledge of empirical acquisition/ extinction parameters regarding behaviors of all varieties and not just those related to language development. The two camps, therefore, continually "talk past" each other with neither camp really listening to the other. The

18

result is a major breakdown regarding transfer of knowledge, as we shall easily see in the coming chapters.

In order to understand the Innateness Camp and the Learning Theory/Conditioning Camp, it is necessary to methodically define the background of each more specifically than has been done above. Let us turn our attention first to the Innateness Camp's heritage: Linguistics.

References

Anderson, S., and Beh, W. (1963). "The reorganization of verbal memory in childhood." *Journal of Verbal Learning and Verbal Behavior, 7,* 1049—1053.

Archer, E. J. (1960). "A re-evaluation of the meaningfulness of all possible CVC Trigrams." *Psychological Monographs, 74,* (10, Whole No. 497).

Brown, R., and Berko, J. (1960). "Word association and the acquisition of grammar." *Child Development, 31,* 1—14.

Chomsky, N. (1957). *Syntactic Structures.* The Hague: Mouton.

Dale, P. S. (1976). *Language Development.* New York: Holt.

Durant, W. (1926). *The Story of Philosophy.* New York: Simon and Schuster.

Ebbinghaus, H. (1964). *Memory.* New York: Dover.

Ervin-Tripp, S. (1961). "Changes with age in the verbal determinants of association." *American Journal of Psychology, 74,* 361—372.

Glaze, J. A. (1928). "The association value of nonsense syllables." *Journal of Genetic Psychology, 35,* 255—267.

Hilgard, E., and Bower, G. (1975). *Theories of Learning (4th ed.).* Englewood Cliffs, NJ: Prentice.

Miller, G. A. (1956). "The magical number seven plus or minus two: some limits on our capacity for processing information." *Psychological Review, 63,* 81—97.

Miller, G. A., and Selfridge, J. A. (1950). "Verbal context and the recall of meaningful material." *American Journal of Psychology, 63,* 176—185.

Mowrer, O. H. (1954). "The psychologist looks at language." *The American Psychologist, 9* (11), 660—694.

Mussen, P., Conger, J., and Kagan, J., (1974). *Child Development and Personality* (4th ed.).New York: Harper.

Riley, L. and Fite G., (1974). "Syntagmatic versus paradigmatic paired-associate acquisition. *Journal of Experimental Psychology, 103* (2), 375—376.

Rock, I. (1957). "The role of repetition in associative learning." *American Journal of Psychology, 70,* 186—193.

Skinner, B. F. (1957). *Verbal Behavior.* New York: Appleton, Century, and Crofts.

Underwood, B. F., Runquist, W. N., and Schulz, R. W. (1959). "Response learning in paired-associate lists as a function of intralist similarity." *Journal of Experimental Psychology, 58,* 70—78.

vonRestorff, H. (1933). "Über die Wirkung von Bereichsbildungen im Spurenfeld." *Psych. Forsch., 18,* 299—342.

Watson, J. B. (1913). "Psychology as the behaviorist views it." *Psychological Review, 20,* 158—177.

Watson, J. B. (1924). *Behaviorism.* New York: Norton.

– 2 –

Taxonomic Linguistics

Definition of the Problem

Following Wundt's early writings on the innate nature or innate predisposition each normal child has to develop language, the reader should recall that a period of disuse or dormancy occurs regarding Wundt's ideas. In the interim between the dormancy and the reawakening of his position, a very interesting movement not directly attached to Wundt (nor Ebbinghaus nor Pavlov for that matter) began taking place. It was the growth of scholarly interest in the field of linguistics. It was a combination of the evolution of linguistics and the reawakening of Wundt's basic position that made the time era perfect in the late 1950s for Noam Chomsky to produce *Syntactic Structures* (1957). This book created a virtual explosion in the interest of scholars in children's language and simultaneously caused a major chasm to appear dividing scholars from one another—e.g., the basic debate between the followers of the Innateness Camp and the Learning Theory/Conditioning Camp.

Linguistics as a Field of Study

According to Dale (1976, pp. 61–62), linguistics as a science has actually chosen two goals for itself. The first is to define a language by producing a very carefully detailed set of rules which describe all aspects of that language and either explicitly or very implicitly tell us if the sentence we deal with is grammatical or is not grammatical. This first goal is no small task since, as you are well aware, the number of languages throughout the world is quite large and the number of dialects within each language can also be considerably varied. Any descriptive system is immediately facing a major challenge as that system attempts to account for all aspects of even a single language if that language is the product of a highly technical, mobile society such as our own. Dale says the second goal is a rather metaphysical one; the linguistic system must discuss language as a "general phenomenon." Dale does not adequately define "general phenomenon," but, unfortunately, we can understand his meaning by simply reflecting upon how much work the first goal will impose upon us. Perhaps we can believe that a descriptive system is quite possible, but at the very same time we fully realize, as in mathematics, physics, chemistry, or any graphic or statistical description of behavior, that "description of" and "reality of" may be two very different issues. For example the words you are reading on this page are nothing more than conventionally accepted stimulus patterns to which you ascribe some "recognition" and upon which you confer the status of "more or less meaningful." There is nothing innately meaningful regarding the shape of a letter or word other than perhaps the innate recognition that the shape of the letter or word does not look like the shape of other letters or words. Even some argument could be made here that such a small innate reaction pattern is itself learned. In short, the first goal should be quite difficult to conquer, and the second may be almost impossible to achieve because it asks us to build a system which is "isomorphic" with the underlying reality the system seeks to describe. This attempt at isomorphism requires us to ask if it is even possible for any human being or any computer programmed by a human to write a linguistic system which touches the "absolute reality" of the language. For example, to say $E = MC^2$ is the formula that generates atomic fission is not necessarily even remotely close to the reality of the actual act of seeing atomic fission. Is then Dale's second goal for linguistics actually impossible or at least highly improbable of achievement?

In order to achieve the second goal, it would, at least at first glance, seem necessary to achieve the first goal, a carefully detailed description of the language itself. Numbers of attempts have been made; many have established stepping stones to the next higher level of descriptive adequacy. The term "grammar" can be used safely here as referring to the end product of any systematic attempt at rigorous linguistic description. To say a child speaks or writes "grammatically" means specifically that what the child has produced is capable of being described using a conventional, existing set of rules defined by the language users to which s/he is most closely allied. An "ungrammatical" sentence is merely one which cannot be described by the language rules which define "grammatical" sentences for that group of language users in question. And there lies the "Catch 22." If any sentence is produced which is not definable by the rules of a given linguistic system, that sentence should be incapable of producing any "sense" or meaning in the person to whom the sentence is presented. Such an immediate rejection by a listener/

reader is actually rarely the case, however. This ability of humans to tolerate enormous variations in sentence form and meaning forces a virtually intolerable, insolvable problem upon a linguistic system; it must somehow carry enough rules or flexibility to create rules to recognize and allow us to process extremely high degrees of variation in normal, daily language use as well as for any of our formal attempts at presenting materials through, say, writing or lecturing. The earliest 20th century grammars used in linguistic analysis woefully failed the test of either carrying a sufficient number of rules or being flexible enough to "create" rules on the spot when a sentence tested the credibility of the system itself. Such grammars were defined as "taxonomic" grammars and seemed most popular between the early 1900s and the late 1950s.

Taxonomic Linguistics/Constituent Analysis Grammar

One of the earliest 20th century grammars of the "taxonomic" variety was known as "constituent analysis," which will be referred to hereon as "CA" for brevity's sake. CA requires the linguist to consider the "natural" groupings into which the words in a sentence seem to fall. In a sentence such as "Chomsky disavows Behaviorism.", it is rather easy to see that the term "Chomsky" can stand apart from "... disavows Behaviorism" since, after all, Chomsky himself is not steadfastedly welded in meaning to either the act of "disavowing" or to "Behaviorism." He is, in short, free to vary his actions and the intended target of those actions. The act of "disavowing" seems to beg for a target. In this case, the target is a direct objective—"Behaviorism." There is something seemingly missing when one says merely; "Chomsky disavows." We find ourselves uniting to see the natural outcome of such a sentence which says to us that an actor (Chomsky) acts upon (disavows) thing or person acted upon (in this case, Behaviorism). CA uses this basic logic to give us a very clear descriptive system, at least in the case of our present sentence.

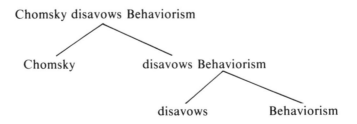

FIGURE 2.1

This simple, present tense declarative sentence in CA terms has one "core constituent" (the sentence taken as a whole), and four "branches" or constituents. The sum of the core constituent and the constituents equals the total number of "constituent components" for any given sentence. Therefore, in "Chomsky disavows Behaviorism." we actually have a total of five constituent components. A quick, simple double check to insure oneself that the correct number of constituent components has been calculated is to multiply the number of words in the sentence by a factor of two and then subtract the number one from the product. In "Chomsky disavows Behaviorism." we have $2(3) - 1 = 5$ constituent components, where 3 is the number of words in the sentence. Incidentally, the "branches" seen in Figure 1 are defined by the lines drawn at the oblique angles from the phrase in the line above to the connected phrase below it:

Chomsky disavows Behaviorism.
|
Chomsky

The branch line may extend down from any word in the phrase segment without causing a change in the meaning of the analysis, but the line is not permitted to cross from one phrase to another. For example:

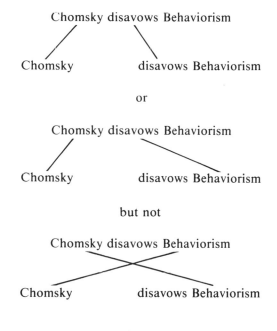

FIGURE 2.2

So far, the example used for CA has been quite simple and has offered no complications as such. But what does the linguist do with a simple sentence which may have multiple meanings, such as "Those are flying planes." This appears, at first glance, to be but one sentence, but closer inspection modifies our perception. We could view "Those" as referring to the target of one's gesturing while standing on an air field. We could be gesturing to separate planes that have no function except to let us simply fly them from other types of planes which are not the type of planes one simply just flies: fighter planes, cargo planes, bombers, etc. If we read "Those" as specifically referring to a set group of planes, we can see that the term "flying" acquires a special meaning as an adjective. If, however, we view the word "Those" as referring to the people who fly the planes, we can see the word "flying" change meanings quickly. For example, we could be saying and gesturing at the same time. "Those (men or women) are flying planes." and mean simply just "Those people," who might be surrounded by a larger group of people, are "flying" planes—not painting the planes or refueling them. There is little debate here that saying "They" would be more communicative (and would force us more quickly to accept "flying" as a verb). But there is also no debate that "Those" can be used in place of "They" by most native English language processors without any major confusion resulting if the referent of "Those" is in front of the person receiving the message. Is CA capable of producing enough rules to account for this?

The answer is in the affirmative, but it is a clumsy solution. It would appear as follows:

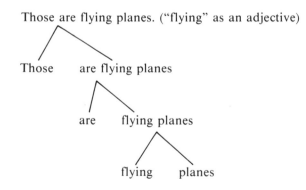

Those are flying planes. ("flying" as an adjective)

Those   are flying planes

are   flying planes

flying   planes

(Total of seven constituent components)

FIGURE 2.3

24

The solution is as follows for "flying" as a main verb (MV):

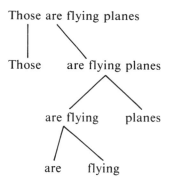

(Total of seven constituent components)

FIGURE 2.4

In both interpretations, the number of constituent components remains the same. The diagrams differ considerably. We may have met Dale's first goal of describing what we see, but it was somewhat time-consuming and never defined the parts of the sentence for us by telling us which word was the subject, which was the direct objective, or which word could serve as adjective or main verb. In short, we know how the phrases are grouped. Have we achieved Dale's second goal of using the linguistic system to produce an explanation for this language utterance as a "general phenomenon?" By no stretch of the imagination have we done so, nor, for that matter, can we as long as we use only CA. Perhaps a more powerful descriptive system can help us.

Phrase Structure Grammar

The system one step more powerful than CA is Phrase Structure grammar (PS). To be considered "more powerful," it must account for all that CA can and then go beyond CA. Let us begin by defining some notational terms here before we actually attempt a PS analysis. There are some disagreements as to exactly which notations should be used in all cases, but we will surely be on safe enough grounds as long as any deviations are not too severe and we hold our notations constant. Although there are vitually endless sources one may consult regarding linguistic

25

terminology and principles, the reader would be especially well advised to read Chapter 4 of Dale (1976) and Chapter 1 of Palermo (1978) for discussions that supplement the following.

Chomsky (1957, 1965) has indicated that the 20th century prior, to his own writing, had virtually been dominated by linguists who left CA as a form of analysis in favor of PS. Although he does not seem to find the move from CA to PS objectionable, he is apparently less than pleased with CA in general—especially when it is compared to his own approach. Admittedly, PS grammar does a significantly more detailed job of diagramming sentences and preparing specific rules, as we shall see, but we again must ask Dale's question about the adequacy of any system's answer when the two goals of description and definition of the essence of language are addressed. Let us return to "Chomsky disavows Behaviorism." and see how PS grammar assails the problems. First, we must agree on the symbols to be used before any attack may be launched. We will assume the following as given:

S = sentence (or corpus)

NP = noun phrase, which must have in it at least one noun or pronoun and any additional number of modifiers so desired as long as the modifiers pertain specifically to that noun or pronoun.

VP = verb phrase, which must at least include a VI or an Aux + MV, and which may include optional NPs as direct or indirect objects. Prepositional phrases are also optional.

N = noun (either "count," i.e., rugs, bats, cookies, etc., or "mass," i.e., sheep, snow, sand, etc.).

Pro = prounoun

MV = main verb, a transitive (action) verb supported by an auxillary (helping) verb.

V = any transitive (action) verb standing along, e.g., an action verb accompanied by no auxillary verb. To be distinguished from a MV, which, unlike the V, must have an auxillary assistant.

Aux = the auxillary verb, which cannot stand alone but which must continually support a MV.

VI = intransitive verb, a verb of being, i.e., is, are, am, was, were, be, etc. VIs stand alone unless they support MVs; in that case, they are appropriately called Auxs.

Adj = adjective

Adv = adverb

Prep = preposition

Conj = conjunction

26

These symbols do not necessarily exhaust all the symbols available, but they do account for the vast majority of them. Using these, we can actually develop four different varieties of PS grammar analyses: (1) the PS marker, (2) the PS tree, (3) the PS rules, and (4) the PS derivation from the rules.

The PS marker attempts to divide the sentence into its component parts by identifying the function of each unit while keeping the word in the context of the words remaining around it. In the case of "Chomsky disavows Behaviorism.", we would write the PS marker as follows:

[S[NP[N *Chomsky*]N]NP[VP[V *disavows*]V-
[NP[N *Behaviorism*]N]NP]VP]S]

One can easily see that NP and VP are used slightly differently from the way one is usually accustomed to using them—especially so for the NP. Technically, in PS markers, a N or Pro cannot stand alone without first having been defined in the context of a phrase. Therefore, this sentence actually has two NPs, but each NP has only one word, a N, in it. This is not true for the VP, which has both a V and a N in it (buried inside the NP). This takes a bit of adjusting to since we are accustomed to using the term "phrase" to refer to more than a single word. Yet, when we stop to think about it, the fact that a phrase may not have only one word in it is a bit arbitrary and actually begs the question as to how a child grows to understand the concept of phrase, which is actually used by most people as a categorizer of meaning regardless of the number of words inside the phrase constraints (boundaries). In short, who decreed that all phrases must contain more than a single word when in some cases a single word may create a more complicated mental process than a group of words associated by the fact we rather arbitrarily define them as fitting into a "phrase." Even somewhat more bewilderingly, we shall soon see that a NP may contain only a Pro. If one clearly understands the preceding argument, perhaps a NP with only a Pro in it is not as arbitrary as would first appear. We simply must remove some conventional habits of defining the term "phrase."

You will recall that the sentence "Those are flying planes." left us with some seemingly unnecessary work in completing the CA. This will again be true using PS markers. We will need two separate markers in order to describe the sentence with its two meanings. As an adjective defining "flying," we will need the following:

[S[NP[Pro *Those*]Pro]NP[VP[VI *are*]VI[NP
[Adj*flying*]Adj[N*planes*]N]NP]VP]S]

As a MV for "flying," the PS marker will be as follows:

[S[NP[Pro *Those*]Pro]NP[VP[Aux *are*]
Aux[MV *flying*]MV[NP[N *planes*]N]NP]VP]S]

PS markers obviously do a better job of informing us of the various parts of speech and how each part relates to the whole, but it is also certainly more work than is the CA. For some readers, the PS markers are actually less useful than the CA diagrams because the latter is less abstract. It does not require the understanding of what any part of speech is defined to be.

PS grammar can also provide us with a graphic diagram system which looks more like a CA analysis and still uses the same notation system seen in the PS marker. The system uses "PS trees." For example, the sentence "Chomsky disavows Behaviorism." will take the following form:

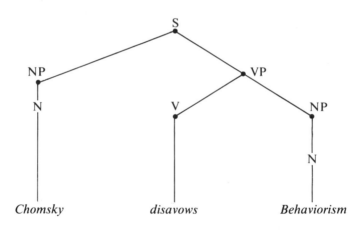

FIGURE 2.5

In the sentence "Those are flying planes.", the following PS trees result:

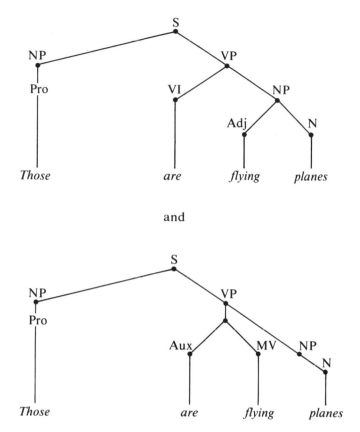

FIGURE 2.6

The first PS tree deals with "flying" as an adjective; the second sees "flying" as a MV. We note here that it is, as it was in the CA analysis and in the PS markers, necessary to construct two separate but highly related diagrams to account for the dual interpretation of the word "flying."

A third PS analysis may be run using what is called the "PS rules." Writing the rules, ironically, calls for a great deal of expertise on the writer's part since the writer must essentially work the rules out from a thorough understanding of the manner in which the language is structured.

Therefore, a novice writer of any language is hardly in a position to write the PS rules and yet understands the fact that the knowledge of how the rules look is really only of major benefit to someone who needs to see them in order to understand the language in the first place. Granted, a proficient user of the language could write the rules for the purpose of cross-cultural comparisons regarding the use of a single idea. Rules could also be written for comparison of one language's structure against that of another when the various languages seek to express numerous ideas in a set of sentences. Also, a novice in the use of any language might profit from seeing the rules of that language after a professional linguist had prepared those rules.

In the sentence "Chomsky disavows Behaviorism." we may write the following rules:

Rule No.		Rule Content
PS 1.1	S	$\rightarrow$ NP + VP
1.2	NP	$\rightarrow$ N
1.3	VP	$\rightarrow$ V + NP
1.4	N	$\rightarrow$ $\begin{Bmatrix} \text{Chomsky} \\ \text{Behaviorism} \end{Bmatrix}$
1.5	V	$\rightarrow$ disavows

FIGURE 2.7

In the Rule No. column, the first number following PS is the number of the sentence in the list of sentences you are supposedly preparing to analyze for that specific linguistic translation. The second number is the rule number itself as it applies to that specific sentence. Therefore, making the comment, "I am having a hard time writing the second rule!" is meaningless to a listener unless the number of the sentence is included. There are just as many "second rules" as there are sentences in the language universe; this point becomes disturbingly obvious as we proceed.

The sentence "Those are flying planes." offers us some initial problems. We actually have two different sentences regarding meaning, but each "sentence" looks like the other. In order to write the rules, one approach would be to painstakingly write a set of rules for each "sentence" and then combine the two sets into one set where such a combination is possible. This is, after all, going to make the analysis at least cosmetically look less cumbersome. For the adjectival use of "flying," we have the following rules:

Rule No.			Rule Content
PS 2.1	S	→	NP + VP
2.2	NP	→	$\begin{Bmatrix} \text{Pro} \\ \text{Adj + N} \end{Bmatrix}$
2.3	VP	→	VI + NP
2.4	N	→	planes
2.5	Pro	→	Those
2.6	VI	→	are
2.7	Adj	→	flying

FIGURE 2.8

In the case of the MV definition for "flying," the rules are as follows:

Rule No.			Rule Content
PS 2.1'	S	→	NP + VP
2.2'	NP	→	$\begin{Bmatrix} \text{Pro} \\ \text{N} \end{Bmatrix}$
2.3'	VP	→	Aux + MV + NP
2.4'	N	→	planes
2.5'	Pro	→	Those
2.6'	Aux	→	are
2.7'	MV	→	flying

FIGURE 2.9

The reader has no doubt noted that the order of the PS rules in Figures 7, 8, and 9 does not necessarily reflect the order specifically seen as the words appear from left to right in the sentence which the rules define. This is apparently due more to convention than to logic, but there is even a case to be made for the latter. For example, the words carrying the greatest amount of content are the nouns in any sentence. We can see in all three sets of rules above that the nouns and pronouns are defined before the verbs, which generally are defined before the adjectives, which are generally defined before the adverbs, the prepositions, the conjunctions, and the articles in that order from first to last. The implication seems to be that Ns, Pros, MVs, Auxs, Vs, and VIs are the most important parts of any sentence. When M. D. S. Braine's (1963) position on language learning is discussed below, we will see that he, at least, will emphatically disagree with what would seem such a safe, non-controversial assumption regarding the importance of nouns and verbs.

Our problem was to state the dual meaning of "Those are flying planes." in one set of rules, not two, if such a task can be accomplished. By the use of parentheses, which indicate that the use of the symbol within the parentheses is optional at any given point, we have the following:

Rule No.	Rule Content
PS 2.1"	S $\rightarrow$ NP + VP
2.2"	NP $\rightarrow$ $\begin{Bmatrix} \text{Pro} \\ \text{Adj} + \text{N} \end{Bmatrix}$
2.3"	VP $\rightarrow$ $\begin{Bmatrix} \text{VI} + \text{NP} \\ \text{Aux} + \text{MV} \end{Bmatrix}$ + NP
2.4"	N $\rightarrow$ planes
2.5"	Pro $\rightarrow$ Those
2.6"	VI $\rightarrow$ are
2.7"	Aux $\rightarrow$ are
2.8"	MV $\rightarrow$ flying
2.9"	Adj $\rightarrow$ flying

FIGURE 2.10

The reader can see the need for rules 2.6", 2.7", 2.8", and 2.9" if the word "flying" is to be adequately defined. This also brings out the rather arbitrary nature of such "rules" if one can simply call a word more or less what one wants when one needs to do so.

The fourth form of PS analysis is known as the "PS derivation" analysis. This is prepared by using the PS rules seen above. For example, in the case of, "Chomsky disavows Behaviorism." we see the following PS derivation structure:

S1	PS Rule No.
1. NP + VP	1.1
2. NP + V + NP	1.3
3. N + V + NP	1.2
4. N + V + N	1.2
5. Chomsky + V + N	1.4
6. Chomsky + disavows + N	1.5
7. Chomsky + disavows + Behaviorism	1.4

The "defining" of the VP in line 2 before defining the first NP is a product of convention. The VP, in this case, has its own NP and, therefore, carries more information (VP → V + NP) than does the first NP alone. In some ways, seeing the VP's full definition allows us to present more information more quickly if we analyze it in line 2 rather than waiting until after the first NP is completely defined. There is nothing that says we must do it this way, but convention is quite emphatic on the issue. If the VP contained only a VI, i.e., VI → is, then the NP appearing first in the sentence (now read as "Chomsky is") would be defined first as a N before the VP would, in turn, be defined as a VI. It is possible to reach a point in linguistic transcription where one cannot easily decide if a NP should or should not be defined before a VP—assuming we are dealing with a present or past tense declarative sentence. Frankly, if the analysis hinges on such a minute issue, the writer is wasting time trying to decide and should choose the linguistic unit farthest to the left hand end of the sentence upon which to base the analysis.

In case of "Those are flying planes." we actually must use the single set of composite rules to produce two separate PS derivations.

S2	PS Rule No.
1. NP + VP	2.1
2. NP + VI + NP	2.3
3. Pro + VI + NP	2.2
4. Pro + VI + Adj + N	2.2
5. Those + VI + Adj + N	2.5
6. Those + are + Adj + N	2.6
7. Those + are + flying + N	2.9
8. Those + are + flying + planes	2.4

If the reader looks very closely at lines 3 and 4 immediately above (and at lines 3 and 4 of the PS derivaton for "Chomsky disavows Behaviorism."), s/he can see that the NPs are defined completely in their "least common denomination" before the substitutions of words begin in the methodical left to right hand manner. The purpose is very clearly to break down the sentence's components until the very most basic units are all that are left standing before absolutely any substituting of real words is allowed. This is not an issue of convention in any sense. Trying to substitute at the same time one is defining in another part of a sentence is prone to result in error in either substitution or defining but most probably in the latter.

The use of "flying" as a MV results in the following derivation:

S2	PS Rule No.
1. NP + VP	2.1"
2. NP + Aux + MV + NP	2.3"
3. Pro + Aux + MV + NP	2.2"
4. Pro + Aux + MV + N	2.2"
5. Those + Aux + MV + N	2.5"
6. Those + are + MV + N	2.7"
7. Those + are + flying + N	2.8"
8. Those + are + flying + planes	2.4"

It can be seen that the last derivation carries just as many lines (8) to accomplish making "flying" a MV as did the preceding in making "flying" an Adj. The derivations are similar to each other in places and quite disimilar in others. In all cases, however, the PS rules must be defined before any writing of a PS derivation can occur since, as a point of logic, the writer has no way to derive anything if s/he has no foundations. The reader may at this point wisely ask what possible purpose there is in writing a PS derivation in the first place. The answer is best seen in view of one's interests. If, for example, the reader wishes to study cross-cultural issues in language, writing a PS derivation could easily show how two or more language cultures using not quite the same PS rules might actually produce PS derivations of very different forms. Comparing two entirely different languages in which both tried to express the same idea could show very interesting agreements and disagreements in both the PS rules and the PS derivations.

Constituent Analyses and Phrase Structure grammars have one major drawback; each is incapable of describing sentences in a manner which shows more similarities than dissimilarities in those sentences. For example, we have seen that "Those are flying planes." requires two Constituent Analysis diagrams, two sets of PS markers, two sets of PS trees, two sets of PS rules in order to create one overall set of rules, and two PS derivations in order to describe the sentence's dual meaning. If that is not frustrating enough, please note that there is absolutely nothing in CA or PS to tell the reader that a certain way of writing a sentence is grammatical and a certain number of other ways does not produce a grammatical sentence. For example, the PS rules for "Trees can grow out of cracks in concrete walks." are identical in form. Only the PS derivation tells the "correct" order and then only if someone writing the derivation seems to have "a priori" knowledge of what is and what is not grammatically possible (see Chomsky, 1965, for further discussion of this issue).

34

Until 1957, the preceding forms of analysis were the only ones available except for a rather minor attempt known as "Markov grammar" which set for itself the task of determining mathematically what the probability of finding a certain part of speech would be in any given part of a sentence if one knew the parts of speech of the words preceding the one to be predicted. This system had seemingly few followers, perhaps because the system was both highly mathematical in nature and highly technical/time consuming. With the development of high speed computers in the 1970s and 1980s, the field of Markov grammar may become of some increased interest. The CA, PS, and Markovian systems were all taxonomic. They were purely descriptive, and approached every single sentence as if that sentence had nothing in common with a preceding one already painstakingly analyzed. For each sentence in that language's universe of possible sentences, there was created a structural description requiring more space than the sentence itself. Logic decreed that the number of linguistic structures needed would have to be nearly infinite if the number of sentences one could possibly produce in any sophisticated language was nearly infinite. But there was even a larger problem at hand. Children, whom taxonomic linguistics had seemingly almost forgotten, rarely spoke in "complete" sentences when they were in or just out of infancy. How did a linguist write the linguistic analysis for such a "sentence" as "Milk!". The analyses could only give us the most superficial of interpretations. For example, the CA and PS analyses of "Milk!" look as follows:

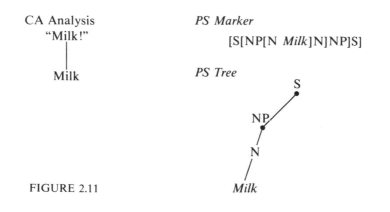

CA Analysis
"Milk!"

Milk

PS Marker

[S[NP[N *Milk*]N]NP]S]

PS Tree

S

NP

N

Milk

FIGURE 2.11

(Here even the formula for calculating the total number of constituent components falls short since $2W - 1 = 2\,(1) - 1 = 1$ total constituent component—which is clearly not the case.)

35

Using one word is actually less of a problem than when two words are used without necessarily being expressed in order; this is a very frequent expression technique used by children whom have left the "one-word stage" at 10—12 months of age and have gone on to the "two-word random production" stage at 18 months or so. The one-word stage usually qualifies the single word as a "holophrase," which literally means "one-word sentence" in which the listener has to guess at the verb and/or whether the noun spoken is actually a subject or a direct object of some unspoken subject and verb. At 18 months, we really do not know if we are listening to a subject—direct object or direct object—subject order or, for that matter, if the child's use of the terms is intended as what we perceive as a noun in our own definition of parts of speech (Bloom, 1970). For example, take the following sentence uttered by an 18-month-old:

"Milk Cow!"

This offers a serious linguistic challenge since we really do not know if the child means to use "Milk" as a verb or as a noun. We do not know if the "cow" is the subject of the milking, is the object of the milking, or, for that matter, has anything whatsoever to do with "Milk" other than as a paired-associate response (see Chapter 1). If we make what seems a "reasonable" guess from the context the child is in, we will reduce our uncertainty, but we reduce it only to an extent which is still unknown to us. The "one sentence" we think we are listening to may actually be only one, but then again it could just as easily be two separate thoughts. If the reader has the time and energy, s/he may wish to write the CA, PS markers, PS trees, PS rules, and PS derivations for all the possible ways the two-word "sentence" above could be interpreted. Please feel free to see it as a possible five-way interpretation!

Transformational Grammar (An Introduction)

Noam Chomsky (1957) is generally credited with starting the modern movement in language development which essentially combined all that was known about linguistics up to that date with the basic assumptions of Wundt (see above) that children had the innate ability to form language given at least a minimally stimulating environment. The book was *Syntactic Structures*; it was admirably short-winded but made a number of significant points that put it well on the way toward meeting both of Dale's (1976) goals of achieving (1) sufficient description and (2) defining language as a "phenomenon" in and of itself. The grammar being proposed was called "Transformational Grammar," which we will abbreviate as TG. Chomsky was writing in a time period when all who were interested in linguistics essentially believed even something at least as complex in appearance as PS grammar was still insufficient. It was difficult to fit the assumptions of any of the taxonomic linguistic models to the apparent growth of and interest in child psychology in our country, e.g., the rediscovery of the work of Jean Piaget (1955), who was (as apparently was Wundt) a believer in the Kantian notions of an "a priori" mental structuring within each child that would, if properly stimulated, sort and categorize/classify natural events into a view of reality the child at that age level could understand. Speculation was that the child could hypothesize about what was "good form" in language. It was speculated that children would learn a language in ways other than through simple classical or operant conditioning, but we must quickly note that not all people accepted this latter idea (Mowrer, 1954, and Skinner, 1957). All observers did agree, however, that it was apparent that children cross-culturally seemed remarkably consistent in their approaches to language learning. Many, following Jean Piaget's modern lead, went so far as to speculate that the child was not a "miniature adult" as had been apparently assumed by most prior to Piaget's increase in popularity. Sentences produced by children at all ages seemed remarkably infinite in variety yet hauntingly similar at the same moment. The linguistic system of the late 1950s and on needed flexibility, needed to reflect how people actually talked and not just how they should talk, and needed to be defined within some general biological framework separating humans from non-humans. Chomsky's *Syntactic Structures* attempted all that and more (DeVito, 1970, pp. 44—47).

References

Bloom, L. (February, 1970). *Semantic Features In Language Acquisition.* Paper presented at the Conference on Research in the Language of the Mentally Retarded, University of Kansas.

Braine, M. D. S. (1963). "On learning the grammatical order of words." *Psychological Review, 70,* 323—348.

Chomsky, N. (1957). *Syntactic Structures.* The Hague: Mouton.

Chomsky, N. (1965). *Aspects of the Theory of Syntax.* Cambridge, Massachusetts: MIT Press.

Dale, P. S. (1976). *Language Development.* New York: Holt.

DeVito, J. (1970). *The Psychology of Speech and Language.* New York: Random House.

Mowrer, O. H. (1954). "The psychologist looks at language." *The American Psychologist, 9* (11), 660–694.

Palermo, D. (1978). *Psychology of Language.* Dallas, Texas: Scott.

Piaget, J. (1955). *The Language and Thought of the Child.* New York: World.

Skinner, B. F. (1957). *Verbal Behavior.* New York: Appleton, Century, and Crofts.

– 3 –

LANGUE AND LANGUE-PAROLE

Transition to Transformational Grammar (TG)

This entire chapter is devoted to considering Chomsky's TG, which though a form of linguistic analysis, goes well beyond Dale's (1976) first goal of achieving an adequate linguistic description of a language and comes, according to its proponents, to grips with Dale's second challenge of treating the language as if it were a general phenomenon. Discussing the actual mechanics of TG as we did Constituent Analysis (CA) and Phrase Structure grammar (PS) would take us far afield; the interested reader is encouraged to pick virtually any modern linguistic text as a source. The TG notations that are used in this chapter are suggestive and by no means seek to do justice to the full TG system. Perhaps the best course the reader could possibly find if s/he is interested solely in linguistics is Chomsky's own classic, *Syntactic Structures* (1957).

Assumptions

Rather ironically, *Syntactic Structures* in and of itself does not clearly set forth the assumptions Chomsky makes about the language learning process. It was eight years later in 1965 when he wrote "Methodological Preliminaries," (Chapter 1 of *Aspects of the Theory of Syntax*) that we are first shown his assumptions in perhaps as clear a fashion as they have ever appeared. Even then, close reading is required since many of his most subtle points are made in a language other than English.

"Methodological Preliminaries" states that no ultimate answer regarding the origins of language is being proposed; there is only an attempt to achieve descriptive, and not explanatory adequacy. TG is proposed as an ideal analysis of the "pure" speaker/listener relationship. In other words, the TG system will not, at least at first, attempt to determine where such variables as IQ, socioeconomic class, race, or motivation/reinforcement fit into the development of language. This is not, however, to say that such concerns will never be addressed sometime in the future. The philosophical approach is one of rationalism/mentalism's searching for what is assumed to be the child's innate ability to develop language. Introspection, the process of observing/reporting one's own thoughts and memories, is to be heavily relied upon. This is not to say empiricism will never be called upon, but it is to say that seeking empirical proof in 1955 is considered rather presumptuous. ("Empiricism" here and throughout this book is understood to be experimental empiricism. The reader should understand that rationalism/mentalism must use some form of empiricism in general or there would be nothing to think about. Experimental empiricism, however, goes beyond the general concept in order to produce laboratory, controlled data—usually of a mathematical nature.) In fact, TG may never really seek empirical proof since, as we shall see when we systematically review J. J. Katz's "Mentalism in Linguistics" (1964), assuming empiricism is science's only means of proof is purely an assumption which may or may not actually be true. In short, TG could be perfectly accurate in its statements and yet never, hypothetically, be capable of a shred of empirical proof. Without "stealing the thunder" of Katz, we should pause here a moment to digest, if possible, exactly what the last line implies. It is saying essentially that the "proof of the pudding need not necessarily lie in the tasting," but rather the proof may lie solely in the intent of the cook. That is generally a foreign argument for most readers/scholars of modern Behavioral Science. British Empiricism, starting with John Locke, left a very strong set of rules for us to follow regarding the preparation, conduct, and manner in which scholarship should occur. In the earliest elementary school levels in the Western world, students are conditioned to believe what they can empirically verify. To read that a scholar of Chomsky's caliber seeks to convince us that empirical proof is seeking an answer to "the wrong question" is usually a bit hard to accept. We will see Katz attempt to ease us into acceptability, so, at least for the moment, we will pay our dime and take our ride on Chomsky's train of thought.

Chomsky at one point in his chapter makes what appears to be a rather subtle (but potentially confusing to the reader) substitution in terms. He claims that the taxonomic linguists have spent far too much time looking at only empirical proof for their models. We can grant him that point since taxonomic linguistics, as we saw in the previous chapter, really was interested only in "surface structure," which is operationally defined as that utterance (be it a complete sentence or not) which is actually produced orally or in writing and which does not remain in the shadowy recesses of one's thoughts. It is also true that taxonomic linguists are just that—linguists and not what Chomsky calls them in his article, Behaviorists. The term "Behaviorists" is a very specific term with several specific meanings which all apply only to psychology, not linguistics, as a field. Granted, both taxonomic linguists and Behaviorists are interested in "surface structures," but it is a serious error to use the terms interchangably since most taxonomic linguists are not remotely close to being qualified as psychologists and vice versa. Chomsky's interchange of the two terms may be understood somewhat better if one realizes that he has the same argument, e.g., criticizing their "sole concern over only behavior," with both groups of scholars. Unfortunately, Chomsky's broadside hits upon the fact, as we shall see in Braine and Osgood's work, that apparently he did not choose to recognize S-O-R Behaviorism as being distinct, although related, to S-R Behaviorism. S-O-R Behaviorism is concerned in equal proportions with the stimulus (S), the person/organism (O), and the response (R). The O is definitely interested in such variables that may exist in the mind of the language user. The error of Chomsky's substitution becomes more clear as we develop the uses of thought of the Behaviorists in a later chapter.

Chomsky's key point in attacking the use of surface structure as the only proper data of analysis is evidently necessary to allow his next point, which is perhaps the most radical point he made. The actual language phenomenon, which he calls the "langue" and the language as one hears/sees it, which he calls the "langue-parole," are not necessarily even close to being one in the same. The langue is referring to the "competence" of the user, whereas the "langue-parole" is in reference to the "performance" of the user. The "performance" could just as easily be called "surface structure," and, therefore, Chomsky is saying the taxonomic linguists and "the Behaviorists" are interested only in the langue-parole. If TG can actually define both the langue and the langue-parole, it has met both of Dale's (1976) goals for a sufficient grammar, e.g., treating the language as a general phenomenon and providing an adequate description of what has been produced in surface structure.

But merely proposing the existence of both the langue and langue-parole, which, are terms rightfully credited to Saussure, does in no sense solve Chomsky's problem of writing a "sufficient grammar," which by its very definition is a grammar which can do all things for all purposes for all people at all times. Ironically, the langue, which was always omitted in taxonomic linguistic analysis, is not as hard to account for in one sense as is the langue-parole, which is precisely what taxonomic linguistics had so painstakingly analyzed in so many detailed ways. The langue could at first be simply set aside with some brief comment about Wundt and Kant's assumptions that all normal children develop language because they are, "a priori," prone to do so. The structure and function of whatever that "a priori" was could be left to the neurologist or physiologist or anyone else for that matter who wished to understand what psychology and philosophy had always wanted to understand—the human central nervous system. The langue-parole was, however, a very different issue. Since Chomsky was proposing TG as a "universal grammar," all of the world's possible language systems, be they formally or informally known to the users of that language, had to be accounted for using only one grammatical system which could promise ultimate flexibility and comprehensive coverage within a portable system that fit somewhere neatly into one's intellectual capacity to understand linguistic transcription. By analogy, Chomsky was to create the Einsteinian formula $E = MC^2$ for the field of language; it must be as brief but totally complete as humanly conceivable. Such a product would save the linguists the embarrassment of needing to create a separate storage center, perhaps as large as a city library, just to store the linguistic transcriptions of one person's verbal output produced in a lifetime. Taxonomic linguistics could never have hoped for the creation of such a small, flexible package as Chomsky sought. His use of rationalism/mentalism admittedly would be his ally since in itself it is more "portable" for the scholar. His critics would harshly criticize the use of rationalism/mentalism and disavow his belief in language "universals." He would retort by asking these seemingly "hard-headed (empirically-minded)" linguists and psychologists why they themselves were using rationalism/mentalism when they spoke of "motivation in speech," "reinforcement," "IQ," and the "effects of social class"—just to name a few "intervening variables"—when none of these things qualified as the independent and dependent variables a hard-headed scholar prides oneself in studying because of the empirical existence of such independent/dependent variables. But, as Chomsky knew, the burden of proof for their acts was less the issue than was the burden of proof for his proposal. Caught in a time period demanding empirical proof seemed his lot in life. Chomsky, in one sense, flung the challenge to rationalism/mentalism back at his critics by asking them to explain the difficulty in understanding why the following sentences do not read with equal ease:

1. The cat's paw's fur is soft.
2. Soft is the cat's paw's fur.
3. The fur on the paw of the cat is soft.
4. Soft is the fur on the paw of the cat.

These sentences are, from first to last, a left-handed nested, a right-handed nested, a left-handed branching, and a right-handed branching sentence. They are supposedly progressively less difficult to understand as we progress from the first to the last sentence. Nested sentences (also known as "embedded") are several sentences in one.

    a. The cat has a paw.
    b. The paw has fur.
    c. The fur is soft.
    d. (Therefore) The cat's paw's fur is soft.

Chomsky contended that no empirical attempt could explain why the processing time for the four sentences was so different when indeed all four were actually saying the same thing with the same words. Only a rationalistic/mentalistic answer would seem possible—a shrewd, deliberate stroke toward a goal going past sense (empirical) data as that empirical data struggled to catch up or forced itself to change its formulas.

Perhaps the most eloquent defense of Chomsky's use of rationalism/mentalism comes from J. J. Katz in his "Mentalism in Linguistics" (1964). Katz places the anti-rationalism/mentalism movement in language development squarely upon those followers of Charles Bloomfield, a famous, outspoken taxonomic linguist. Bloomfield (1938) had previous to *Syntactic Structures* written an essay which harshly criticized the use of rationalism/mentalism as a tool for proving religious phenomena. He was interpreted by his followers to have said that taxonomic linguistics was unwilling or at least incapable of understanding the mental processes involved in language development and, therefore, should at that point in time reject rationalism/mentalism. Bloomfield's "argument" was persuasive enough to convince such greats in his field as C. F. Hockett (1948) and R. M. W. Dixon (1963). The message was the same from both of these writers: only that which could be seen or heard qualified as scientifically valid linguistic data. Katz believes taxonomic linguistics is far too narrow in its approach; empiricism is definitely not the only way one can know the truth of something, and apparently all that the taxonomic linguists wish to do is discuss empirical proofs. Mentalism is older than empiricism as a method of knowing, it does study cause/effect relations, and it is just as interested in the nature of the stimulus (environment) and response (actual verbal output) as it is in the actual mental processes standing between (mediating) those stimulus/response events. So the reader will not confuse Katz's last statement as defining mentalism in such a way as to confuse it with S-O-R Behaviorism (see above) it is best to note here that the S-O-R

Behaviorists see the inner processes of O to be essentially no less mechanical in nature than they do the S and the R, albeit the O is much more complex and depends on mediation to do its work. Mentalism makes no such claims for the O. In mentalism, the O is "free" to be whatever it wishes to be whether that something is or is not similar to the S and R in the mechanical sense. Perhaps the easiest way to see the distinction is to consider S-O-R Behaviorism as believing the brain is actually just as mechanically organized by the same set of rules in nature as is any other natural thing or event in that universe. The mentalistic position grants us that stimuli and responses are mechanical, but it will not say the brain actually follows the same set of mechanical rules the rest of the universe surely follows. The brain, for the mentalist, is a vast unknown which has perhaps a set of rules governing it that are completely dissimilar from the rules of nature as such. In fact, some mentalists might go so far as to say that "mind" and "brain" may be different in both function and production but yet related regarding the fact that "mind" does at least depend upon the brain for physical support. Katz himself perhaps best brings this point home when he says that Chomsky, at one point in his defense of his own system, did not even have to say that the model for TG was basically neurolgical and that the data in the model was linguistic. After all, as Katz puts it, the model could be made of "cardboard flipflops" and still work just as nicely. In a way, Katz seems a bit hypocritical with this, since he has already proposed (see above) that the mentalist is as interested in the stimulus, the organism, and the response as anyone. Then, he turns to us saying the O could just as well be nerve cells or cardboard or, one might suppose, anything else. In another sense, his meaning is clear; why hamper the publication of a new form of grammar just because we do not understand the neurological substrates which support the model? Katz says Chomsky did not invent mentalism for his own defense; it existed prior to Chomsky and happened to aid Chomsky when he called on it.

Katz says Chomsky's model will show us that it has a sufficient explanation for syntax, semantics, and phonology as well, so it is, therefore, superior to the taxonomic grammars. It will be interesting to see below if Chomsky does all this. If you are betting he cannot, you may be on very safe grounds. Even Katz himself says later in his chapter that syntax is most important and that phonology and semantics are related directly to syntax but not to each other.

Mentalism, as Katz sees it, is actually the best alternative facing us. After all, it is mentalism which seems most easily to be able to borrow facts and concepts from other disciplines in order to create a finished, sufficient product. Taxonomic linguistics and especially Behaviorism are held in place by the need to progress only after rigorous experimentation and consequent data analysis have occurred followed by seemingly endless experimental cross checks. After all that, the moves forward are by inches instead of miles, so Katz sees little profit in such an approach. Mentalism is the correct way, and he is frankly frustrated over the fact no one seems to want to easily let that technique be used. Mentalism is just as interested in studying cause effect relations in language as is Behaviorism, and, therefore, it deserves a chance to be heard without the combined criticisms of the taxonomic linguists and the Behaviorists. Katz, in fact, asks for an apology from taxonomic linguistics and Behaviorism since both have taken some unkind shots at mentalism and have, therefore, caused some scholars to immediately reject it rather than suffer criticism. Katz believed that mentalism would ultimately pull learning, perception, motivation, and any other psychological process of an "intervening variable" nature into a complete model of human cognition. At the moment, let us settle for first things first—e.g., an explanation or at least a satisfactory description of how language develops and functions. We return to Chomsky, who is in complete agreement with Katz (Chomsky, 1968, pp. 75-77).

Chomsky's justifications for proposing his model are positive in nature (Chomsky, 1965).

1. TG will describe surface structures at least as well as all the taxonomic grammars have.

2. TG will be "generative" in nature. It will discuss levels of language processing beneath the surface structure level; it will operationally define an "area" called "deep structure" and an "area" known as the "transformational rules," which mediate processing between the deep structure and surface structure levels.

3. TG will provide excellent "economy"—e.g., it will be a small, portable system which has a sense of eloquent simplicity about it.

4. TG will have the capacity to be flexible and generalizable. We will not need to completely reconstruct the model each time we move from one language to a second or third. It will consider racial and nationality differences in language and be sensitive to all their rules and exceptions to the rules. It will be sensitive to but not overcome by dialectical differences or cross cultural variations in rhythm of speech delivery.

5. TG will make itself applicable to people interested in abnormal language development and normal language development since, for the first time, the nature of language will be formulated in a small enough, captive space to be used as a basis for hypothesis generation. This hypothesis generation has been impossible to date because taxonomic linguistics conveyed the idea that language was too idiosyncratic or too

45

large a field of study to easily permit definition of normal or abnormal language development in any way but the grossest of senses. (This last point is inferred from Chomsky [1965]; he does not specifically state this as such.)

This writer prefers to present Chomsky's TG model as part of a larger model which the present writer infers to exist following the careful study of Chomsky's writings. This "inferred model" goes beyond simple TG and links TG to the processes of simple cognition without doing harm to Chomsky's actual TG model. Developing the larger model provides apparently some improved clarity and understanding of Chomsky's TG model, per se, while at the same time tying multiple loose ends created by placing the model into the O of the S-O-R complex. The inferred model is a four-stage one; Chomsky's TG model is a three-stage one and is proposed to fit at the third stage position in the four-stage model itself.

The Four-Stage Model and TG

The first stage in the inferred model is the INPUT phase. By INPUT is meant all incoming verbal material whether that material is oral or written. For simplicity's sake, the examples used below will deal with oral and written material only. The INPUT phase specifically deals with the person's ability to "sensate" the material coming to him/her as it is seen or heard. If we for convenience's sake assume no difficulties at this stage, the second stage approaches in two separate, but related, forms. The MEMORY CODING phase (Stage 2a) requires the person to take his/her short-term memory (STM) of the INPUT and convert that STM into long-term memory (LTM). Broadbent (1957) has done the pioneer work on STM and LTM and has set the pace for most memory research done since. Broadbent says that each of us has initially a one to two second "first phase" in STM that is virtually a "picture perfect" copy of what has just been sensated. For approximately another 28 seconds or so that "perfect" picture deteriorates. Causes for the deterioration are legion, but perhaps the easiest way of summarizing them is to say that the 28 seconds provide ample opportunity for past experiences to "interfere" with the present sensation while, in fact, that present sensation is being "crowded out" of immediate memory by new INPUT. The term "deteriorate" as used above is not to necessarily be taken literally. If it were taken that way, the reader would be accepting the idea of "decay" theory in memory; the decay theory has been long abandoned. The

46

point simply is that the 30 seconds or so that the individual can more or less accurately preserve what has been seen or heard lasts just that long—30 seconds, unless s/he can process the INPUT one step further into LTM. LTM, unlike STM, is based upon a relatively permanent protein change in the brain—or at least so it is speculated. This protein change is usually accompanied by a different form of coding than is seen in STM; it is a "verbal" coding which is highly dependent upon words and symbols. Once into LTM, the storage process is considered relatively permanent. Since LTM storage has, supposedly like all storage points in nature, a finite amount of space in which to work, the INPUT may be "moved" to a position from which easy "retrieval" is difficult or impossible completely. We will assume here since we are not actually pursuing a full course in cognitive psychology that our INPUT has no such retrieval problems, and therefore, a lengthy discussion of how to retrieve hard-to-find INPUT can be left to the cognitive psychologist. In our inferred model, the Stage 2a is then two-phase stages (STM and LTM) where the INPUT is stored. It is worth noting that LTM may or may not take place; if STM is lost prior to the beginning of the LTM processing (which begins at the end of the full 30 seconds), there simply will be no LTM, but this in no way should imply for our inferred model that the person who received the INPUT will not be able to respond to it. As we shall see, it may mean only that the response may ultimately be made but that the person cannot recall to which INPUT the response is being made. We shall see this more clearly as we complete the fourth stage of the model.

Stage 2b occurs simultaneously with Stage 2a. Stage 2b is defined here as the ESSENCE EXTRAPOLATION phase. This means that the semantic correlates (meaning) of the INPUT is somehow taken from the INPUT and is placed into action as that meaning. You experience this thousands of times daily when you realize that rarely do you recall just exactly every specific word or word's meaning in an INPUT. You "sample" that INPUT, you take the essence of what was said or read, and, through some process yet unknown, seek to put that essence into LTM. Now, how the connection is made between Stages 2a's second phase and Stage 2b's only phase is, again, still far from being known. We do have LTM for essences of meaning and, for some unknown reason, for issues of only the most minute importance. The point here is a fairly simple one: unless the person can derive some meaning (Stage 2b) from INPUT, there simply is not going to be any need for the use of TG in the ultimate four-stage model. TG in the model can survive without Stage LTM, but it cannot without Stage 2b. This will be apparent as we enter the TG phase.

Stage 3 (TG PROCESSING) involves the TG model proposed by Chomsky. It has three subphases; entrance to the TG model comes in from only one direction: through Stage 2b, the ESSENCE EXTRAPOLATION stage. In Stage 3, we are properly in Chomsky's realm—his book *Syntactic Structures* (1957) becomes our guide.

At the base of the TG model lies an "area" of processing Chomsky calls "deep structure." Deep structure uses what he calls "basic strings" of information to establish the most crude, basic beginnings of the sentence that will ultimately be produced in response to the INPUT. This phase is so basic that he wants the "basic strings" to be understood to be fundamentally neurological constructs (recall Katz's comment above that Chomsky needed not commit himself to neurology since mentalism would have just as easily accepted cardboard flip flops). Chomsky, however, quickly removes us from neurology by saying that these "basic strings" can for all practical purposes be called "kernel sentences." He has pulled us back into linguistics (and perhaps not a moment too soon since he is not a neurologist). The "kernel" is defined as the most basic sentence construction the world knows: the simple, present-tense declarative sentence—e.g., "Mike walks.", "I say.", "You do.", etc. As we shall see later, he has a special notation system to describe deep structure more specifically, but it may wait until we intuitively grasp his meaning.

Immediately above the "deep structure" lies a complex area which comprises the second phase of the TG system. This area is known as the "transformational rule" level and is the phase that actually converts the deep structure sentence into the final product one speaks or writes. In a simplified sense, what occurs first is that the deep structure's "simple, present-tense declarative sentence" is introduced to the matrix of rules one has acquired by using one's natural ability to learn the rules after actually having come in contact with an environment stimulating enough to make the person want to acquire the rules in the first place. Rules, according to Chomsky (1965), are not learned through simple operant or classical conditioning but are rather learned through a "creative approach." The rules vary in content and number from culture to culture with the more primitive cultures having fewer rules than the complex cultures. English, for example, is generally conceded to have eight or nine rules that any speaker of that language will eventually have to use. Russian has approximately the same number. The rules lie in what best could be described as a hierarchical grid with the least complex rule sitting in position one in that grid and the progressively more complex completing the hierarchy. The language user has only the innate capacity and desire to "fill in" the existing grid, which is apparently innately present. The actual rules the language user completes the grid which are not innate, but they are the "natural" rules of the language in question— e.g., their "goodness of fit" to the language makes them most economical and generalizably flexible at the same time. The order into which the rules fall is determined by the language user's experience with the language in question. As the deep structure sentence enters the grid, the speaker or writer asks the question regarding what is to ultimately be produced. Depending upon the answer, the deep structure sentence flows through the grid and is transformed by only those rules of relevance to the final output. Upon contact with each rule in this hierarchical grid, the sentence must either be accepted for transformation or must be "passed on" untransformed by that rule to be again accepted or passed on by the next rule in the hierarchy. Technically speaking, the deep structure of any sentence remains just that only as long as it has not yet been processed by a TG rule because it is sufficient in its simple, present-tense form to skip past all the rules in the hierarchy. Skipping past all the rules is not as rare as one might think since much of human communication does deal with the present-tense declarative nature of things, i.e., "The day is beautiful!", or "I am hungry.", or "The work is too hard." If the deep structure does undergo transformation(s), the "kernel" nature of the transformed sentence is still basically left completely intact. For example, someone saying "Why aren't there more beautiful days like this?" is actually basically still saying to us, "It is a beautiful day." We assume the latter despite the seeming greater complexity of the former and may, at times, ask or direct speakers or writers to "get to the point" by asking that a complex sentence be reduced to its least common meaning denominator. On many occasions, however, boiling an idea down to its deep structure level reduces the beauty of the language itself. Shakespeare's *Hamlet* could surely be rewritten "more to the point," but few, if any, read the play who did not understand the point before they started reading.

A case in point regarding conversion from the deep structure through a selected example set of rules is as follows. Assume you wish to say, "What did I say?" We start first by noting in the TG system that the deep structure component of this question is actually "I say what.", which is, of course, a simple, present-tense declarative sentence. Chomsky's specific notation (promised earlier) is as follows:

$$\text{Deep: (Q) + I + say + what + C.}$$

(Q) is a "question morpheme"; the Q is surrounded by parentheses, which make the Q morpheme inactive at this level of processing. C is a marker of tense and/or number which may be used in deep structure or in any transformational rule so desired. The "Q" always occurs at the first of any line, but C is perfectly free to "float" from place to place as it is needed. C is actually a term of rather "magical" power since it may become involved or may not in any line as it is needed. Its rather "magical" nature seems to weaken its descriptive usefulness and destroys any explanatory merit it might have. C simply exerts and functions upon command.

The deep structure sentence is not the same as the final product we desire, so we know that at least one transformational rule is needed here. In English, the first one we would encounter would be the rule that would transform the simple, present-tense declarative into a simple question. The rule can be written as follows:

$$T_{question}: Q + I + say + what + C?$$

This shows us that the parentheses are gone from around the Q, which means it is now "activated." The rest of the sentence is the same as was the deep structure. Admittedly, we do ask questions which sound like "I say what?" and equally admittedly most of us rarely realize the simple nature of what has been processed. But we still are not producing the sentence we wanted to produce in the first place, so at least one more rule must be necessary. It is as follows:

$$T_{wh}: Q + what + I + say + C?$$

This is the "wh" transformation rule and says simply (perhaps far too simply) that we may now move any "wh" word to the front of the sentence despite the position or may, if we must, create a "wh" word to put into the start of that sentence. This rule, like all others, does not explain how such an action occurs; it merely describes the action as occurring. "What I say?" sounds less grammatically sophisticated in one sense when compared to "I say what?", but this is more a cultural bias than a linguistic reality. But we are still short of our final goal, so we seek another rule. It is as follows:

$$T_{do}: Q + what + do + I + say + C?$$

The T_{do} rule, or "do" transformation rule, allows us to put the word "do" in any appropriate place it seems best to fit in the sentence. We now have "What do I say?", which is closer to our goal, but which still leaves us a bit short. The final TG rule needed here is as follows:

$$T_{affix}: Q + what + do + ed + I + say + C \rightarrow$$
$$Q + what + did + I + say + C?$$

The "affix" transformation allows us to add an "ed" to the auxiliary verb "do." It is now possible to state the final product as "What did I

50

say?" It is also not the least uncommon to hear a child say, "What doed I say?" as this rule is being perfected in practice.

Our production of "What did I say?" actually required five steps—one deep structure and four TG rules—to be able to reach the last step, which is known as the "surface structure" production phase and is properly labeled as the third phase of Chomsky's TG model. At any point in the above, we could have easily stopped sentence processing and jumped rapidly into the surface structure, which, of course, is the actual portion we see or hear in the language itself. For example, we could have left deep structure with what we had and never accepted processing by any TG rule and would have still produced a perfectly acceptable, grammatically accurate, simple, present-tense declarative sentence. We would simply have accepted a "pass" on each rule as we approached it. Figuratively, it could be shown as follows:

Surface Structure: "I say what."

T_{affix}: PASS

T_{do}: PASS

T_{wh}: PASS

$T_{question}$: PASS

Deep: (Q) + I + say + what + C.

Even receiving a "pass" on any of the above rules requires some small amount of mental processing time, but a "pass" in no sense could require as much processing time as actually undergoing the transformation through the use of the rule. It would also be just as easy for us here to have been processed through the $T_{question}$ and T_{wh} rules and then received a "pass" on all remaining rules. This is especially satisfying to see because it means that each of us is clearly able to say or write something beneath our ultimate capacity to use all the rules in our competence if we so choose, but in no way does it at the same time allow us to "pass" on rules we do not have in our knowledge of the language. Therefore, judging a person as a "less competent" language user just because s/he said. "What I say?" instead of "What did I say?" is a gross error in Transformational logic since we do not know whether the person voluntarily chose to "pass" rules s/he fully understands and did not feel like using at that moment because of need to save time or because of lack of reinforcement from his or her immediate language community. It brings Chomsky's point that performance and competence are not necessarily the same home to us more clearly than when we first saw it.

Once the rules of the language are "learned," the hierarchy remains fixed but generally flexible enough to withstand any necessary changes in the language's structure. For example, we can see the very same hierarchy used again from above with now a new sentence which does not require all five processing steps to reach surface structure. We wish to say "Does Mike smoke?". We proceed as follows:

Surface Structure: "Does Mike smoke?"
T_{affix}: Q + do + es + Mike + smokes + C? →
      Q + does + Mike + smoke + C?
T_{do}: Q + do + Mike + smokes + C?
T_{wh}: PASS
$T_{question}$: Q + Mike + smokes + C?
Deep: (Q) + Mike + smokes + C.

We can see here a "pass" on the T_{wh} rule and, finally, C's use in the T_{affix} rule to save us from the embarrassment of non-agreement in tenses between the auxiliary verb "does" and the main verb "smoke." The processing time for this sentence would probably be less than for our previous example since the two sentences are comparable in length and the latter uses one less transformational rule. Being processed through a rule is more time-consuming than taking a simple "pass." It would seem logical that taking a "pass" at the lower, simpler level of rules would save less time than taking a "pass" at the higher, more complex levels, but this is not an empirically proven fact—yet. A word of caution might also be added here regarding the making of cross-cultural comparisons/conclusions solely on the basis of number of rules used in a language. Two cultures whose languages have exactly the same number of rules may be decidedly different in complexity regarding structure/function since we know that the content and hierarchy defining any language's rules depend upon that culture's needs both past and present. It most probably is safe, however, to say that a language which has only four or five rules is "usually" not as sophisticated as a language with more rules. A case in point is our use of the two examples above; neither goes beyond four or five rules, and yet we have sophistication. Still, since English has eight or nine rules, it is obvious we can surpass the sophistication of "What I say?" with little effort on our part. A culture whose language uses fewer rules than English or Russian can apparently survive at that level of language processing quite nicely or would be trying to develop the rules it needed. Whether English or Russian (or any of the world's many other equally complex languages) goes beyond eight or nine rules in the future is pure speculation. We will recall from Chapter 1 that G. A. Miller cites the normal human memory span as being effectively "seven plus or minus two" units. Whether a TG rule is a "unit" is perhaps debatable, but Miller's point is still clear. How many TG rules a language can actually build is not a simple question of asking a computer to "generate" all the rules it possibly can and then forcing the populace to commit those rules to memory. There must be a useful, workable limit to the number of rules per language. This is precisely Chomsky's (1957, 1965) argument used against the Taxonomic Linguists; they had pushed the demands upon human memory storage and retrieval of useful rules to almost infinity, e.g., there were different sets of rules for every different sentence, and the total number of producable sentences was virtually unknown. The PS rules in another language may have only the slightest, most coincidental similarity to any other language's rules. Similarity is not the issue for PS; it is the fact that languages do have rules—no more or no less. It is generally unnecessary to state that Chomsky's TG rules do not really explain anything but merely stand as descriptions which appear in a form making one question the symbolic notation system being used, e.g., what is (Q) in reality? No one would expect the reader to believe there is a real (Q) floating somewhere inside one's head. And yet (Q) is no less real for transformational grammarians than E in $E = MC^2$ is for the theorists who invented the atomic bomb. If Chomsky had contended that (Q) or C or any other symbol was isomorphic with the neural underpinnings of that language system, we would perhaps have a serious complaint about his presumptuousness. Although he did say the system was neural, he also quickly said that the data was linguistic, which is a perfect description of (Q) or C or any other symbol or rule he uses. His system presumably defines a set of rules whose neural bases are still as unknown today as they were in 1957 and 1965.

What we can fault Chomsky's model on are in the areas of semantics and phonology. Chomsky's TG model is absolutely most easily geared to attack questions about a language's syntax, which deals with questions of word order in a sentence judged to be either grammatical or ungrammatical. Chomsky (1957, 1965) says meaning (semantics) is in "deep structure," but he fails to expand upon this to any extent. We will see in the material dealing with O. H. Mowrer in the chapter on S-R Behaviorism that the simple, present-tense declarative sentence buried in deep structure is a very natural area to which to attach meaning. Chomsky apparently does not want to use (or perhaps did not see) the implications of Mowrer's model, which precedes Chomsky's by three years. We will not overlook the implications, however, as we pursue the writings of the Behaviorists. Regarding phonology, there seems to be nothing to say. Chomsky was not then and is apparently not now interested in phonology, which is part of descriptive linguistics. This is perhaps understandable since phonology is a part of the domain he would call "surface structure," and that domain was the least of his apparent interests. All of this puts Katz (1964) into something of a sad position considering the fact he concluded that Chomsky's model was a "sufficient" grammar accounting for the syntactic, semantic, and phonologic aspects of language. Chomsky's TG model may account for syntax, but even that is an open dispute for the Behaviorists.

Rather recently, McCawley (1968), Fillmore (1968), and Bloom (1970) have gone into greater depth regarding the "deep structure" aspects of TG. So as to separate their work from that of other transformational grammarians, they have used the phrase "case grammar" to describe their interests in how the deep structure itself is based upon rules that determine how the subject and verb in that simple, present-tense declarative sentence will interact. An analysis of the actual grammar here is unnecessary since so many linguistics books already do a very satisfactory job. In principle, it is interesting for us to note that Bloom's (1970) research seems to indicate a lack of consistency in how infants form cases and use them. The question to be asked is whether these "inconsistencies" are just that or whether there is actually yet a deeper level of analysis that must be made into the various deep structure functions. Science thrives on inconsistencies. In any case, calling "case grammar" a grammar, per se, seems a bit perfunctory. Perhaps it would better be considered a part of TG at a level TG did not originally care to explore. By labeling "case grammar" and actual "grammar" one receives the mistaken impression that it is a full-fledged grammar capable of standing in contrast to TG, which is far more sophisticated in its scope. The revelation that deep structure was itself possibly based upon rules came as early as the writings of Bever, Fodor, and Weksel (1965). These authors assaulted the work of M. D. S. Braine, an S-O-R Behaviorist, by saying that Braine's contention regarding the importance of the simple, present-tense declarative sentence was bogus because children and adults alike most probably had rules which underlie even that simple starting point. Although they rather effectively caught Braine off guard, as we shall later see, they also may have at least set the stage for Fillmore, McCawley, and Bloom to attack Bever, Fodor, and Weksel's own champion—Noam Chomsky himself.

As a point of review, you should recall that Chomsky's TG model actually occupied only the third major stage in the four-stage model being proposed. The production of the surface structure at the final phase of his TG model could easily be seen as the last phase of the entire model if one were to eliminate all of the fourth stage. After one has gone through all the TG rules, has not one done it all? Unfortunately, the answer is negative. Stage four in the total model will be referred to here as the OUTPUT/MEMORY RECHECK stage. We can easily enough understand the term OUTPUT. It means simply articulating orally or in writing the surface structure produced in the last phase in the TG model. This is a rather mechanical area for analysis purposes and is in the domain of speech theory and therapy, as well as the area known as "composition" in writing. What makes this fourth stage unique is the fact that MEMORY RECHECK has been added. It is contended here that the speaker or writer rechecks his/her memory storage (Stage 2a) as the OUTPUT is being made so as to monitor the correctness or "goodness of fit" of the OUTPUT. Such a feedback system keeps the OUTPUT relevant to what the person recalls of the original INPUT. Without such a feedback system, the speaker/writer could not efficiently proceed with his/her communication attempts. The proposed four-stage model would indicate that a person could successfully go through the first three major stages, and produce an OUTPUT, but then question the adequacy of the response because for some reason either the INPUT never went into LTM, did not complete STM, or was actually lost from LTM after some physically or psychologically oriented interference occurred. One could conceivably have an answer for a question that was never asked quite the way it was answered or one could make a response to a comment which has only a resemblance to the comment actually made in the second place. The Stage 2a memory coding processes might conceivably be in perfect working order and still allow the speaker or writer problems if the person who made the original INPUT appears to forget his/her comment while the person formulating an answer is rechecking an accurate memory storage during his/her OUTPUT. The answer was perfect, but the person who originally produced your INPUT cannot reinforce you because they have lost their own Stage 2a. A blank stare might be your only reward for a perfect OUTPUT/MEMORY RECHECK on your part.

If Chomsky's critics were upset with him in the late 1950s and early 1960s (as some are still quite upset today) because he separated the "langue" (competence in a pure language model) and the "langue parole" (language as it was seen or heard – the performance), then this proposed four-stage model should displease them even more because it actually goes not so much beyond Chomsky, but rather around and about him. Unlike taking Chomsky's model as the only significant portion in the communication process, this four-stage model wants to expand the language user. One can easily see how various language problems would at least descriptively fit into such a four-stage model as this one. For example, a person with problems in memory storage would not infrequently be in a position where the only way to know if the OUTPUT was correct or appropriate would be to closely watch the reactions of the person with whom one speaks or writes. Those with ESSENCE EXTRAPOLATION problems would possibly create incorrect deep structures, which could be followed by superb stage-three processing but finally followed with a disheartening stage-four MEMORY RECHECK, e.g., saying to oneself, "I knew I wasn't saying that right! I guess I really didn't remember." All processing stages could be perfectly intact and yet a child from a language culture using only three TG rules would find his/her OUTPUT laughed at by these children using eight or nine rules. The tasks of finding where the model believes learning disabilities, mental retardation, and brain trauma show their greatest disruptions would seem useful, immediate research goals. Questions regarding breakdown in the model due to disease, injury, and age are still very much in need of answers. Haunting theoretical questions exist in abundance. Does "case grammar" best fit into analysis at Stage 2b, ESSENCE EXTRAPOLATION, or does it better fit in the analysis of the deep structure itself as Chomsky defined that deep structure?

In a sense, it was Noam Chomsky himself in his book *Language and Mind* (1968) as cited by Dale (1976, pp. 102–103) who essentially calls us back to think about exactly what is being proposed. He says we have really three major goals facing us in any attempt to prepare a sufficient grammar. We must better define the basic unit of linguistic analysis we propose to use. The point is well made since all experimentation leads to data analysis. Are we defining the phoneme, the grapheme, the morpheme, the word, the sentence, or perhaps the paragraph as our basic unit? Ebbinghaus used CVCs and called each one a single unit. We are afforded no such luxury when using real language. We must define the biological components of the language system. This means an in-depth, continuous neurological analysis of the human central nervous system. This is a large order since the very basic questions that produced psychology as a science were related to questions of neurology/biology. These questions are in some cases no closer to being answered now than they were 100 years ago: defining consciousness, self, feelings, etc. We are to finally write the sufficient grammar, which takes into account all we know about points one and two above. We must conclude that Chomsky himself has not written what would appear to be a "sufficient grammar" since no one yet has defined the basic unit of analysis and no one knows the precise bioneurological principles involved. In that sense, only time will prove Chomsky right or wrong in what would appear to be his own "trial balloon." Following the 1957 publication of *Syntactic Structures*, he found an entire camp of theorists ready to tear his system apart by showing the system to be based upon false assumptions regarding the nature of man. We speak here of the Behaviorists and now turn our attention to them in the next chapter. The diagram below of the proposed four-stage model serves as our summary and the beginning point against the Behaviorist barrages.

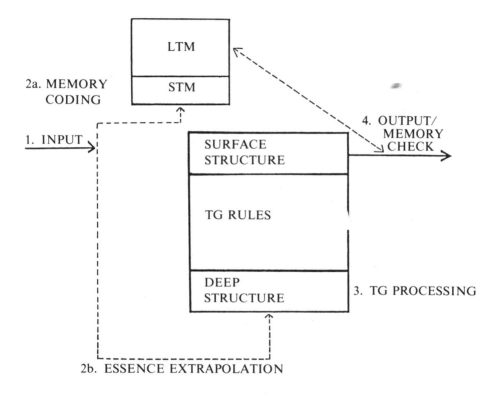

FIGURE 3.1: Four-stage language model with Chomsky's transformational grammar at the third stage.

This model is more useful to the student of language development than are any of the taxonomic grammars, but it can perhaps be challenged regarding its mentalistic origins and its apparent inefficiency regarding the handling of semantics and phonology. Perhaps the Behaviorists can assist us in resolving these short-comings, or perhaps they will dismantle our model and start again. We will surely see the Behaviorists take aim at the concept of the "langue," which our four-stage model is based upon (or at least strives to define more accurately), but we also see the Behaviorists differ substantially among themselves as to just how much emphasis each proposed model should have upon the "langue-parole."

References

Bever, T., Fodor, J., and Weksel, W. (1965). "Theoretical notes on the acquisition of syntax: A critique of 'contextual generalization.'" *Psychological Review, 72* (6), 467–482.

Bloom, L. (February, 1970). *Semantic Correlates in Language Acquisition.* Paper presented at the Conference on Research in the Language of the Mentally Retarded. University of Kansas.

Bloomfield, C. (1938). "Linguistic aspects of sciences." *International Encyclopedia of Unified Science,* Chicago (11231).

Broadbent, D. E. (1957). "A mechanical model for human attention and memory." *Psychological Review, 64,* 205–215.

Chomsky, N. (1957). *Syntactic Structures.* The Hague: Mouton.

Chomsky, N. (1965). *Aspects of the Theory of Syntax.* Cambridge, Massachusetts: MIT Press.

Chomsky, N. (1968). *Language and Mind.* New York: Harcourt.

Dale, P. S. (1976). *Language Development* (2nd Ed.). New York: Holt.

Dixon, R. (1963). *Linguistic Science and Structure.* The Hague: Mouton.

Fillmore, C. (1968). "The case for case." In E. Bach and R. Hams (Eds.), *Universals in Linguistic Theory* (1–88). New York: Holt.

Hockett, C. F. (1948). "Biophysics, linguistics, and the unity of science." *American Scientist, 36,* 556–572.

Katz, J. J. (1964). "Mentalism in linguistics." *Language, 40* (2), 124–137.

McCawley, J. D. (1968). "The role of semantics in a grammar." In E. Bach and R. T. Hams (Eds.), *Universals in Linguistic Theory* (124–169). New York: Holt.

– 4 –

S-R BEHAVIORISM

Empiricism vs. Rationalism/Mentalism

In the preceding chapter we discovered that Transformational Grammar (TG) had essentially been conceived through the use of the philosophical approach known as rationalism/mentalism. We saw Chomsky and Katz defend the model against predictable criticisms, but we did not actually see the criticisms as such. The criticisms come from the awakening of psychologists, not linguists, who will be classified as belonging to the Learning Theory/Conditioning Camp attributed to I. P. Pavlov in Chapter 1 of this book.

Before looking at specific positions, it is necessary to understand the philosophical assumptions underlying the "scientific method," which is supposedly the basis of the Learning Theory/Conditioning Camp.

First, it is assumed that the principles proposed by the British Empiricists (starting with John Locke and progressing through modern complex statistical/computer analysis) are still quite acceptable today. These principles essentially can be reduced to the general guideline statement that a scientist is allowed to accept as proof only that which is verifiable through the senses, e.g., that which is seen, heard, tasted, touched, or detected by smell. Second, it is assumed that the sensory data one is using for proof will be gathered, categorized, and interpreted.

The scholar/scientist is placed into a specific problem-solving approach which has both good and bad features. One's research is usually not going to be ambiguous in its appearance because all the terms and processes are operationally defined. Yet, the very act of using operationalism means that some terms and processes will be defined in an apparently very artificial fashion. "Learning" is equal to that observable performance which is the direct result of practice. By using the five steps, we may replicate any study we can afford to try, but the study may appear quite trivial since it attempted to choose as its topic only that aspect of behavior which is controllable. There may appear to be no need to re-run a study which so carefully pursued knowledge of the "tip end of a gnat's eyelash." Another problem centers around the question of just how many of these very small but highly scientific studies must one accumulate before one says that all is known that can be known about a process taken as a total process. A perfect case in point is in the writings of Bloomfield in the late 1930s as seen in Katz (1964, p. 125):

> . . . we can distinguish science from other phases of human activity by agreeing that science shall deal with events that are accessible in their time and place to any and all observers (strict behaviorism) or only with events that are placed in coordinates of time and space (mechanism), or that sciences shall employ only such initial statements and predictions that lead to definite handling operations (operationism) or only terms as are derivable by rigid definition (physicalism).

Katz (1964), ironically, prefers to interpret this statement as not being a limitation upon investigation because Bloomfield has also said on page 231 of his 1938 book (according to Katz, 1964, p. 125):

> These several formulations (behaviorism, mechanism, operationism, and physicalism), independently reached by different scientists, all lead to the same delimitation, and this delimitation does not restrict the subject matter of science but rather charcterizes its method.

But here specifically lies the problem. How can a scientist pursuing the truth of an issue believe, in any sense, that Bloomfield has in his above paragraphs freed him/her to grasp large "chunks" of areas to explore? Bloomfield clearly does not say that any scientist can study any given "portion" of an area s/he wishes. All he says is that the issue, just the issue, is open for investigation. This brings us to the crossroads of a dilemma. If a scientist pursues an area, that pursuit will undoubtedly be in small, measured, ultraconservative steps. The findings will be small, measurable, and perhaps seemingly trivial. Psychology's Behaviorism accepts this as par for the course and trusts that ultimate truth will come by adding up the small pieces. The Learning Theory/Conditioning Camp accepts Behaviorism. Innateness Camp scholars (see previous chapter) are not willing to accept Behaviorism's slavish adherence to small, measured moves since the Innateness Camp, as especially can be seen through its use of rationalism/mentalism, wants to see far, far more of the holistic process in language; and frankly, believes that perhaps the sum of all Behaviorism's "small pieces" may never add up to anything of significance. As Katz (1964) clearly explains, rationalism/mentalism wishes to, in a sense, "get on with it" and is willing to shake loose the bounds of empiricism at times if making a bold move, e.g., Chomsky's model ultimately makes a major breakthrough. Behaviorism, too, is quite interested in making "breakthroughs," but the definition of "how" is quite different from rationalism/mentalism's approach. A "breakthrough" comes only after hours of tedious empirical research produces a novel hypothesis which, after being tenaciously empirically pursued, proves to be the door to a new field of investigation. Behaviorism says its critics who use rationalism/mentalism lack caution. Behaviorism's critics say it moves too slowly and often down dead-end streets. Let us turn our attention to S-R Behaviorism's contributions to the Learning Theory/Conditioning Camp, and then let us think about the major issue of whom we agree with regarding an approach to language development and function.

The S-R Behaviorists' Assumptions

The assumptions underlying S-R Behaviorism have been reviewed in Chapter 1. The reader is referred to that chapter to prepare for a better understanding of the positions cited below. By no means are O. H. Mowrer and B. F. Skinner the only S-R Behaviorists with an apparent interest in language development and function. They are very probably the two best known authors in the field and are representative of their respective lines of thought today for their followers. Ironically, both Mowrer and Skinner's efforts occurred in the 1950s, and neither has written pointedly toward this field since that time. By no means may we merely assume either has actually lost interest; their behavior has simply decreased regarding the addressing of issues in this field. Was the behavioral decline due to a lack of reinforcement, or was it due to their individual beliefs that enough had been said. For Mowrer, the lack of reinforcement may have been the cause. For Skinner, perhaps assuming he believed he had said enough would be the wiser course. The reader should keep these questions "in mind" as we proceed.

O. H. Mowrer and First vs. Second Signal System Conditioning

We saw in Chapter 1 that I. P. Pavlov had clearly proposed a "second signal system" to account for language function, which his "first signal system" clearly could not do with its rather detailed principles of classical conditioning. Mowrer (1954), writing three years before Chomsky produced *Syntactic Structures* apparently chose to either reject or at least ignore Pavlov's advice by using the first signal system as the "launch point" in the battle to understand language outside the Human Verbal Learning and Innateness Camps' domains.

To fully appreciate the definition of the first signal system, one should read I. P. Pavlov's own works, e.g., *Lectures on Conditioned Reflexes* (1928), or pursue Chapter 3 of Hilgard and Bower (1975). For our immediate purposes, we may define the first signal system in general terms as being that process which occurs when some type of "neutral" cue (meaningless written or oral word, sound, or visual stimulus pattern) is presented in some contiguous manner (associated with) a stimulus pattern which is not neutral. If this association is rigorously defined, we can see five separate patterns develop. They are as follows:

1. *Traditional or classic classical conditioning:* This pattern presents the neutral cue to be called a "conditioned stimulus" (or CS) so that one-half a second elapses following the termination of that CS and the onset of the non-neutral stimulus pattern from now on to be called the "unconditioned stimulus" (or UCS). The CS and UCS may vary in regard to time, length, and intensity or quality, but the one-half second interstimulus gap is always the same.

2. *Delayed classical conditioning:* This pattern has the CS preceding the UCS in such a fashion as to let the last one-fourth of a second of the CS overlap the first one-fourth of a second of the UCS's presentation. Aside from this, the CS and UCS are allowed to vary in length of time, intensity, or quality as is so desired.

3. *Trace classical conditioning:* The CS again precedes the UCS, but this time the length of the time gap between the termination of CS and the onset of the UCS is greater than one-half second. There is theoretically no limit on how long the gap may be, but it is safe to say that the association between CS and UCS becomes progressively harder to establish as the gap's length is increased. As the gap length is increased, the probability that unwanted associations will occur systematically increases. For example, if a CS is defined as the word "skunk" and the UCS is some pungent odor, separating the end of the CS from the beginning of the UCS means that any other word of a neutral nature may appear between "skunk" and that UCS. If the interfering word is closer to the UCS than is "skunk," the word "skunk" may never be paired with the odor.

4. *Simultaneous classical conditioning:* The CS and UCS are presented for the same length of time, at exactly the same time, causing a perfect overlap between the CS and the UCS. The presence of two signals at one time serves little communicative use, and the person involved cannot attend to both signals at the same time. So, attention is generally shifted back and forth from CS to UCS and back again if the CS is attended to at all.

62

5. *Backward or reversed:* This is the last of the first signal system's association types. In this type, the UCS actually precedes the CS and, therefore, puts the CS at a distinct disadvantage since the onset of the CS does little but tell the person that the UCS has been terminated (usually for at least one-half a second).

If the preceding five patterns are ranked for difficulty of causing an association between the CS/UCS, the order from least to most difficult is (a) traditional classical conditioning, (b) delayed, (c) trace, and (d) simultaneous and backward classical tied for most difficult. If resistance to extinction is what is produced in the form of behavior that persists after reinforcement is withdrawn (in this case, the reinforcer is always the UCS), then the most to the least resistant association to extinction fall into the following order: (a) traditional or classic classical conditioning, (b) delayed, (c) trace, and (d) simultaneous and backward tied for least resistant. What is usually graphed in either learning the association (acquisition) or trying to reduce the behavior caused by such an association now left unreinforced (extinction) is the strength of the conditioned response (CR), which is produced by the CS as that CS gains or looses its association with the UCS. For any of the five types of classical conditioning acquisition or for extinction, the general curve shapes are as follows:

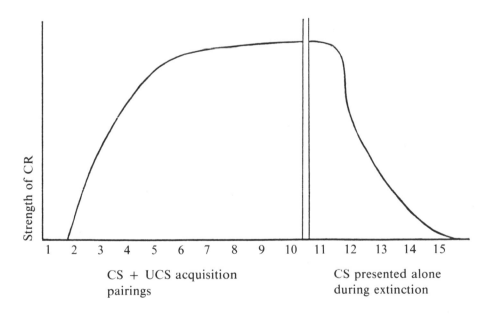

FIGURE 4.1

If we assume above that the CS is our word "skunk" and the UCS is a foul odor, our pairings of the CS and UCS would produce a CR (your reaction to the CS) which would grow as seen above on the acquisition side. You can easily see that the strength of CR grows rapidly, or, we could say, the growth is negatively accelerated. It grows rapidly at first and then progressively less so. When the actual odor (UCS) is withheld, the process of extinction begins with the observable s-shaped decline in the CR. If we at some point in extinction reintroduce the UCS, the extinction ceases, and relearning of the CS/UCS association progresses again to some point where we decide to start extinction a second time by again withdrawing the UCS, and so on. Admittedly, the above does not cover all the complexities of the first signal system, but it will meet our needs quite nicely regarding O. H. Mowrer's (1954) proposal, which now becomes our chief interest.

Mowrer's entry into the field of language development came as something of a surprise to many S-R Behaviorists simply because they, as a group, had had no particular interest in language. Mowrer was aware of this and seemed to be groping for a starting point in his article "The Psychologist Looks at Language" (1954), when he cites Bloomfield's 1938 criticism of psychology's seemingly total lack of interest in language phenomena. Mowrer, interestingly, does not correct Bloomfield by citing work done from the late 1800s through 1954 in the Human Verbal Learning Camp. Rather, he picks Bloomfield's comment as a starting point to launch his own model, which will be based on the one thing Ivan Pavlov asked his followers not to use—the first signal system.

Mowrer assumes from the start that there are acutally four types of communication possible. They are the "thing-thing," "sign-thing," "thing-sign," and "sign-sign" types. The "thing-thing" type occurs when an "action" is associated contiguously with a second "action." For example, if you bump into a bookshelf, the chances are good the shelf and the books on the shelf will react (communicate) with you by perhaps falling or causing you at least to shift your attention to them to see if falling will occur. There is nothing "symbolic" in any sense here; lower animals can engage in this type of "communication" as easily as humans. Still, it qualifies as being important to us because it readily can demonstrate the first signal system in so much as the first action has undoubtedly produced cues (sounds) which can act as CS's which may be associated with the second action in the "thing-thing" sequence. We can see that the second "thing" must produce some kind of action which makes the stimuli from that second action take the form of a UCS. If this did not happen, the first action's cues (CS's) would only be associated with the second action's stimuli (more CS's). If you review the

64

five-part definition of first signal system conditoning presented above, you will see no example in which conditioning first occurred solely based upon one CS's being associated with a second CS. (The reader should quickly note here that not all learning theorists necessarily limited themselves to the first signal system's dictates, e.g., E. C. Tolman (1932) made himself famous by proposing S-S learning (sign-gestalt) where for all practical purposes the S-S could be read as CS-CS.) If we return to our bookshelf, we can see Mowrer's point. Assuming that bumping the shelf caused a "rattling" sound to occur which was followed one-half second later by the sharp pain of a book's crashing upon your head, the CS becomes the "rattling" sound, and the UCS becomes the pain itself. Naturally, we could just as easily use any cue for the CS as long as the CS begins as meaningless (neutral) and can be learned as a "signal" predicting or recalling the presence of the UCS. We can see that from the five definitions of the first signal system conditioning that the strongest "thing-thing" association could occur using traditional classical conditioning and that the strength of the connection would rapidly weaken as we drop from delayed to reversed and/or simultaneous classical conditioning. There is little question here that Mowrer's point is easily verified; after all, Pavlov's entire first signal system model is based on just such associations as exemplified above but, of course, using strict laboratory controls. "Thing-thing" communication is not Mowrer's chief interest; he searches for bigger game.

In "sign-thing" communication, Mowrer assumes more his own line of thought. If "sign" is defined specifically as a word of any language and if the "thing" is defined, as above, in the form of an action's stimuli, it should be possible by analogy to "thing-thing" communication for us to produce a "sign-thing" communication which helps us lighten our burden of so many "things" to carry. Making the burden lighter is precisely what Mowrer proposes to do. He speaks of the ultimate purpose of any language being in the amount of "inertia" that language can produce. Here the reader needs to exercise caution; "inertia" is a very specific term as Mowrer uses it. He refers not to the idea of creating a human population of indolent people. He refers to making the communication process as free of unnecessary elements as is possible. For example, if we can teach a person the meaning of the word "duck" without continually having to produce a falling book from a library's shelf, then one has succeeded in lightening the communication burden. Let us return to our library and its falling books to pursue this problem. In the "thing-thing" form of communication, the cues produced by the rattling of a bookshelf were followed by the actual falling of a book or two, which acted as pain producing stimuli. The order of events was "thing" precedes "thing" or CS precedes UCS. In "sign-thing" communication, we can still easily call the CS a set of cues that will alert us to the presence of a UCS, but here the CS becomes a word rather than a rather natural set of stimuli such as cues produced by a rattling bookshelf. The point is crucial; "signs" are arbitrary, symbolic constructions which may act as CSs, whereas cues produced by a rattling bookshelf are not arbitrary or symbolic in any sense. The rattling phenomena does not actively symbolize its own rattling behavior because there is no device present to construct any element of arbitrariness. Now if we propose to place the word "duck" as a sign into the sequence of events, we could easily establish a strong contingency between that word and the pain of receiving a falling book, but this time we have a symbolic CS preceding a UCS. The association built between "duck" and the pain could be established using any of the first three methods in teaching first signal system conditioning, but, for efficiency's sake, we would be best advised to use the classic/traditional technique. Inertia is produced because the word "duck" is generally going to mean the same thing, e.g., produce the same CR of jumping back or covering one's head, no matter what environment the person finds himself or herself in. The specific rattling which set the specific cues (things) in motion on the bookshelf may, however, produce far less generalizability for itself because those cues are very definitely not arbitrary or symbolic in any sense. The CS "duck" becomes more useful to the person in the general press of daily affairs because of its symbolic nature. Mowrer would seem to have a problem in a small sense, since the CS "duck" is not just paired to the pain of falling objects for most of us. The "duck" may also be a CS producing the CR of looking up to see a feathered fowl pass. The problem of having one CS ("duck") associated with two very different UCSs is less serious than it might seem and in no sense violates Mowrer's claims. The context in which the CS is produced is the critical saving grace. Ones yelling, "Duck!" while walking through a dimly lighted cave is rarely going to cause the listener to cast an upward glance as in hopes of bagging ones limit. In a duck blind, one rarely needs to fall to the floor to protect oneself from falling ducks. Behavioral confusion is apparently a relatively direct function of how many different UCSs are attached to a single CS presented within a given environmental setting.

Mowrer's third form of communication is "thing-sign" communication and apparently forces us into a Pavlovian "backward" or "reversed" first signal system paradigm. The UCS (thing) precedes the CS (sign). This paradigm has already been cited as producing very poor contiguous associations. The signal (CS) is redundant. The UCS has already passed before the CS appears. Frankly, having the CS follow the

UCS simply tells the person that the UCS is over. Since CSs serve best to tell us that something of significance is coming, reversed conditioning is ineffective. In the case of our rattling library bookshelf and the pain of the falling book, to detect the CS proves of little value to our throbbing head. An exception to this exists, however, if the UCS is highly negatively traumatic, e.g., all possible CSs following the UCS are heightened in associative potential. This would be quite rare at best. Positive UCSs followed by CSs yield even worse associations than do negative UCSs associated with their CSs. If the pain of a falling book (UCS) has been felt, the CS "Duck!" is not totally ambiguous. If an actual feathered fowl has just passed before one yells "Duck!", little real ambiguity results. From the nature of the difficulty of conditioning reversed associations, it should be fairly easy for the reader to conclude that the most effective way to teach an association is by putting the CS in front of the UCS rather than behind it despite the correlated increase in CS ambiguity which may occur if the same CS is associated with different UCSs.

The ultimate level of communication is the "sign-sign" form; it creates the greatest inertia. In this form, one CS precedes a second CS but only after the second CS in the sequence has first been paired with a UCS that has resulted in "sign-thing" communication. For example, assume the word "Hey!" (CS_2) occurs one-half second before you hear the word, "Duck!" (CS_1). If CS_1 had been associated in a "sign-thing" order to the UCS of pain produced by a falling book, the CS_2, with repeated pairings with CS_1, will begin to act as a signal telling the person to prepare to receive the painful UCS after the word "Duck!" has first been heard. Symbolically, the chain of associations looks as follows:

$$CS_2 + CS_1 + UCS$$
"Hey!" "Duck!" pain of falling book

In this chain, it would be a very safe assumption that the strength of CS_2 to "elicit" a CR would probably be less than the strength of CS_1 since CS_1 is so much closer to the UCS. Such is indeed the case. "Hey!" is less directly connected to the UCS than is the signal "Duck!". Mowrer uses some very specific terminology here to indicate the flow of the associative strength. The actual direction of the flow is from right to left if we move from the strongest to the weakest end. He uses the phrase "first order conditioning" to describe the connection made between the CS_1 and UCS. "Second order conditioning" describes all other associations e.g., CS_2's connecting to CS_1, a CS_3's connecting to CS_2, a CS_4's connecting to CS_3, etc. As we move from the UCS to the left, we engage also in the dual processes known as "predication" and "attenuation." Predication specifically refers to the process of transferring meaning from the UCS through the CSs. Attenuation describes the process of how predication weakens as it flows from right to left. In our example, the strength of CS_2 is directly dependent upon the strength of CS_1, which is directly dependent upon the strength of the UCS. We might pause briefly to note that it is possible in this "sign-sign" communication pattern for the UCS to precede the CSs in question, e.g., UCS + CS_1 + CS_2. In this case, "Duck!" would precede, not follow "Hey!". "Hey!" would be in CS_2's position and would undoubtedly be far weaker than in the case of CS_1 "Duck!". We should be aware that this arrangement of UCS + CS_1 + CS_2 is just an extended case of reversed classical conditioning and is, consequently, not going to produce a "sign-sign" communication pattern nearly as strong as one where CS_2 + CS_1 + UCS is used. By using our knowledge of the five first signal system paradigms, we can safely say that the "thing-thing," "sign-thing," and "thing-sign" communication patterns are all under Mowrer's phrase "first order conditioning." Only when two CSs are being associated (even in a chain longer than two CSs) can we use the phrase "second order conditioning." In the case where we have CS_2 + CS_1 + UCS, both predication and attenuation move from right to left in second order conditioning. In the case of UCS + CS_1 + CS_2, both predication and attenuation move from left to right.

To summarize the above points using the example, "Hey! Duck!", we may conclude the following:

1. If "Duck!" has not been in association with a UCS, then pairing "Hey!" with "Duck!" will produce no meaning for "Hey!" because the association of the two CSs has no reinforcer (UCS) to support it.

2. If "Duck!" has been associated with, in this case, a painful UCS, "Duck!" itself becomes a CS through the process of being "sign-thing" (first order/predicated) conditioned to the UCS.

3. If "Hey!" is associated by "sign-sign" (second order/predicated) conditioning to "Duck!", which has undergone first order conditioning, then "Hey!" will derive some meaning from "Duck!", albeit this meaning will be weaker than the meaning of "Duck!". Therefore, "Hey!" may produce a general sense of alertness in the listener, but it should not necessarily produce actual ducking behavior as should the word "Duck!".

4. The process of transferring meaning from the UCS to its CSs usually, but not always, occurs in a right to left hand direction and is specifically known as predication. As predication progresses, attenua-

tion increases. "Hey!" receives less of the falling book's produced pain than does "Duck!".

5. All the above points fall under Pavlov's first signal system.

The fifth point may cause the reader to ask if simultaneous classical conditioning plays any role in Mowrer's system. Apparently its role is overlooked. It would offer Mowrer the embarrassment of trying to determine whether first or second order conditioning was occurring or if something altogether different from first and second order conditioning were at hand. For example, let us assume that the pain of the falling book, the word "Duck!" and the word "Hey!" all reached the listener simultaneously and with equal attention-holding force. What does the person attend to—especially if the time period is too short to allow attention shifts among the two CSs and one UCS? In the world of daily events, it is very highly improbable that such an event would occur in the first place. It is so improbable, Mowrer cares not to pursue it. He has a good point.

So far, Mowrer has actually stayed on safe grounds, and his analyses may make us want to ask if Pavlov really meant to throw out the first signal system as a sufficient explanation of language development. Mowrer uses the sentence "Tom is a thief." to illustrate his system using a simple, present-tense declarative sentence. The process is lengthy for him. He shows first order conditioning/predication occurring between "thief" (CS_1) and the act of our experiencing thievery (UCS). Second order conditioning/predication/attentuation all occur as the meaning of "thief" (CS_1) is transferred to "Tom" (CS_2) through the intransitive verb "is," which effectively acts as a plus sign between CS_2 and CS_1. Time is spent discussing how "Tom" could be associated with "thief" and any other number of CSs without causing us problems in defining "Tom." Mowrer specifically sees two Toms: one is a linguistic Tom, and the other is the physical Tom. He uses the symbol r_T to denote the linguistic Tom where "r" is an internal reaction to "T," which stands for Tom. The physical Tom is symbolized as R_T, where R is an outwardly observable reaction to Tom as a real, living person. It is, therefore, quite conceivable that a person can have many "internal" reactions to Tom as he "exists on paper." For example, we could label Tom with the term "thief," with the term "priest," with the term "pauper," and perhaps even with the term "poet" and have little, if any, conflict in our perception of the linguistic Tom. But we might also feel some conflict if our concept of "priest" does not allow us to believe that thievery is part of the priesthood. In such a case, Mowrer falls back upon R_T to save us undue stress. Perhaps Tom has been labeled a thief despite the fact he is a priest. Perhaps the reality of it all is just that: he is a thief. We can still see R_T and forgive him a host of conflicting labels. "Oh, yes, Tom is a thieving priest, but if you really knew him as I do . . ." We must note that C. E. Osgood (1963) does not accept Mowrer's thinking, which Mowrer labels as the "semantic mediation" process. Osgood sees the label as being the "real" part of anyone. For example, you see Tom through the cloak of his labels; if any of the labels conflict, the conflict is quite stressful to the observer: "How could you steal, Tom? You're a priest!" Resolution of the conflict occurs if a label is removed. "Despite the fact you once were a thief, Tom, you are an exceptionally fine priest today." We should note that perhaps no conflict would exist for a person if s/he firmly believed that all priests were actually thieves in the first place. "Of course, Tom is a thieving priest! Are there other kinds?" Perhaps both Mowrer and Osgood take stands which need some tempering. Perhaps the labels do dominate our thinking for a greater period than Mowrer would admit, but then Osgood should accept the fact that the real, physical person eventually does separate himself/herself from those labels if the conflict caused by the labels is too great. Perhaps the question of r_T and R_T is a moot issue to Mowrer's system as a whole. Is there more significant criticism?

Unfortunately, the answer is in the affirmative. Mowrer's "Tom is a thief." allows the transfer of meaning through the use of the intransitive verb "is." We can rather easily see a problem if we substitute a transitive verb into the sentence.

Let us assume the sentence reads "Tom shot a thief." This is a simple, past-tense declarative sentence with the transitive verb being "shot." If we accept Mowrer's analysis as used in "Tom is a thief.", we see no initial stage problems. "Thief" can act as the CS, and the UCS must again be natural. So far, it reads as CS_1 ("thief") plus UCS (action). If "Tom" is to qualify as CS_2, we are going to have to engage in second order conditioning (CS_2 "Tom" plus CS_1 "thief"). The problem is quite apparently in the use of the "plus" (for "is") versus the use of "shot." In no sense can we simply predicate the meaning of "thief" if "shot" is used since the sentence does not now say that the meaning of CS_1 can be directly transferred to CS_2. Police occasionally shoot thieves. Tom has done so, so maybe Tom is a policeman. Thieves also occasionally shoot thieves, so, since Tom shot a thief, perhaps Tom is a thief after all. Or perhaps Tom does not qualify as any of the above. Granted, Tom's having shot a thief does connect him to "thief" in a sense, but in no way is he necessarily equated to the meaning of thief. We see similar problems if we say that "Tom knows a thief." or that "Tom hangs thieves." Considering the fact that typical daily use of the language is filled with past-tense sentences we must admit Mowrer's model has a small problem. He does not solve it in his article, nor does he do so at a later date. He also does not solve the problem of a more subtle nature dealing with the use of the present-tense intransitive verb versus the past-tense intransitive verb. For example, "Tom was a thief." is closer in meaning to "Tom is a thief." than it is to "Tom shot a thief." Undoubtedly, second order conditioning occurs when the meaning of "thief" is transferred through "was" to "Tom," but somehow in that transfer we understand that something, perhaps a "debt to society," has been paid or that at least Tom quit doing the act that we really preferred him not to do. Mowrer does not account for this problem. Mowrer's model also falls short regarding the use of normal syntactic patterning as seen in languages which are very highly dependent upon inflectional endings rather than word order when it comes to expressing an idea, e.g., Russian or Latin. In Latin, "Mary hit Paul.", "Paul hit Mary.", or "Hit Mary, Paul." are equally acceptable to us as long as we understand the inflectional endings which direct the flow of action from one person to another. If Mary actually hit Paul, the inflectional endings will tell us despite the word order's appearance. Mowrer's system does not discuss the problem. In one respect, Mowrer's model could be criticized regarding its assumption that the major purpose of all second order conditioning is to cause "inertia," which was defined above as generally being that state of affairs which exists when communication has reached its ultimate level of efficiency and ease. He seems to be drawing a conclusion regarding the still heatedly debated "nature of man" issue, and, yet, he really has no empirical proof. If the purpose in developing language was to ultimately produce inertia, then people who were exceedingly good friends and knew each other's habits well should eventually talk only upon the rarest of occasions. Such is obviously not the case as casual observation shows us. But perhaps we are unfair to Mowrer. Perhaps the motive or reinforcement for talking (as we will see in B. F. Skinner's writings) is separate from the issue of efficiency altogether. If one wishes to deliver a message efficiently, one seeks just those words which make the message seem "to the point." On the other hand, producing large numbers of messages may have no bearing upon the efficiency of each message within the total; all the parts may be necessary despite their number if the full message is to be effectively presented. Good friends talk a great deal, not because they are inefficient; they speak often because they are prone to have many issues in common and perhaps most significantly because they can so efficiently transfer many messages in a relatively short time span. A message receiver's chronic need for reclarification or representation of any message (but especially ones of seemingly simple content to the speaker) is hardly reinforcing to that speaker and usually decreases efficiency.

The problem with Mowrer's model lies squarely in its lack of sufficiency. It does not address phonology and is, quite frankly, a model oriented toward semantics rather than syntax. If the semantic emphasis is credited as being a significant contribution, which is very probably true, we must remain mute regarding its virtue as a syntactic model. Mowrer has in no way accounted for either the variety of human sentence production nor for the process which underlies our seemingly immediate understandings of sentences vastly differing in syntactic structure, yet, which have the same general idea buried deep below their apparent surface dissimilarities. He seems to acknowledge the system's shortcomings toward the end of his article when he says that no language model is sufficient unless it has a complete method built into it for the analysis of semantics. The reader receives the impression that Mowrer has almost said that the purpose of the entire article was solely one of proposing a meaning analysis; this is quite surprising, since a careful reading of the article's introduction reveals no such specific direction. The article seems to simply begin by pursuing language as that "general phenomenon" referred to in Chapters 2 and 3 of this book. Aside from this, we can see strengths in what he says since there have been no challenges to the Pavlovian first signal system. Without some kind of concrete, physical experience (whether directly or vicariously through any of the mass media) first order conditioning simply cannot occur; if first order cannot, second order cannot. This principle could and should adorn the walls of all our nation's classrooms. As long as we avoid the sticky problem of the transitive verb and as long as we accept Pavlov's ideas as we look at the simple, present-tense intransitive verb declarative sentence, we are on solid ground.

We are on some solid ground with Mowrer. There is an enticing connection between O. H. Mowrer's model and that of Noam Chomsky. The two theorists did not use the same methodologies. By no means would the two theorists claim to have proposed models which overlap. That is precisely the point. Their models are very nicely, mutually compatible at the places where each is the weakest, e.g., Mowrer assists Chomsky on semantic deficiencies in Chomsky's model, and Chomsky provides Mowrer with the syntactic principles Mowrer never quite got around to addressing. The connection lies squarely in Chomsky's comments that "deep structure" is based upon the simple, present-tense declarative sentence and Mowrer's quite sufficient explanation of how meaning is transferred from thing to sign within that simple, present-tense declarative. Chomsky (1957, 1965) leaves us no doubt that "meaning" is in the deep structure processing area of his three-stage TG model. But it is also equally true that he does not even begin to describe the actual processes underlying the transfer of meaning; Mowrer cannot propose a "deep structure" analysis himself for his own model, because his model is not one that has multiple levels, such as is Chomsky's. So there we have it: the perfect connection and natural support point for a S-R Behaviorist and a Transformational grammarian. Let us see how this might work. In Chapter 3, we saw the syntactic transformations Chomsky's system could make with the deep structure sentence "(Q) + Mike + walks + C." The TG analysis then seemed to rather breezily skip into the various transformational rules, finally yielding a perfectly grammatical "Did Mike walk?" in surface structure. If we ignore the S-R Behaviorists' cries of dismay over our pushing Mowrer's "surface structure" analyzing model down into the dark recesses of the "neuro-logically-defined" deep structure, we can see that "walks" is actually CS_1 with the actually experienced action of walking being defined as the UCS. "Mike" is in CS_2's position and should receive predicated, albeit attentuated, meaning from transfer originating at CS_1. Mowrer's model can in no sense change the word order to make syntactic variation possible in surface structure since he, Mowrer, is dealing with the "surface structure" level when he does his semantic analysis. By agreeing at the start that language can be processed below the surface structure level, Chomsky has opened the door to our moving of Mowrer's model. It is extremely worthy of note that the "case grammarians," Fillmore (1968), McCawley (1968), and Bloom (1970), were and still are looking at the development of meaning within the deep structure, and, yet, they do not devote a reference to the possibility of an S-R Behavioristic answer to their problem. This casts rather strong support for the claim made in Chapter 1 of this book regarding the fact that linguists will be linguists and psychologists will be psychologists with neither party necessarily borrowing from each other nor perhaps seeing that there is really any-thing to be borrowed. Such problems lead some scholars to believe the one salvation scholarship may ultimately have is in the use of very sophisticated computer programs which can store data from many disci-plines and, on command, produce the common features all the data have despite the origin of that data. In no sense does this grant the com-puter scholastic potency; it merely grants the computer "King-of-the-Mountain" position for storage/retrieval efficiency for the type of data discussed above.

There is potentially considerable utility in the merger of Mowrer and Chomsky at the deep structure level. Assume that a child is missing the experience needed to produce a UCS stimulus pattern. Assume further that the teacher has required that a sentence of considerable syntactic complexity be produced as in an answer to a question the teacher has asked. Let us further assume the answer is produced but that it really seems awkwardly stated. If we assume that the semantic components of any sentence's deep structure interact with the TG rules, we could now see where the "awkwardness" may have come from; the meaning of the proposed answer at the very basic deep structure level was insufficient to assist the syntactic processing stages in the TG model. How, for example, do we know that we cannot grammatically say, "Did steak prefer John?" Our knowledge in deep structure processing clearly tells us we cannot have a "meaningful" situation where an inanimate "steak" "prefers" an animate "John" since steaks' actions are limited to lying in place while growing cold and decayed. "John" may also lie in one place and grow cold up to a point, but it is doubtful we will see him decay. He certainly has his ability to "prefer" things; he has produced actions (UCSs) demonstrating his ability to "prefer" on numerous occasions. Our responding student should and must "know" through the interaction of syntax and semantics that an immediate correction in the sentence production process is necessary if s/he starts to say, "Did steak prefer John?" A person who can say or write "Did steak prefer John?" and seriously believe this is a grammatical sentence does not have a syntax-related problem (at least not at this level of processing); it is a semantic-related issue. The "inferred four-stage model" proposed in Chapter 3 would neatly profit from placing Mowrer's model into the 2b ESSENCE EXTRAPOLATION Stage or at least into Chomsky's deep structure of TG PROCESSING. Unfortunately, the ultimate exploration of how Mowrer's model allows us to connect meaning to the 2a Stage, MEMORY CODING, and the fourth stage's MEMORY RECHECK remains unknown.

B. F. Skinner's Operant Conditioning

Better known by far for his contributions regarding the development of language than O. H. Mowrer, B. F. Skinner classifies himself yet today as an S-R Behaviorist. Skinner's work in operant conditioning became best known initially in his *Behavior of Organisms* (1938). Skinner stated in that book that he was not anti-Pavlov in any sense unless, of course, one was trying to use Pavlov to explain all aspects of all behavior. It was ironic that he held this position because he himself received just such a criticism from Chomsky (1959). Skinner in 1938 perceived classical conditioning as describing very adequately those aspects of behavior which were strictly reflexive. Operant conditioning was concerned with larger, molecular behaviors that involved such actions as arm/hand movement, leg/foot extension, talking, listening, writing, or virtually any other learned behavior that did not require itself to be limited to such atomistic concerns as seen in classical conditioning. Skinner rarely indulges in speculation about the workings of the central nervous system. Perhaps this avoidance is due to his having had to change a position in the early 1970s that he had cherished since at least 1938. In 1938, he had claimed that classical conditioning was under the domain of the "autonomic nervous system." Operant behaviors fell under the domain of the "peripheral nervous system," which controlled voluntary movements. It was a convenient and seemingly necessary distinction at that time since no one had ever operantly conditioned anything except simple key-pecking behaviors in pigeons or bar presses by rats under any form of laboratory control. Besides, such a splitting of the central nervous system made it a bit easier to believe classical and operant conditioning were indeed very separate forms of learning. We note here that few learning theorists accepted his rigid theoretical distinction between the two learning types. E. L. Thorndike (1898) had preceded Skinner with such a proposition that there were two forms of learning: one was called "classical" and one was labeled "connectionism," which definitely looks like operant conditioning in the Skinnerian sense 30 years before Skinner. Otherwise, Skinner could rarely find any major learning theorists who would agree to his distinction. Scholars in learning theory such as Clark Hull (1943) did not wish to split classical from operant; E. R. Guthrie (1952) and W. K. Estes (1950) said all learning was classical; there was no such thing as operant conditioning. K. S. Spence (1956), one of Clark Hull's most articulate followers and a contemporary of Estes (who was one of Guthrie's followers) leaned toward saying all learning was classical. With such prominent scholars taking issue with Skinner, one would assume he would have dismissed his position. He refused. Ironically, none of the scholars who agreed with Guthrie or Estes or Spence cast a vote in favor of O. H. Mowrer's interpretation of language development; nor did they cast a vote against Skinner's (1957) *Verbal Behavior,* which took the basics of *Behavior of Organisms* and combined them with some excellent empirically based operant conditioning research he had conducted across at least a 20-year time span. Skinner chose to describe, if not actually explain, language development, as if it all were based from beginning to end upon operant conditioning. Mowrer could have his first signal system in classical conditioning and see how he would best explain why he was trying to use a form of learning controlled by the autonomic nervous system to explain such complex behaviors as were seen in language learning. Skinner did not need to use Pavlov's warning about the futility of employing the first signal system as an explanation of language so he, Skinner, could dismiss Mowrer. Mowrer had "dismissed" himself by relying upon a form of behavior which had a neurological foundation that could control only such things as heart rate, blood pressure, and gastric secretions. Miller (1969) convincingly demonstrated operant control of heart rate, brain waves, blood pressure, and a host of other "autonomic-based" behaviors. In one sense that was a bit stress-producing for Skinner's assertions that classical and operant were vastly different systems, but on the other hand it also made an interesting supportive point for his *Verbal Behavior.* After all, Miller had put more things under operant control. Mowrer's (1954) work is not referred to in Skinner's *Verbal Behavior,* which did not appear until three years after Mowrer had stated his case. In order to understand *Verbal Behavior,* we must understand Skinner's eight operant conditioning paradigms, and we must define his basic five schedules of reinforcement with special emphasis being placed upon the first five schedules. Our reference for the eight paradigms comes from the synthesis of Skinner's work done by Hulse, Egeth, and Deese (1980, p. 18); our source for the five schedules will be Ferster and Skinner's (1957) *Schedules of Reinforcement.* Please keep in mind that the data presented in these sources is most usually based upon observations of behaviors other than verbal behaviors. First, we must see the eight operant paradigms.

Skinner believes that each of us finds him/herself in a position which can change from moment to moment. In some instances, we are asked to produce behavior, and in others we are asked to withhold our responses. In some settings, we will receive cues regarding what to do or not do. We will receive reinforcement of either a positive or a negative nature in all cases. Perhaps the easiest way to see all the paradigms is in this manner:

Paradigm Type	Nature of Cues	Reinforcement Type	Behavior Must Be
1. Reward Training	No Cues	Positive	Produced
2. Discrimination Training	Positive Cues	Positive	Produced
3. Escape Training	No Cues	Negative	Produced

Table continued

Paradigm Type	Nature of Cues	Reinforcement Type	Behavior Must Be
4. Avoidance Training	Negative Cues	Negative	Produced
5. Punishment Training	No Cues	Negative	Withheld
6. Discriminated Punishment Training	Negative Cues	Negative	Withheld
7. Omission Training	No Cues	Positive	Withheld
8. Discriminated Omission Training	Positive	Positive	Withheld

Assume a child walks up to you and says, "I'm lost! If you help me find my way home, my father will give you some money!" Clearly, the child is asking you to do something in a manner which is rather specifically laid out by the verbal cues present here. The cues appear to be quite positive; the words used are not in the least threatening and are actually quite promising (assuming you are interested in the money in the end of the offer). The child promises a positive reinforcer in the form of the money referred to during the verbal cuing. If you are to receive the reinforcement, you clearly must take the child home. You must produce, not withhold, efforts in order to be reinforced. If you do help, you are reinforced positively; if you cannot, you are simply left unreinforced. This child has put you into a discrimination paradigm. Assume the same child approaches a day later and says, "I'm lost again! If you don't help me find my home, I'll tell my father to have you arrested!" The child has provided you with some unfortunate but clearly negative cues; action is sought from you. If you do produce, the child promises not to harm you. The child has put you into an avoidance training paradigm. Assume a short time period passes before you see the child again. Assume this time that you start the conversation first by saying, "Well, we meet again! Today, I want you not to say a word to me about anything! I really didn't appreciate your trick you played last time!" You have provided what seems to be negative cues; you are asking the child to withhold verbal behavior. If the child does, you seem to be saying you will not punish him/her. If we read the chart, we find that this is a case of discriminated punishment training. During "round four" with this child, you and s/he meet on a street corner as s/he comes home from school and you from work. This time neither of you says a word; you stare blankly at one another. Finally, you give in and say, "Well, how are you today?" The child instantly screams, "Police!" The analysis of this meeting is a bit more complex than in the above examples. The child has, operationally speaking, provided you with no cues to prompt your question. You produced behavior anyway and were immediately punished for it. To remove this punishment, you apparently must withhold any comment (and should have apparently done so from the start). The child has you in a punishment paradigm; there is no warning, behavior must be withheld, and, if it is, you are free of punishment and are negatively reinforced for your withholding. The concept of "negative reinforcement" is a bit difficult to understand wherever it is used. Negative reinforcement refers to achieving a state of neutrality; it is freedom from pain and/or discomfort, but in no sense is it a "rewarding" state, e.g., no one has specifically given you anything positive in the form of a reward (positive reinforcer). There is nothing "happy" about being negatively reinforced; if, however, you can achieve a state of neutrality through being negatively reinforced, you may then be allowed to pursue something that is positively reinforcing. For example, if you do withhold further comment to the child in our fourth example, the child may simply walk away and leave you in a position to pursue something quite rewarding. It was mentioned above that this fourth example was a complex one. We have, so far, overlooked the fact that technically you had put the child into one of the eight paradigms when you asked the child how s/he was. Assuming you asked the question in a positive, friendly fashion, you were apparently expecting a response and were seemingly ready to positively reinforce such a response. Or, in other words, we could read this as "positive cue is given, promise of reward is present, and behavior is to be produced." You had put the child into a discrimination paradigm before the child let you know by his/her actions just exactly who really was in charge of the meeting. Exactly which paradigm one is in at any given moment is defined by the person's environment (the S-R Behavioristic assumption); how the person sees that environment is a joint junction of past training, sensory capacity, and the species specific/genetic predisposition of the person in question. Skinner (1974), in his book *About Behaviorism* repeatedly allows the use of "perception." However, he is interested only in what is finally produced or withheld and is not at all interested in the mental

78

processes which produced the behavior itself. This 1974 position is an interesting tempering of a rather blunt approach he proposes in Chapter 19 ("Thinking") of *Verbal Behavior* (1957). He states in that chapter that thinking is the same thing as behavior itself. He does not in 1957 give one the "freedom" to think one way and to perform another way as he seems to do in 1974. Still, his basic point is the same in 1957 and 1974: performance counts. This brings us to the next major contribution of the Skinnerian system: the systematic manner in which performance may be counted for S-R Behavioristic interpretation purposes.

It is impossible to "graph" anything in the eight conditioning paradigms unless one speaks strictly about behavior. That behavior is not only determined by the training paradigm itself. It is equally determined by the frequency of reinforcers involved in the paradigm. For example, on the intuitive level, let us say we are watching the behaviors of two six-year-old twins who have been placed into an avoidance training paradigm. The teacher says to each, "If you can't add this column of numbers correctly, I'll keep you during recess until you can!" If we assume the first and second twin dutifully perform but that the second twin is kept in during recess anyway, the chances are good that a similarly-stated threat will have a lesser impact upon the second twin. The reason for this is apparent; the first twin was reinforced (negatively in this case) and the second twin was not. Behavior in any paradigm increases as a direct function of the amount of reinforcement, quality of reinforcement, and, obviously from our above example, the frequencey of reinforcement. Quality and quantity of reinforcement are less well documented than is frequency of reinforcement, and at all times the "perception" of the reinforcement is critical as well (Premack, 1965). Ferster and Skinner (1957) have spent extended periods of research time demonstrating what the basic behavioral curve shapes are for the various schedules of reinforcement irrespective of quality or quantity considerations. Skinner's contention is that the basic curve shapes seen below are always going to appear generally as they do regardless of the type of behavior being operantly conditioned; they are "transituational." The curve shapes appear regularly for both the time when behavior is being learned and when behavior is declining due to lack of reinforcement. We refer to the gain in behavior through reinforced practice as "acquisition;" we refer to the decline in behavior caused by an absence of reinforcement during practice to be "extinction." On any graph, they are separated by a "double line bar." The "basic five" schedules are graphed below. We could use any example of any kind of behavior we wished, but let us choose behavior operationally defined as the number of times per trial a person says a plural noun in a sentence; we will assume the plural nouns are reinforced according to the following operational definitions:

1. *Continuous reinforcement* (CRF): Each time a plural noun is said it is immediately reinforced.

2. *Fixed ratio* (FR): The person must say a specifically experimenter-predetermined number of nouns before the person is reinforced, e.g., FR_5 means five plural nouns, FR_{15} means 15 plural nouns, etc.

3. *Variable ratio* (VR): The number of required plural nouns varies from reinforcing to reinforcing event, e.g., sometimes 5 plural nouns are needed, sometimes 10, and, then again, perhaps it may take only 3 on an occasion. The sum of the required amounts is calculated ($5 + 10 + 3 = 18$), and that sum is divided by the number of amounts in the series (3). Therefore, this is a VR_6 sequence since 18 divided by 3 equals 6, which is the average number of required responses which must be emitted before a single reinforcer is given. The required number of responses needed before a reinforcer can be delivered is randomly presented to the learner so no specific "patterning effect" will develop, e.g., a $5 - 10 - 3$ sequence could be followed by a $10 - 3 - 5$ or a $3 - 5 - 10$, etc.

4. *Fixed interval* (FI): In this schedule, only one response is required, but it must occur within a specific time interval if reinforcement is to occur. In that one sense, it differs from its untimed cousin, CRF. Usually, responding just once during a specific time period is very difficult to do since the person tries to "outguess" the length of time by which the interval is defined. This is especially true for people who cannot judge time easily or, even more so, cannot easily estimate how much time it will take to complete a single response as in writing a research paper where the paper is called "one response." Usually, the person starts responding very slowly as if s/he knows the interval is far from being over and then very rapidly speeds performing so that by the end of the time interval the performance is at a very high level. This is described as "positive acceleration" since the performance rate becomes progressively faster until the reinforcement occurs at the time interval's close. After each reinforcement, the person drops the level of performance back to a very slow rate. Unlike FR schedules, which show the behavior increasing at a very fast linear rate just prior to reinforcement and then show absolutely no performance at all until the next linear increase, FI reinforcing will keep the person performing immediately after reinforcement has passed. This "post-reinforcement pause" in the FR schedule is quite unique to that schedule alone. The post reinforcement pause tends to increase geometrically in length up to a limit as the number of responses required to earn a reinforcer is increased linearly.

FI does not show this relationship since only one response needs to occur during the fixed time interval if reinforcement is to be achieved.

5. *Variable interval* (VI): In this schedule, the number of required responses remains at one, but the time interval varies from a point determined by the experimenter. For example, sometimes it may require only five seconds from the last time reinforcement occurred until the opportunity arises for a second reinforcing. If the person has responded at least once during that five second period, the reinforcement is granted. If no response has occurred, the reinforcement is not given, and the person must wait for the next time period to elapse. If, let us say, the selected time intervals are five seconds, ten seconds, and three seconds, we can average those periods (total of 18 seconds divided by three chosen intervals) and, in our case, have a VI_6 schedule. This averaging process to determine the schedule's subscript number is exactly the same as is used for the VR schedule with the exception that VR is concerned with the number of responses varying, while VI is consistently concerned only about varying the time intervals in order to achieve one response per interval. In VI, the person may respond as many times as s/he wishes, but only one response is needed to gain all the reinforcement that is available for that interval. This is not so for the VR schedule; one may respond as frequently as one wishes since s/he "knows" reinforcement is contingent upon the number of responses being greater than one for any reinforcement to occur.

All the preceding can be shown in graphic form as follows:

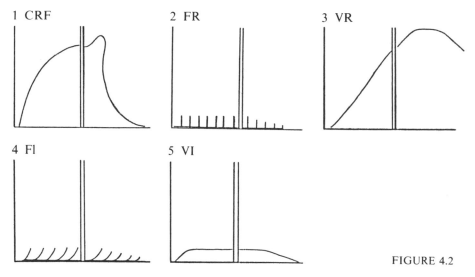

FIGURE 4.2

81

Let us use our knowledge of the eight basic training paradigms and the basic five reinforcement schedules to predict some behavior. Two identical twins live in the same house with parents who pride themselves on their "even-handed" discipline. Let us say that the twins have broken a window by kicking a football through it and are now preparing to share the blame. Twin 1 says she will try to "talk her way out of it." Twin 2 says she will just wait to see how Twin 1 does before choosing a coping strategy. The mother asks, "Which one of you broke the window, or were both of you in on this one?" Twin 1 perceives this as an avoidance training paradigm. The cue to "explain yourself" is apparently negative in tone. It is going to be desirable to avoid being punished (negative reinforcement), and it certainly is time to speak up (behavior is to be produced). The mother says, "You have ten seconds to come up with an answer!" In this avoidance conditioning paradigm, the mother has set a ten second (fixed interval) for the production of the simplest explanation possible. Twin 1 starts speaking slowly and then as the ten seconds tick past, she grows faster and faster in her statements. At the end of the ten seconds, the mother says quite neutrally, "I see; go on. I can wait another ten seconds." Again the first twin's performance "scallops." The behavior starts very slowly and then becomes gradually more and more positively accelerated. If mother extends the time interval again by ten seconds, the same scalloping will probably occur. It will continue to occur until either mother removes the threatened punishment or Twin 1 removes it by stalling its coming. Twin 2 may imitate Twin 1's behavior if mother is appeased. We can see from this example that clearly what was said (quality) is less the issue here than is how much and how frequently "it" was said. This should not be much of a surprise to us since we saw above that Skinner is least interested in the quality of behavior. "Quality," per se, is not graphable and is open to a host of subjective definitions as we pass from culture to culture.

Readers interested in such further pursuits have a host of books and journal articles to choose from. The authors of *Principles of Behavioral Analysis,* Millenson and Leslie (1979), have done a superb job in summarizing much of the material in this area.

By this point, if not considerably before, the reader should ask for an answer to how all the preceding actually fits into language development as such. After all, none of the eight operant paradigms nor none of the five schedules of reinforcement is specifically labeled as language-oriented principles. This is precisely Skinner's major point as is seen in Chapter 19 ("Thinking") from his *Verbal Behavior.* There is no significant difference among any of the behaviors produced by people that cannot be reduced to the descriptive principles seen in operant or classical conditioning. There is no need for a special field of investigation known as the psychology of language development and function. Or, perhaps we could also say there is no more need for a special study of language development and function than there is for the entire, global field known as "behavior analysis." So what then is "verbal behavior"? Skinner's answer is quick and simple; verbal behavior is essentially the interaction humans have on a symbolic level. It is no more or less than any other form of behavior. It certainly requires no distinction between the "langue" and the "langue-parole" because it is simply all "langue-parole." Language is what we see in written form, what we hear people say, and what we see expressed in art, music, and dance when those endeavors are symbolic in nature. There are basically two fundamental splits in language which are legal areas of academic pursuit: the first area deals with "mands," and the second area deals with "tacts." Mands come to us in the forms of questions or "commands"—e.g., I ask or tell you what to do by putting you into a training paradigm (hopefully it will be a discrimination paradigm) which cues you symbolically to produce (or sometimes withhold) behavior. For example, "Say! Can you tell me what time it is?" stands as a question requiring a response. Ignoring it will probably produce a command such as "Please tell me what time it is!" Tacts, on the other hand, are statements which require no answers or action as such, but they (the tacts) may actually produce a verbal response of a manding type. For example, while walking down the hall you say, "Isn't it a beautiful day today!" Albeit, this is a question in one sense, it requires no answer and, therefore, is not a mand. The speaker knew it was a beautiful day as he or she perceived it and simply was saying just that and no more to the listener. If we had thought the speaker was actually asking us a question, we would probably have been less than rewarding in our answer since life is usually filled with matters more pressing than the confirmation of another's personal concern over such a seemingly trite issue. Tacts stand alone and are sufficient in and of themselves and are, consequently, very easy to ignore since they do require nothing from us other than an occasional nod of the head or jotting down of a scrawled note to indicate attention is being dutifully paid. How frequently and under what circumstances one "mands" or "tacts" depends upon which of the eight paradigms for training one is in and which of the 13 schedules of reinforcement is operable. It is no less, and it definitely is no more, than that. Each of the training paradigms, of course, does assume that there probably has been some past conditioning in your history which possibly affects your present attempts at being conditioned, but this is implicit in the very definition of the eight training paradigms. We need no special "four-stage inferred models" (see

Chapter 3), no deep structures/transformational rules, and we may dispense apparently with the abstract second signal system. Skinner's system also saves us the apparent need to understand such fields as Taxonomic Linguistics and human verbal learning. In short, Skinner's system saves us the time and effort of understanding anything but operant conditioning, which, admittedly, is a large field in and of itself.

All of this apparent simplicity of description sounds well and good for the moment, but we soon find Skinner himself having to add a few extra terms to describe events that would otherwise have no "explanation." For example, it is well known that children often practice developing certain kinds of sentence structures by orally rehearsing those structures in the presence of no one but themselves. This is not the same process adults use when they "talk to themselves;" in the case of adults, the content of the sentence usually is the concern, e.g., stating a problem aloud so as to better find a solution. Children, of course, do heavily depend upon orally self-presented instructions to direct their activities, but they also use the oral messages to practice their syntactic structures. Skinner labels this process of solitary self-rehearsal as the "explanation" of the process itself. Unfortunately, this is not the only place where this occurs. We see the term "ruttening" used to label the process where one word is attached to a second, a second is attached to a third, a third to a fourth, etc., in order to "explain" syntactic growth. Ruttening is defined as "intraverbal chaining," which apparently refers to the process of stringing words together from the start to the end of a sentence. But the assignment of the label "ruttening" solves no problems for us. In fact, it rather complicates issues because we see here the disturbing implication that perhaps learning syntax is a process of merely adding one word to a second to a third and so on, until we have strung together a left to right hand sentence. This sounds suspiciously like Ebbinghaus' serial recall position with an addition of the description of how reinforcement for practicing will increase behavior. However, one can easily see from reading Skinner that he is not taking Ebbinghaus' side; Skinner does not even once mention the serial position effect by name or implication. Another term that Skinner uses that seems to lack explanatory power is "synonomy." This term is called upon to "explain" behavior in which very specific, familiar stimuli suddenly and unexplainably produce perfectly contradictory results. For example, the speaker in question has always asked a friend, "How are you?" when the two of them passed in the hall. The friend has always responded very positively and has been continually reinforced each time by the speaker. However, when the question is routinely asked one day, the answer is not positive nor cheerful. All the past history of conditioning would indicate that the response would be a positive, friendly one. In order to explain this, Skinner invents the term synonomy to stand for the process which takes place when a highly reinforced stimulus suddenly stops producing the desired response on one or more occasions.

Skinner ventures to a limited extent into the world of reading, but again we see the usual extremely heavy reliance upon the 13 schedules and the 8 training paradigms. Reading is establishing a "textual response pattern" based upon very heavily reinforced practice where the person sounds out the words and phrases, e.g., uses an "echoic operant." We are reinforced for reading and writing and using correct grammatical rules through the use of positive reinforcement. We use "editing" rules, which are based upon negative reinforcement, in order to learn what is not an acceptable exception to a rule. A child is ready to read or write when the past history of conditioning has established the necessary prerequisites for reading and the environment is prepared to reinforce the child for appropriate responses. If a child does not read when the environment tries to reinforce him/her, it is due to a lack of the necessary prerequisite spells. There is, of course, no mention of the need for cognitive stage changes as prerequisites for reading (Elkind, 1979). Skinner treats reading as he does all other aspects of language. Reading is behavior—no more and certainly no less.

Apparently Skinner remains relatively in agreement with his 1957 position as seen in *Verbal Behavior* because there is no evidence to show that he was disturbed by a rather scathing attack from his arch enemy (on the language scene only), Noam Chomsky. It would be 1970 before another S-R Behaviorist would rise to the defense of the principles Skinner believed in so wholeheartedly. But before we see the 1970 defense, let us look in depth at Noam Chomsky's challenge.

Chomsky's Rebuttal

Chomsky reaction to Skinner's *Verbal Behavior* came in 1959 in an article entitled, appropriately enough, "Review of Skinner's *Verbal Behavior*." From a timing perspective alone, it is interesting to note that Skinner could have just as easily critiqued Chomsky since both *Verbal Behavior* and *Syntactic Structures* had appeared in 1957.

Chomsky makes it perfectly clear at the beginning of the review that he has selected B. F. Skinner rather than any of the other Behaviorists because Skinner states his case clearly enough that his position's nullification will easily be understood by almost any knowledgeable reader in the field. Such a position is perhaps all well and good except for the fact, as we shall soon see, Chomsky drifts from Skinner's position at times to either intentionally shoot at other positions or unintentionally because he is not a learning theorist and has, therefore, confused various and sundry positions with that of Skinner's. The evidence would appear stronger for the latter.

For starters, Chomsky is quick to demonstrate that Skinner's research (dealing with the 8 operant training paradigms and 13 schedules of reinforcement) is almost exclusively conducted with and is, therefore, fundamentally applicable to infrahumans. This Chomskian comment is quite correct in at least as far as it goes regarding the fact that most of Skinner's early research was conducted exclusively with infrahumans. Chomsky's comment that the data produced from such studies is applicable only to the infrahumans is not necessarily so. Chomsky clearly evidences his lack of understanding of the purpose of Skinnerian behavioral analysis—e.g., at no place in Skinner's writings will the reader find Skinner saying that the only possible important principles of learning are those he sets forth; Skinner merely sets forth what he has actually found. Chomsky asserts that the importance of Skinner's work in learning theory has been eclipsed by the writings of the cognitive psychologist Harry Harlow, who was quite instrumental in the 1950s and the 1960s in demonstrating certain learning phenomena not easily explainable by operant conditionings—or at least such was claimed by Harlow. To accept Chomsky on this point seems risky since time and further research generally have not pushed Harlow to the same place in learning theory prominence as B. F. Skinner, albeit it should be hastily added that cognitive psychology has grown rapidly since Harlow's initial work became public. We may at least let Chomsky's comment stand on that issue, but it would seem unwise to accept Chomsky's comment at face value. Let us simply grant it as being Chomsky's opinion.

The entire concept of reinforcement seems to offer Chomsky ample ammunition to hurl at Skinner. Reinforcement, as Chomsky sees it, is a perfectly useful concept when it comes to describing some behaviors, but by no means will it account for all behaviors. Reinforcement, according to him, actually "explains" nothing since it is circular to say that one did what one did because one was reinforced. One could just as easily then turn and say that one was reinforced because one did what one did! This is circular reasoning, a tautology. There is no evidence to show, as far as we can see upon close inspection, that Skinner ever did say he was "explaining" anything. If anything, his own writing indicates his belief that description comes first, and explanation comes far later.

Chomsky does not wish to accept the concepts of "shaping" and "successive approximations," since they apparently are descriptive terms only. Again, a simple Skinnerian defense can be made since "shaping" and "successive approximations" are descriptive, not explanatory, processes. Chomsky attacks the use of "mands" and "tacts" from a reinforcement viewpoint and shows an interesting problem. "Mands," according to Chomsky, satisfy needs when the mands are met; all things that are reinforcing are "drive reducing" (or meet needs). Therefore, since "tacts" do not meet needs gratification in any sense, "tacts" cannot be reinforcers and are, therefore, impossible to explain from a reinforcement perspective. It is truly a beautiful argument flawlessly executed in form. Unfortunately, Chomsky is misinterpreting the initial premise. Skinner did not at any time say that the only things that were reinforcing were drive state reducing. The position that all reinforcers must demonstrate drive reduction and can do nothing but reduce drives is actually the position of Clark L. Hull (1943), who was a classic learning theorist in every sense of the word, but was definitely not a Skinnerian. Of course, Skinner did believe that things that reduced drives were highly reinforcing, but then again, so were things which occasionally increased a drive or held a drive stable after it had reached a point of satisfaction to the person. Why were there tacts? The answer was simple for Skinner; they existed because they had reinforcing value—e.g., people enjoy being greeted with a cheery "How are you today?" even though the listener knows perfectly well that this question does not explicitly or implicitly give one the right to start a lengthy discussion related to one's actual state of being. The answer to the question is "Fine!", whether or not one really is.

Chomsky's failure to accept Skinner's concepts of "shaping" and "successive approximations" is a subtle issue passed over a bit summarily above. Skinner's assumptions are that the growth of language occurs in gradual, equally measured bits or, simply, "successive approximations." Chomsky is not unaware that children do show growth patterns which may appear to the untrained observer to develop precisely in that fashion. But that is to the untrained observers. Actual close inspection does not quite indicate this (Brown, Cazden & Bellugi, 1969); there are rather rapid increases followed by periodic slow, rehearsal periods. Chomsky sees the TG rules being developed by each child coming into play in some time frame which is anything but slowly approximating of some end goal. He says rules are learned in a creative, dynamic fashion—which obviously is not descriptive of operant conditioning phenomena. Or then again, is it? We can grant the fact that most operant conditioning does not occur in only a few attempts (trials). In fact, most studies attempting to condition even the simplest behaviors are very time consuming and tedious for the learner and the experimenter. However, relatively recent research has demonstrated that apparently operant conditioning can occur quite rapidly under precisely appropriate conditions. The "phenomenon" is known as "autoshaping" and occurs as follows (Brown & Jenkins, 1968). As the reader reviews the procedures involved in "autoshaping," it is apparent that actually both Chomsky and Skinner are placed in rather awkward positions: Chomsky is placed on the defensive because he has to show operant conditioning to be a slow, tedious learning process and Skinner because he has no ready explanation to account for why autoshaping occurs as rapidly as it does. The procedure is as follows: A hungry pigeon is placed into an empty "experimental space" (Skinner box) with an illuminated disc (which is to be pecked at) at one end of the box. The disc is illuminated for eight seconds, and then a feeder opens allowing the pigeon to eat freely for a very brief moment. Then the feeder is closed, and the process of illuminating the key and following the open feeder is reenacted again and again. Since the pigeon does not have to actually peck the key to cause the feeder to open (reinforcement is not contingent upon pecking behavior), one would logically assume key pecking would never develop to the key. One would be in error with such a prediction. Not only does the pigeon peck the key, but the behavior starts virtually on the very first trial and becomes extremely rapid after only a couple of additional attempts. Apparently, as the explanation goes, pigeons are species-specifically prone to peck at anything reminding them of food. The illuminated key in this case acts as a conditioned stimulus (CS), and the food acts as the unconditioned stimulus (UCS). When the illuminated key is on, the pigeon produces a conditioned response (CR) of pecking. Aside from the fact this appears to be a classical conditioning experiment inside an operant setting and aside from the fact that using Pavlov's "classic/traditional" method might have produced even more efficient conditioning than did this "delayed" conditioning design, we have on our hands a case of extremely rapid conditioning of associations which the pigeon was species-specifically prone to develop. By admittedly crude analogy, is it even fair for us to dare speculate that perhaps humans are species-specifically prone to make language associations at a speed of development which would make ordinary operant conditioning appear far too slow to account for it? But, be it extremely fast if it is developed in that fashion, must we construct the term "creative" or the term "dynamic" to describe it and, perhaps, by using such terms, make it sound as if it is something totally different from absolutely anything seen in the conditioning literature? Chomsky apparently leads us to believe that is his preference. It could safely be predicted Skinner would not find it his preference.

Chomsky does critique Skinner's use of other technical terms which Skinner invented to "explain" various phenomena in language development. Specifically, Chomsky is especially critical of Skinner's "synonomy," "echoic operant," "automatically self-reinforcing," and "textual response," which is the phrase Skinner coined to "explain" the process of reading. Perhaps even "textual response" can be excused in light of Skinner's use of the phrase "magical mand" to describe what a speaker is doing when requesting that a person commit some obviously absurd, possibly self-injurious act—e.g., "Oh, go jump off a building!" or "Go take a flying leap at the moon!" There seems little danger that anyone would accept such an offer at face value, and the offer is usually made out of sarcasm and anger. Chomsky's point is perhaps less an issue than he would have it be since there undoubtedly is some amount of reinforcement coming from the facial expression or sense of shock/dismay the receiver shows when the magical mand hits. Still, it is a bit artificial and actually "explains" no more than any of the other terms Chomsky is less than pleased with. Chomsky's (1959) critique can really be seen in the form of five summary points:

1. Skinner's use of operant conditioning principles to "explain" language development is of no value to the serious student of language. Skinner effectively tells us nothing of value.

2. Saying that each of us "shapes" our behaviors in order to "successively approximate" end goals—e.g., mature language development, is a hollow description of a very complex procedure which exists inside the central nervous system and, therefore, must be described and explained inside that central nervous system. Saying that the person goes about memorizing sentence frames and then simply substitutes words into those frames is not a sufficient explanation of that process. (It is interesting to note here that Chomsky misses Skinner with criticism and actually hits M. D. S. Braine, whose position is based upon the generalization of sentence structures and the substitution of content words. Braine's work occurred several years after this 1959 critique by Chomsky and was based to a great extent upon the principles of operant conditioning set forth by Skinner, but yet did not limit itself to just those principles. Braine is classified as a S-O-R Behaviorist, so the Chomskian criticism of Skinner seems perhaps to attribute to Skinner something he never actually proposed.)

3. Chomsky contends that Skinner makes no effort to discuss how the child learns rules. Chomsky further contends that any discussion of rules in linguistics rapidly brings us to a discussion of "operational" vs. "obligatory" rules. We must grant Chomsky his point here. Skinner does

not discuss any special rules for language since Skinner obviously does not see language as being a special field of study in the first place. Chomsky seems to be saying, in so many words, that the rules at issue are the TG rules. Since Skinner discusses nothing below the "surface structure" in language, TG rules have no place.

4. Skinner, according to Chomsky, has completely removed the "contribution of the speaker" from the entire language process. (We are here at a philosophical impass between the two writers. Skinner would have us see the nature of science as staying out of issues within the "Black Box," the central nervous system, since we cannot even yet clearly define the most basic neurological processes which cause behavior to occur. Chomsky would ask us to free ourselves of such artificial scientific straightjackets and make some seemingly shrewd intuitive guesses as to what actually does happen inside the central nervous system—e.g., let us discuss the contribution of the speaker. The full debate was discussed at length at the beginning of this chapter; the reader is referred back to that point for reconsideration of this issue. Let us merely note that Chomsky uses it as a criticism; we will not pass judgment as to the criticism's acceptability, nor are we saying that it is merely an issue of "personal choice" on the reader's part. Rather, it would appear to be an issue beyond proof or disproof of this point. This issue's resolution would seemingly affect all aspects of human performance.)

5. The last point is a rather interesting one, since it is based upon some speculation using a computer. It is predicted that it would actually take a language learner approximately 120 years of listening seven days a week 24 hours per day to merely hear only once the entire repertoire of sentences the average English-speaking six-year-old can produce. Logically, if each sentence had to have multiple rehearsals in order to be learned, we would readily escalate far beyond the 120 years if we were talking about achieving even minimal competence. (This criticism on Chomsky's part seems just a bit hypocritical since he has already criticized Skinner for relying too heavily upon generalization among sentence types with the substitution of various words from sentence to sentence (point No. 2 above). The fifth criticism makes it appear that Skinner has proposed that each sentence is uniquely different from any other and, therefore, there is no generalization from sentence to sentence. The predicted amount of time to learn the number of sentences the average six-year-old can produce is, therefore, seriously suspect and most probably inflated. But there may be even a larger issue at hand here. How does Chomsky know exactly how competent a six-year-old is considering the fact he does discuss "competence" not "performance"? We are, in short, back to the mentalist/rationalist vs. the empiricist viewpoint.)

90

Chomsky's 1959 critique was widely heralded as a victory for the TG position and a sound thrashing for Behaviorism (at least S-R Behaviorism in particular). MacCorquodale (1970) says this in defense of Skinner. The reader should note that the year is 1970, which makes MacCorquodale's defense appear a bit late in coming, but, then again, can we determine exactly what made MacCorquodale assume it was time to defend Skinner in the first place? The answer is probably in the negative; speculation, however, could be made. If the reader thinks back to the reason O. H. Mowrer (1954) decided to have "psychology look at language," we can see his citation of Bloomfield's criticism of psychology as having had no interest in the field. We can recall that the Bloomfield criticism was some 20 years before Mowrer responded. Mowrer seemed to be grasping at straws regarding a starting point for his own work; Bloomfield was at least an anchor point. MacCorquodale has 11 years behind him; what better thing to say in introducing your own ideas than that you are defending one of the profession's best-known scholars, B. F. Skinner, even if that person, nor perhaps any other S-R Behaviorist for that matter, has not asked for a defense. No matter the motive, a defense is worth a review—and a critique.

Skinner's Defense

MacCorquodale (1970) grants Chomsky a "quick victory" in his 1959 article and notes that many of Chomsky's followers seemed to jump on the bandwagon by surpassing Chomsky's critique in venom if not in content or logic. But they, like Chomsky, all seem guilty of some serious misinterpretations of what Skinner has actually said.

For starters, MacCorquodale clearly points to Chomsky's agreement to attack Skinner's and only Skinner's position. It is obvious that Chomsky has let M. D. S. Braine's position become Skinner's. It is also clear to MacCorquodale that Chomsky does not understand that Skinner never said that all things which are reinforcing are also drive reducing and, in fact, must be drive reducing to be reinforcers. MacCorquodale prefers to see Skinner's position as being an "untested hypothesis." It is an elaboration upon research Skinner published using animals. Skinner has been misinterpreted by his critics. At no place, according to MacCorquodale, does Skinner ever say that reinforcement is necessary for the learning of any language. Skinner's use of technical terms is easily defended in light of the hypothetical construct building of Noam Chomsky. Skinner discusses genetics, Mediational Behaviorism (S-O-R Behaviorism), and neurology as well as anyone, according again to Mac-

Corquodale. MacCorquodale sees, in short, Skinner's position having been totally misinterpreted. The partial criticisms qualify as quick, cheap victories and no more. Chomsky and his followers build a "straw man" in the form of Chomsky's critique of Skinner's position. As Mac-Corquodale sees it, only time will verify Skinner's thinking and reduce Chomsky's mentalistic/rationalistic creation to mere speculation.

These criticisms of Chomsky's position qualify as rather curious if not occassionally off-center. When MacCorquodale says B. F. Skinner never said reinforcement was necessary for language learning, one is left wondering if perhaps MacCorquodale is referring to a B. F. Skinner we do not know. Of course, Skinner says reinforcement is necessary for learning. After all, the eight operant paradigms are based squarely on the assumption that reinforcement of some variety is at work, if the paradigms are to operate in the first place. Secondly, reading Skinner's *Verbal Behavior* hardly leaves the reader with the impression Skinner is stating a "hypothesis," or is merely elaborating on past research which he clearly marks as research done on other behaviors. To the contrary, the impression is given that this book is the answer. It does not appear to be an elaboration; it is an analysis of a new form of behavior, albeit the principles of analysis are the same ones used in much of Skinner's other analyses on other forms of behavior. Does it discuss such variables as mediation, neurology, and species-specific (genetic) differences? According to MacCorquodale, it does so; but, if it does, it must be admitted that it is "well-hidden" in the book. Perhaps we should label this last point "wishful thinking" on MacCorquodale's part. We can see in the writings of MacCorquodale a rather deep-seeded need on his part to vindicate Skinner by filling in all the gaps Skinner left open—usually on purpose. The question here is who, Chomsky or MacCorquodale, is more guilty of having burned the "straw man." The larger question is, of course, whether anyone really needed to defend B. F. Skinner in the first place.

The question of any defense of a position against any other position is a basic part of science itself. It is assumed that any growth in the field must occur at the "expense" of some position and its followers. How high the price will be of releasing one's grip from a model depends upon the strength of that grip at its start. Those who accepted Chomsky's rebuttal of Skinner truly believed the issue was a closed issue. But for those in the Learning Theory/Conditioning Camp who knew that S-R Behaviorism is not the only form of Behaviorism, the issue was far from decided.

92

References

Bloom, L. (February, 1970). *Semantic Features of Language Acquisition*. Paper presented at the Conference on Research in the Language of the Mentally Retarded, University of Kansas.

Bloomfield, C. (1938). "Linguistic Aspects of Sciences." In *International Encyclopedia of Unified Science* (11231). Chicago.

Brown, P. and Jenkins, H. (1968). "Autoshaping of the Pigeon's Key-Peck." *Journal of the Experimental Analysis of Behavior, 11*, 1—8.

Brown, R., Cazden, C., and Bellugi, U. (1969). "The Child's Grammar from I to III." In J. P. Hill (Ed.), *Minnesota Symposium on Child Psychology* (28-73). Minneapolis, Minnesota: University of Minnesota Press.

Chomsky, N. (1957). *Syntactic Structures*. The Hague: Mouton.

Chomsky, N. (1959). "Review of Skinner's *Verbal Behavior.*" *Language, 35* (1), 26—58.

Chomsky, N. (1965). *Some Aspects of the Theory of Syntax*. Cambridge, Massachusetts: MIT Press.

Elkind, D. (1979). "Beginning Reading: A Stage-Structure Analysis." *Childhood Education, 55* (4), 248—252.

Estes, W. K. (1950). "Toward a Statistical Theory of Learning." *Psychological Review, 57,* 94-107.

Ferster, C. and Skinner, B. F. (1957). *Schedules of Reinforcement*. New York: Appleton, Century, and Crofts.

Fillmore, C. (1968). "The Case for Case." In E. Bach and R. Hams (Eds.), *Universals in Linguistic Theory* (1—88). New York: Holt.

Guthrie, E. R. (1952). *The Psychology of Learning*. New York: Harper.

Hilgard, E. and Bower, G. (1975). *Theories of Learning* (4th ed.). Englewood Cliffs, NJ: Prentice-Hall.

Hull, C. L. (1943). *Principles of Behavior*. New York: Appleton, Century, and Crofts.

Hulse, S., Egeth, H., and Deese, J. (1980). *The Psychology of Learning* (5th ed.). St. Louis, Missouri: McGraw-Hill.

Katz, J. J. (1964). "Mentalism in Linguistics." *Language, 40* (2), 124-137.

MacCorquodale, K. (1970). "On Chomsky's Review of Skinner's *Verbal Behavior.*" *Journal of the Experimental Analysis of Behavior, 13,* 83—100.

McCawley, J. D. (1968). "The Role of Semantics in a Grammar." In E. Bach and R. Hams (Eds.), *Universals in Linguistic Theory* (124—169). New York: Holt.

Millenson, J. and Leslie, J. (1979). *Principles of Behavioral Analysis* (2nd ed.). New York: Macmillian.

Miller, N. E. (1969). "Learning of Visceral and Glandular Responses." *Science, 163,* 434—445.

Mowrer, O. H. (1954). "The Psychologist Looks at Language." *The American Psychologist, 9,* 660—694.

Osgood, C. E. (1963). "On Understanding and Creating Sentences." *The American Psychologist, 18,* 735—751.

Pavlov, I. P. (1928). *Lectures on Conditioned Reflexes*. New York: International Publishers.

Premack, D. (1965). "Reinforcement Theory." In D. Levine (Ed.), *Nebraska Symposium on Motivation* (123—188). Lincoln, Nebraska: University of Nebraska Press.

Skinner, B. F. (1938). *The Behavior of Organisms*. New York: Appleton, Century, and Crofts.

Skinner, B. F. (1957). *Verbal Behavior*. New York: Appleton, Century, and Crofts.

Skinner, B. F. (1974). *About Behaviorism*. New York: Knopf.

Spence, K. W. (1956). *Behavior Theory and Conditioning*. New Haven, Connecticut: Yale University Press.

Thorndike, E. L. (1898). "Animal Intelligence: An Experimental Study of the Associative Processes in Animals." *Psychological Review Monographs Supplement, 2* (8).

Tolman, E. C. (1932). *Purposive Behavior in Animals and Men*. New York: Appleton, Century, and Crofts.

– 5 –

S-O-R BEHAVIORISM

M. D. S. Braine on Contextual Generalization

Martin Braine's model was offered in 1963 in an article entitled "On Learning the Grammatical Order of Words." It was based squarely upon operant conditioning principles as presented by Skinner, but it surpassed Skinner in many ways. Braine, as an S-O-R Behaviorist, had to go beyond simple S-R Behaviorism by making an attempt to put the organism (0) back into the formula. Braine does just that but, in the process, produces a model which does not speak of transformational rules as does Chomsky's, nor does it put the major emphasis upon the learning of the "main words" (the contentives) as does Skinner's system (and Chomsky's as well). Braine places great stress upon the process of stimulus generalization (Sgen).

The process of Sgen is quite simple: once a rewarding stimulus pattern has been identified, a subject will respond to it and similar stimulus patterns in order to continue gaining that reinforcement. The correlary is that responding decreases disproportionately more rapidly as stimulus patterns become progressively less similar to the originally-reinforced stimulus pattern. These Sgen principles hold for sound perception as well as for visual stimulation. With the preceding in mind, we are ready to pursue M. D. S. Braine's position.

To describe Braine's model, let us look at the sentence O. H. Mowrer was fond of analyzing: "Tom is a thief." A case could be made for saying that the most important aspects of it are its shape and the small words that hold that shape together. We could just as easily say "Mike is a thief." or "Linda is a princess." or anything else we wish as long as we keep the sentence framework the same and as long as we keep "is a" in the same place relative to the sentence's beginning and end. We can see that memorizing such a simple sentence frame would seem easy enough and that all we would need to do is commit to memory as many nouns as possible to "stuff" into the beginning and end positions when we had a need to communicate. But why must we memorize only one sentence frame? What if there were a limited number of general frames which would meet our needs and those of our neighbors? Why not even assume the length of the frame would be expanded or contracted from its original starting point so all possible flexibility could be achieved in our system? Also, let us assume that the number of those apparently critical "small words," i.e., is . . . a, is limited to a workable size which would allow easy memorization. If all these elements were placed into one model, would we have something that would reinstate the importance of the organism's central nervous system while at the same time saving us the problems of explaining and defending either the simplicities of a Mowrer or a Skinner or the complexity of a Chomsky? But how could we first experimentally justify it? That was Braine's problem.

In 1963, Braine attempted to achieve experimental progress by devising a five-part study. In the first subexperiment, he used 16 children ranging in age from nine years six months to ten years five months. This subexperiment was designed to determine if the mere position of a word in a sentence could serve as a "functional stimulus." Or, it could also be stated that the purpose was to determine if a sentence frame as a whole could be memorized.

The materials were CVC nonsense syllables (see Chapter 1) which had been placed into the form of three simple sentences. They were similar to "KIV BEW," "JUF MUB," and "FOJ YAG." Each child was required to memorize the first two sentences and then received a Sgen test in a modified multiple choice format. The Sgen test could read as follows:

1. FOJ ———— (KIV, BEW)
2. (MUB, KIV) ———— YAG
3. (JUF, BEW) ———— YAG
4. FOJ ———— (MUB, JUF)

Each child was asked to simply read each line and "choose" the proper CVC to fill in the blank. No instructions as to how to pick a choice strategy were given. The results were clearly in support of a contextual generalization (Sgen) approach. Approximately 78 percent were filled correctly as follows:

1. FOJ BEW
2. KIV YAG
3. JUF YAG
4. FOJ MUB

96

The probability of this occurring solely by chance was less than one in a thousand. Clearly, the children must have "known" what to do regarding making a choice, and, yet, only one child said the purpose was clear. The children reported that it "sounded right" or that they had "heard it before" despite the fact they had never specifically *seen* the lines before. Braine concludes they had shown Sgen and, therefore, had engaged in the process of "contextual generalization." Learning the position of words within a sentence as well as the general shape of the sentence served as a "functional stimulus." He further concluded that contextual generalization was an auditory and not a visual process because none of the children said it "looked right." It is also a "temporal" and not a "spatial" process. What was neither justified nor even part of the subexperiment's domain is his conclusion that any two-year-old child could probably engage in contextual generalization since it is not an intellectual/cognitive task but is simply perceptual in nature. When we review the study to see where the two-year-olds were, we find none. When we seek convincing proof that he has evidence showing us that perception has actually ever been split from intelligence or cognition, we find none. His comment qualifies as wishful thinking; it cannot even support itself as an acceptable hypothesis since it has no supportive evidence upon which to build. Yet, the reader is left with the conclusion he has support, and we do not easily see that the next three experiments seem to take the "perceptual base" as a foregone conclusion. The fifth subexperiment finally addresses this issue to some extent, as we will see.

The second subexperiment is clearly more sophisticated than the first. The children range in age from nine years seven months to ten years seven months. This time, we have both a control and an experimental group, and each group has 16 subjects. The experimental question is whether knowing an absolute position in a sentence is preferable to knowing the relative position one word has to a second within the same sentence.

The sentences used in this subexperiment are those used in the previous one with the exception that GED would precede JUF in line two, GED would precede FOJ in line three, and POW would follow BEW in line one. This effectively means the sentences now read much as follows:

LINE 1. KIV   BEW   POW
       2. GED   JUF   MUB
       3. GED   FOJ   YAG

Both groups of 16 children each were asked to memorize the first two lines, but the instructions varied from group to group. One group, which will be referred to as the control group, was always given GED and POW and had only to recall the other CVCs in the two lines. The second group, the experimental group, had to memorize all the CVCs including GED and POW. It was hypothesized that being forced to memorize GED and POW would assist that group when it came to handling the rigors of the generalization test using the third line seen above. The contextual generalization test read as follows:

TEST LINE 1. GED FOJ ——— (KIV, BEW POW)
            2. (MUB, KIV) ——— YAG
            3. (GED JUF, BEW POW) ——— YAG
            4. GED FOJ ——— (MUB, GED JUF)

The correct answers to these lines are the same as in the first subexperiment with, of course, GED and POW added where appropriate. The prediction that the experimental group would do significantly better than the control group was confirmed. Braine concluded that forcing attention toward the fixed positional cues (the "absolute position" cues) was a superior strategy regarding the promotion of contextual generalization. The control group had memorized relative positional cues and did not use GED and POW to good advantage during the generalization test. Very interestingly, when Braine followed the generalization test by asking each child to recall as many sentences as possible when s/he was simply handed all the CVCs, there were no significant differences to appear. Unfortunately, this argument falls short of being convincing since the number of CVCs was certainly not an issue when the contextual generalization test proved itself in the hypothesized direction. Careful consideration of the preceding may lead us to the tempting, albeit not necessarily well-warranted, conclusion that contextual generalization may apply more to a receptive process in language than it does to an expressive process. This would translate as contextual generalization could be of assistance during reading or listening, but it is of no particular value when generating language during writing or speaking. These are speculative comments, but they would seem worthy of further pursuit. It is interesting to note that the experimental group was headed toward superior recall over the control group, but being headed in the predicted direction is not the same thing as having reached significant differences.

Subexperiment three addresses the question of whether contextual generalization holds true both within and between/among entire phrases. The "within" issue had been demonstrated to Braine's satisfaction in the first two subexperiments. The subjects were 24 children ranging in age from nine years eleven months to eleven years one month. The experimental procedure here is considerably more complex than in the first two experiments, but the results are readily understandable. Within the limits of this subexperiment, it was demonstrated that not only do subphrases within major phrases fall under the principle of contextual generalization but the major phrases within each sentence also fall under the principle of contextual generalization. The results held despite the number of subphrases within a major phrase, the number of major phrases within each sentence, the length of the subphrases or major phrases, the length of the words comprising the subphrases and major phrases, or the phonetic components of the words. Braine admits this conclusion is based upon a very limited number of nonsense syllables representing words.

Subexperiment four is a repeat of the first subexperiment with the purpose now being to more carefully control the procedure. In the first there was no particular effort made during the teaching of the first two lines to allow the children to see as many "negative" instances as they did "positive." For example, lines one and two could read as "KIV BEW" and "JUF MUB," and those lines were continually repeated until it was time for the generalization test. A critic could well argue that the children chose as they did on the contextual generalization test only because they had so often repeatedly seen the "correct" associations and had so rarely experienced anything that was not correct. This problem was controlled for in subexperiment four: the data indicated agreement with the findings of the first subexperiment. Contextual generalization was upheld; the absence of "negative" instances in subexperiment one had not been a confounding variable.

So far, all that has transpired in the first four subexperiments seems straightforward enough, albeit the conclusion that the process of contextual generalization probably works with children two years old has no experimental support, and the conclusion that contextual generalization is auditory/temporal rather than visual/spatial seems warranted only if we accept the introspective reports of the children. Subexperiment five seeks to address the first of these concerns, but the second concern stands at the close of the five subexperiments.

Subexperiment five is in essence a repeat of the first subexperiment with a change in materials and subjects of a reduced age level. The children were two nursery school boys and girls ranging in ages from four years two months to five years zero months.

The materials in this subexperiment were adapted to meet the age restriction of the children. Instead of CVCs, animal pictures/sounds were used. Although Braine tries to make this experiment appear as a perfect-as-possible parallel to the first one, the use of materials such as animal pictures/sounds does offer some procedural changes. First, the children are taught the association between pictures and the appropriate sounds. For example, a picture of a duck is associated with the sound of "Quack!"; the picture of a kitten is associated with the sound "Meow!". We are told that apparently a pig is used and a cow, but we do not know what other two animals comprise the list. After the sounds are correctly associated with the pictures, each child memorizes two two-word sentences in the form of two animal pictures with one picture being either above or below a blank space into which a match is to be placed. The idea of using "above or below" instead of "left to right" (as was used in the first subexperiment) came from Braine's assumption that children could more readily conceive of up/down than left/right at the nursery school age level. Apparently, the original first two lines now become the picture of a cow placed over the picture of a kitten, and the second line now becomes the picture of a pig above the picture of a duck. By analogy, this is "KIV BEW" and "JUF MUB," respectively. The contextual generalization test is a perfect parallel to that in subexperiment one, but we are not told what the two test pictures are, e.g., the pictoral parallel to "FOJ YAG" is missing in Braine's writeup. Since we are using children of such young ages, several minor adjustments have to be made to allow data collection to transpire. The results were astonishingly close to those of the first subexperiment's. For example, 75 percent of the contextual generalization blanks were accurately filled here vs. 78 percent for the older children of subexperiment one. Neither position (up/down vs. left/right) was a "preferred" position regarding accuracy of blank completion in either subexperiment, albeit in subexperiment one there was more of a tendency for the right-side blank to be more accurately filled (not statistically significantly so, however). Braine concludes that contextual generalization is at work with the language development of the nursery school children. In some respects, the findings of this last subexperiment qualify as very surprising. The last subexperiment is not as well controlled as the preceding four. There seems to be no rigorous control for the familiarity level of the materials, and yet his data shows only two children on the nursery level learning the animal picture/ sound associations without error. Exactly two children learned the CVCs without any errors. In short, he probably could not have matched his two sets of materials better in the two subexperiments if he had tried, albeit we can only draw that conclusion because the results are so very similar.

But has he actually demonstrated contextual generalization on the two-year-olds level? Obviously, he has not. In fact, one is hard-pressed to suggest appropriate learning materials to use with two-year-olds if it is necessary to use pictures/sounds of animals on nursery school children. It is quickly noted that no one has concluded that contextual generalization cannot/does not occur in two-year-olds. All that is being said is that Braine has not actually demonstrated it at that level.

Braine is too much of a scientist to conclude that two-year-olds actually do use contextual generalization. He is, however, willing to conduct a rather lengthy discussion at the end of his five subexperiments which is admittedly speculative but is nevertheless, fascinating from a logic perspective. He leaves the nonsense syllables and the animal pictures/noises for a discussion of real English words and sentences, albeit he does not restrict his comments only to English. Any language which is highly dependent upon syntactic rules which stress word order would be included here in his speculations.

Braine contends in his speculations that the sentence frames in English are limited in number to an approachably small number. He likewise believes that each frame can be "stretched" to whatever length is necessary in order to accommodate the content of most ideas. What actually holds the frames in a stable but still flexible stance are the reasonably few "closed class morphemes" which exist in syntactic systems concerned with word order, e.g., English, French, Italian, German, as opposed to Russian or Latin. These closed class morphemes (or "functors") can, in English, be listed as the following, albeit this list does not necessarily exhaust the total of all examples in each classification:

1. Articles: a, an, the
2. Prepositions: up, down, between, across, etc.
3. Pronouns: he, she, it, they, them, we, us, our, your, his, her, their, this, that, these, those
4. s, es: when that s or es indicates a plural noun or indicates the presence of a present-tense transitive verb
5. Intransitive verbs: is, are, was, were, am, be
6. Auxillary verbs: was, were, has, had, have, is, are, am, been
7. Specific ending for adverbs: ly
8. Noun and verb endings: once, ence, ment, mant, ize, er, ing, ed
9. Conjunctions: because, but, and, however, therefore, nevertheless, albeit, thus

Each closed class morpheme is used to signal either the beginning or ending of a "primary unit or phrase." Each primary unit is composed of an "open class" word or set of words, e.g., nouns, verbs, adjectives, or adverbs. Open class words are also frequently referred to as "contentives" for rather obvious reasons. In the sentence "Tom is a thief.", the primary units, Tom . . thief, are held in place within the frame of the sentence by the closed class morphemes "is a." From Braine's perspective, what is actually "heard" by the language receiver is "_is_", and then all that is left for that reader or listener to do is to simply fill in the blanks. Since the open class morphemes are considered virtually infinite in number, the receiver of any message must be prepared, perhaps most by context cues, to see certain words as being a "more probable fit" than others. Because of our experiences with names, we expect in advance that Tom may be some things and not others, e.g., he could be a thief or the local alley cat, but he will not be an onion or a telephone post. Braine contends that we begin to "think in frames" and hold the closed class morphemes as tightly in place as possible so as to limit uncertainty when attempting to analyze input. You are prone to accept "_is a_," but not "_ _ is a," which appears admittedly ungrammatical. "It is a_ _?" is somewhat less immediately appealing than is "_is a_," but it is still quite acceptable on grammatical grounds. By analogy, William Shakespeare apparently had to first think to himself, "To_ or not to_; that is the_!" before he found the appropriate content words with which to fill in the blanks. It would indeed be interesting to contemplate how many of the people writing in or before Shakespeare's time had thought of using the same frame and closed class morphemes but simply could not find the "right" content words to fill the blanks.

Critics of Braine's model were quite vocal in their disagreement. Bever, Fodor, and Weksel (1965a) in "On the Acquisition of Syntax: A Critique of 'Contextual Generalization'" leveled serious criticisms at Braine's model and, in turn, caught a critique from Braine (1965) in his "On the Basis of Phrase Structure: A Reply to Bever, Fodor, and Weksel." Bever, Fodor, and Weksel, unlike some authors we have seen so far, do a very accurate job of summarizing Braine's position before trying to tear it apart. They grant him the point that anyone reading his model will understand that he puts very heavy stress upon memorizing sentence frames and closed class morphemes. They credit him with the assertion that he said intonation helped in establishing natural word/ phrase barriers in any sentence. This credited assertion seems to logically fit Braine's system, but one is very hard-pressed to find where Braine actually said that himself in his 1963 article. Bever, Fodor, and Weksel seem less interested in challenging the mechanics of Braine's contextual generalization than they do the apparent "tempting prediction" Braine seemingly wishes us to make regarding how a two-year-old could use the model to acquire language. This point was noted by

Braine in the fifth subexperiment of his 1963 article. He had no proof then that a two-year-old could use the system; he did not empirically prove that any two-year-old could because of the problems of finding any two-year-olds who cooperate in such studies for anything longer than a few seconds. Bever, Fodor, and Weksel are in possession of data that comes from a generative grammar approach, e.g., Transformational Grammar. Bever, Fodor, and Weksel contend the child has no one to model who is using the simple sentence frames Braine claims all of us memorize. Adults, to the contrary, are fond of stringing together long chains of words which may cause several simple frames to be overlapped. This is easily varified when we see in Chapter 1 the work of Miller and Selfridge in 1950 on approximations to English; fifth-order approximations were most common among adults, who are usually prone to use sentences with more than five words in them.

Of all the sentence frames, Bever, Fodor, and Weksel believe the child is least likely to receive, and yet, ironically, may be the most important, is the simple, present-tense declarative frame itself. They claim that sentence type is actually itself a very complex construct which has rules underlying its frame. It is interesting to hear them say that because as it was pointed out in Chapter 3, case grammar (McCawley, 1968; Fillmore, 1968; Bloom, 1970) makes exactly the same point albeit three years after Bever, Fodor, and Weksel made theirs. At no time does one see the names of Bever, Fodor, and Weksel attached to case grammar as such, however. Bever, Fodor, and Weksel inadvertently seem to also criticize their philosophical leader, Noam Chomsky, with their criticisms of Braine since it is true of Chomsky that he places very heavy stress upon the function of the simple, present-tense declarative in his model's deep structure phase. But this issue as criticized by Bever, Fodor, and Weksel is minor in comparison to the strength we see placed behind their last major shot at Braine. They clearly contend that there is no satisfactory proof that syntactic systems which stress word order absolutes and fixed word positions within fixed sentence frames produce more rapid language learning than we would see in syntactic systems which do not stress such absolutes. If this is true, it is a telling criticism. The problem here is finding an adequately controlled method which would allow us to make such comparisons easily. We can readily guess that syntax, semantics, and phonology are interactive, so finding one language which uses syntactic rules heavily dependent upon word order absolutes and finding a second language which is heavily reliant upon syntactic rules which have little concern over word order still leaves us with two languages very dissimilar regarding semantics and phonology. Therefore, comparisons become quite strained at best. The work of Dale

(1976, p. 29) leads us to the conclusion that Bever, Fodor, and Weksel are in error; inflections develop during the period when children are already using two to three word sentences. Many inflections will not be used consistently until the child is already using four word sentences. This would cause one to wonder why any language would want to become (or remain) inflected in nature since children apparently wish to start with some rule defining fixed word order. To date, there is no research available to answer that question. This information was apparently unavailable to Braine in 1965 when he wrote his critique of Bever, Fodor, and Weksel's critique. Braine's most effective comment is simply that Bever, Fodor, and Weksel cannot prove that the simple, present-tense declarative is not the basis of language development; he also refutes their claim that he said the child receives many daily examples of the simple, present-tense declarative. According to Braine, the child receives just enough examples to allow that "which comes naturally." Braine has a point regarding the research support's not being there for Bever, Fodor, and Weksel's comments about the innatability of the basic simple, present-tense declarative. But that was at that time. In 1968 both McCawley and Fillmore and Bloom in 1970 essentially validated the position of Bever, Fodor, and Weksel on the instability of the "kernel" sentence during the very earliest stages of language development. The development of that basic sentence type is apparently very heavily involved with the child's development of semantics, e.g., the child is seeking some way to make the association between any action or set of actions he/she has observed and the symbolic representation of that action itself. It is difficult to determine exactly to whom the victory goes in this interchange of critiques. Bever, Fodor, and Weksel (1965b) critiqued Braine's (1965) critique of their original critique. In what seemed to be the dying moments of the debate, Bever, Fodor, and Weksel (1965b) stated they could still not accept Braine's original (1963) assumption that the simple, present-tense declarative sentence was indeed the very most basic level of linquistic analysis.

The question as to whether M. D. S. Braine is more or less correct than Bever, Fodor, and Weksel or any other group of Transformational Grammarians is still perhaps a question just as full of fire and fury as it was when the original debate started. To say that Braine's model is completely wrong seems to deny what we see as children's beliefs regarding the "understandings" they have from taking content from context. How many children (and adults) have read the following lines from Lewis Carroll's (1906) "Alice in Wonderland" and said that they "understood?" It is a fine testimonial, as are the Dr. Seuss books, to Braine's contextual generalization model.

JABBERWOCKY

'Twas brillig, and the slithy toves
   Did gyre and gimble in the wabe;
All mimsy were the borogoves,
   And the mome raths outgrabe.

"Beware the Jabberwock, my son!
   The jaws that bite, the claws that catch!
Beware the Jubjub bird, the shun
   The frumious Bandersnatch!"

He took his vorpal sword in hand:
   Long time the manxome for he sought—
So rested he by the Tumtum tree,
   And stood awhile in thought.

And as in uffish thought he stood,
   The Jabberwock, with eyes of flame,
Came whiffling through the tulgey wood,
   And burbled as it came!

One, two! One, two! And through and through
   The vorpal blade went snicker-snack!
He left it dead, and with its head
   He went galumphing back.

"And hast thou slain the Jabberwock?
   Come to my arms, my beamish boy!
O frabjous day! Callooh! Callay!"
   He chortled in his joy.

'Twas brillig, and the slithy toves
   Did gyre and gimble in the wabe;
All mimsy were the borogoves,
   And the mome raths outgrabe.

—Lewis Carroll

C. E. Osgood on Understanding
and Creating Sentences

Charles Osgood was no new-comer to the psychology of language when he presented his S-O-R Behavioristic model to the American Psychological Association during his presidential address in September of 1963. His reputation as a "conservative" thinker had preceded him; for example, his article entitled "A Behavioristic Analysis of Perception and Meaning as Cognitive Phenomena" (Osgood, 1957) had made it clear he had little interest in creating psychological models which required the invention of mentalistic constructs. This idea was underscored by his article entitled "Psycholinguistics" (Osgood, 1963b) in which he criticized those who find it necessary (or convenient) to invent terms and constructs to discuss linguistic events which could just as easily be explained on a "lower level." Osgood (1963a) places himself scientifically/philosophically in a position to see Chomsky, Greenberg, and Jakobson on his left and psychologists such as B. F. Skinner, O. H. Mowrer, and John Carroll on his right. He finds G. A. Miller usually in a position close to his own and, not infrequently, out in front of him. He is, in short, deeply involved in the field from all its different directions. He readily accepts the contributions made by O. H. Mowrer (1954) and by B. F. Skinner (1957) and M. D. S. Braine (1963) and yet seeks to expand. He perceives S-R Behaviorism's efforts to explain or describe language as being comparable to the creation of the "kiddiecar." His proposed model will be the "Model T" since "at least it has the advantage of putting the driver inside" (Osgood, 1963a, p. 741). It is a safe prediction the driver will look quite dissimilar to any Noam Chomsky would create. By reviewing the writings of each, it is clear that Braine and Osgood were a "good fit" to each other, albeit Braine was almost solely interested in syntactic development whereas Osgood was prone to use semantic issues as his launch point into the discussion of syntax.
Symbolically, Osgood's (1963a) model appears as follows:

$$Sr - sR$$

The S defines the actual sensory input from the environment; the R is the observable response made by the language user. The critical components, however, are the r and the s, both of which are internal components. Neither is even hinted at in Skinner's (1957) writings and are mentioned strictly by inference in Mowrer's (1954) work. The r and the s are, effectively, the O in the S-O-R Behavioristic model. As they are developed, both r and s play key roles in a sophisticated view of the O.

Both r and s are under all of the laws of general behavior theory which govern the S and the R, or, in other words, the "inner" world of information processing is the same as the outer regarding issues such as stimulus generalization, acquisition of habits, and extinction of habits. The r and s function under the same laws of probability as do the S and R. This makes the nature of human language development and usage mechanistic and "frees" us from such ambiguous, unvarifiable concepts as "free will," "free choice," "free decision," and "volition" or "intent." Due to the seemingly infinite number of association possibilities in the human central nervous system, the concept of "human nature" is by error granted "freedom." In reality, this "freedom" is only that part of human behavior which science has yet to define from known, predictable probabilistic associations. In no sense does Osgood believe this "cheapens" the status of humans or degrades the highest achievement of humans, e.g., the development of the sentence, but it certainly does place maximum stress upon science to "prove its case probabilistically."

Osgood begins by saying that we already know many descriptive things about language functioning: meaning. We know that meanings generalize to words having similar sounds/shapes and that meaning is less strong as the word becomes less like the word to which the meaning was originally attached; this process is known as "semantic generalization" (Osgood, Suci & Tannenbaum, 1957). We also know that words have both denotation and connotation where denotation is defined as a very specific set of elements (markers) which tell us objectively what the word does mean. Connotation refers to the "subjective," emotional aspects of words. Connotation can be subdivided into three aspects: evaluation (the goodness of a thing), potency (the strength of a thing), and activity (the amount of movement produced by a thing) (Osgood, Suci & Tannenbaum, 1957). Meaning generalizes on both the denotative and connotative levels. Aside from its "semantic generalization" function, word meaning has a "semantic satiation" function, which means meaningful words lose their meanings temporarily when repeated many times in sequence, whereas words with no apparent meaning neither lose nor gain meaning with simple sequential repetition (Lambert & Jakobovits, 1963). "Semantic generalization" and "semantic satiation" are involved in all language-behavior based activities, which includes all behaviors except for perception and motor learning. Perception is most probably a form of S-S learning, and motor learning is a form of R-R learning. At first glance, one might be repulsed by the assertion R-R learning has no verbal component—especially if the reader has any familiarity with the work of Luria (1959), which stresses the connection between verbal commands and motor performance especially in the behavior of preschool children and aphasics. Osgood refers to the association of muscle movement but does not stress verbal components in it.

Within any grammatical sentence, there are two mutually compatible processes occurring. One is convergent, and the second is divergent. The convergent process is concerned with "control," whereas the divergent process concerns itself with "choice," where choice is defined in the probabilistic sense. The convergent process works from left to right; the divergent process works in a vertical manner. The convergent process is described essentially by Markovian probabilistic rules; the divergent process is definitely not described by such rules. Let us suppose the word "chair" has been presented to you. According to Osgood's model, the stimulus is perceived on several levels simultaneously. Convergently, you attempt to find a suitable second word so as to chain words into a left to right sentence; divergently, you think of as many words as possible which are related to the stimulus word but by no means are related in the sense that they complete sentences. For example, "chair" convergently produces the verb "is" so as to complete a sentence. "Chair" divergently produces "desk," "table," "write," etc. According to Osgood, both processes occur simultaneously and with equal processing speed.

We note there is one problem that Osgood has perhaps overlooked. Research by Brown and Berko (1960), Ervin-Tripp (1961), and later by Anderson and Beh (1968) and Riley and Fite (1974) leads us to question his assertion of simultaneously complex convergent and divergent processes. All of these studies indicate that children when presented with a single word tend to produce associations to that word which reflect cognitive, qualitative changes in the child's thinking. Brown and Berko use the terms "heterogeneous" and "homogeneous" to describe a cognitive association pattern which Ervin-Tripp defines with the terms syntagmatic and paradigmatic respectively. Brown and Berko and Ervin-Tripp apparently agreed that children under seven years of age prefer making heterogeneous (syntagmatic) word associations, whereas children over nine prefer homogeneous (paradigmatic). Children ranging in ages from seven to nine seem to show a mixed preference with no clear pattern. Riley and Fite demonstrated that a cognitive shift from syntagmatic to paradigmatic preference was dependent upon the difficulty of the task. Children preferred making syntagmatic word associations even at age nine years if the words appeared in complex, abstract sentences. On the other hand, this same study showed that if the task were fairly easy (simply "free associating"), paradigmatic shifts were evident as early as seven years of age. If we allow ourselves to draw the analogy that syntagmatic associations are essentially convergent Osgoodian associations whereas paradigmatic associations are essentially Osgoodian divergent associations, we can see Osgood's assertion treading on very thin ice regarding the supposed equally complex and simultaneous timing of convergent and divergent processes. As long as sentence complexity and abstractness are always kept developmentally slightly ahead of the child's reach, the child should continue to prefer syntagmatic (convergent) processing strategies to paradigmatic (divergent) processing strategies. By no means is it being said here that children absolutely cannot perform paradigmatically while performing syntagmatically. It is merely curious that they prefer one over the other at various ages, and it is challenging to attempt to understand how children can demonstrate a clear behavioral performance difference of one over the other and still be thinking about both types of word association with an equal amount of simultaneous rigor. What is an example of a "syntagmatic" association? It is defined as responding with a different part of speech after a stimulus word is provided. Given "chair," the child responds with "is," for example. On the paradigmatic side, "chair" would produce a response of the same part of speech. For example, "chair" produces "desk," "table," or any other noun.

The basic expression of his model was Sr − sR. The simultaneous convergent and divergent processes must occur on the r level (decoding level). The S has triggered in the r both processes simultaneously. Literally, unless the S is completely novel to the receiver, the decoded portion becomes defined on a personal level which is rich with a past history of experiences through conditioning of both a classical and operant variety. The actual end products, e.g., that word or set of words produced on both the convergent and divergent levels, becomes the actual encoded stimulus (s) which will produce some observable response (R). In some cases, the R may appear highly improbable to the observer; careful behavioral analysis of the person's past experiences should, however, show us that the given response R was highly probable for that person under the given set of environmental circumstances and with the given set of reinforcers present. Admittedly, this complicates the picture since this "mediational stage" (r − s) is not something directly observable. Osgood complicates this by stating that there is no way to assure ourselves that the r and s even use the same "units" of linguistic analysis. In fact, it is more probable they do not. How close the decoding and encoding units are to appearing like one another under specific environmental circumstances is most probably best described as an interaction between one's past history of conditioning, the circumstances themselves, and the demands placed upon the system's neurological underpinnings. It is also tempting to say Osgood also included a

109

comment concerning our need to recognize cognitive stage changes as they affect the process. However, he did not.

The actual R produced from the first S's being decoded and then encoded can itself act as a S for the word following it. When it does act as a S, decoding and encoding again occur before a second R is produced. The process of Sr − sR → Sr − sR → ... continues as long as is needed until a sentence is "created." The entire chain of processes including the S, convergence, and divergence in r, s, and R phases are defined as strictly mathematically probabilistic. What appears as "free or random association," "slips of the tongue," or "grammatical errors" are defined as such only because the community of language users surrounding the speaker or writer generally agrees that what has been spoken or written is highly improbable. In short, the culture defines what is "acceptable" and reinforces the acceptable to make it more highly probable of occurrence. In his presentation of this model before the American Psychological Association, it was interesting to note that he senses the probability of losing some of his audience due to his model's obviously heavy emphasis upon probability. He demonstrates his sensitivity by stating that complexity is the price for the highest human achievement, producing a sentence. He also seriously doubts that this model is either subtle or sensitive enough to be sufficient and begs us to brace ourselves as we prepare to dive from yet a higher altitude. Before departing, however, he has two specific criticisms to send toward Chomsky's Transformational Grammar Model.

First, Chomsky in *Syntactic Structures* (1957) stated his rejection of the Markovian form of analysis because he said it meant that processing could occur only on the convergent level (left- to right-hand direction). Osgood admits to using a Markov-like analysis but also adds the divergent process discussed above. Second, Osgood says Chomsky is openly critical of Skinner (Chomsky, 1959) because Skinner did not discuss how language rules are developed. Osgood believes that discussing rules of any kind is a question of determining probabilities. As Osgood knows, Chomsky does not discuss probabilities.

Osgood builds a rather solid case for his general position that a Markovian model is not useless despite Chomsky's position. He cites research done by Johnson in the early 1960s to show that the probability of making an error in the process of selecting a word to fill a phrase is less than the probability of error seen when we move from the end of one phrase to the beginning of the next. For example, in the sentence "Tom is a thief.", the probability that we would necessarily pick "Tom" as the word to begin our sentence with is much less than is the probability we would pick the word "is" to follow "Tom." The article "a" is highly probable following a verb. The word "thief" is a noun which most probably follows "a," so the probability of error is reduced to a point less than that for selecting the word "Tom." After all, when we started the sentence with "Tom," we had absolutely nothing to decrease the probability of error except the context cues which preceded "Tom." Those cues were in a separate sentence. The Markovian chain of left to right hand probabilities shows decreasing probabilities of error through to the last word itself.

To make the model actually work, Osgood says we need three more things: (1) the Word Form Pool, (2) the Semantic Key Sort, and (3) the Cognitive Mixer. Each of these qualifies less as a "thing" than it does as a "process." The Word Form Pool has two functions: (a) it acts "reflectively," e.g., it allows us to see or hear the word that has just been read or spoken, and (b) it has a memory function. The two phases allow us to take any word spoken or read and in a gestalt-like fashion add to that word any "parts" we believe are missing. The Word Form Pool thereby reduces uncertainty as to what was read or heard by providing "closure" and "unitizing" the input. By closure, we are referring to filling in (or perhaps occasionally discarding) parts of any stimulus pattern. By "unitizing," we are referring to decreasing the number of "loose ends" of the stimulus pattern so it may be smoothly processed in the next stage. Unitization does not necessarily mean discarding ambiguous parts of a word, but such may actually happen in order to produce the desired end product. For example, the word "TAE" will usually be read as "THE" if it is in the appropriate context. The Word Form Pool "polishes it" to make it better fit where it belongs. With enough of the stimulus changed, the Word Form Pool may simply be unable to make the word fit at all. For example, "EAT" will probably never look like "THE" no matter how many contextual cues are provided. The products of the Word Form Pool are actually words, not morphemes. Osgood claims on the basis of research data that the morpheme is not the simplest unit for language analysis since morphemes may actually have longer processing time than do words. For example, in the word "MOTHER" the two morphemes are "MO" and "THER." The entire word is recognized far more quickly than are either of its morphemic parts. Since the Word Form Pool seeks ultimate efficiency, the word becomes the basic unit for further analysis. Even though Osgood cannot define the underlying physiological processes the Word Form Pool bases itself upon, he can say the word can be "completed and polished" in the space provided simply because D. O. Hebb had already demonstrated that recently stimulated neuron chains act as "revivaboratory circuits" (Hebb, 1949). Or, in other words, the stimulation simply does not activate any nerve cell or set of cells in such a manner as to cause only one reaction.

Words in the Word Form Pool float without association to one another. Each word in the pool is meaningless. When a word leaves the Word Form Pool because its probability of being the next word in the sentence has made it a prime candidate to be "called up," the word enters the Semantic Key Sort, which causes the word's meanings to become activated. Meaning takes two forms inside the Word Form Pool: "Denotation" refers to specific, objective meaning. "Connotation" is the subjective feeling aspect of meaning and also includes how widely we allow the objective meaning to generalize. It might be added here that each word from the Semantic Key Sort not only undergoes the denotative convergent/divergent processing discussed above, but it also undergoes a form of connotative meaning analysis. The connotative system is best defined as having three component parts: (1) the evaluative component makes a judgment as to the goodness of a word, (2) the potency component makes a judgment regarding the strength or weakness of a word, and (3) the activity component makes a judgment as to the speed of action a particular word contains. All the connotative elements of meaning are best described in this book's chapter on semantic development and specifically detailed in Osgood, Suci, and Tannenbaum (1957). The Semantic Differential Technique (Osgood, Suci & Tannenbaum, 1957). was specifically devised to measure the three dimensions of connotative meaning listed above and has been successfully used in cross-cultural comparisons of certain words and phrases. But if one is keeping score, we know now that meaning analysis in the Key Sort takes place on the denotative level (convergently and divergently) and on the connotative level (evaluation, potency, and activity) simultaneously. Osgood wishes to use the symbol "r_m" as the label for the entire processing sequence's output that emerges from the Semantic Key Sort.

The question could easily be asked here as to how all this discussion of semantics and generalization on the convergent and divergent levels explains any part of the development of syntax. Osgood has a quick response to this. The very essence of snytactic development may actually lie in semantic processing. For example, what determines precisely what word will occur at which position in a sentence? It surely must be heavily, if not entirely, based upon the flow of meanings from word to word. It is a flow of probabilities, and it is, therefore, possible for us to conclude that syntax is definable via a Markovian grammar model. Considering the fact that Case Grammar (McCawley, 1968; Fillmore, 1968; & Bloom, 1970) leads us to the conclusion that the earliest analysis level in syntax is on the semantic level, Osgood may have hit the target dead-

112

center with his comments which appeared three years prior to the development of Case Grammar Analysis. Osgood is, however, unwilling to state that he firmly believes that all syntactic growth can be traced to semantic underpinnings. To the contrary, he asserts that there is needed at least a third element to combine with and support the Word Form Pool and the Semantic Key Sort. The third element is the Cognitive Mixer. The description of the Cognitive Mixer's functions as well as its mechanics is the most ambiguous part of Osgood's model. He cites the fact that the Cognitive Mixer has one function that has been researched; it seeks congruity among meanings within a sentence. This is surely a process far beyond the capacity of the Semantic Key Sort since the Key Sort only has to retrieve various stored meanings and has no responsibility for any possible conflicts in those meanings as the meanings interact in the Cognitive Mixer. The very term Cognitive Mixer surely is a classic oversimplification. Osgood fears the possibility that people may attempt to build a "little linguistic" inside each of us to do the processing of the products of the Key Sort. This is "unthinkable" for him since it would explain nothing and would perhaps actually impede our progress toward an explanation. Realizing the limits of the profession's growth in the field of cognitive psychology, he abandons further comment regarding the functions of the Cognitive Mixer.

Osgood asks if the complexity of his position has in any fashion made it less appealing, e.g., especially to the S-R Behaviorists such as those followers of O. H. Mowrer and B. F. Skinner. He offers no apology, and in fact, he says the probability is quite high that the proposed model with its Markovian emphasis is hardly more than a very crude "successive approximation" to the actual process it attempts to merely describe. Considering the fact that the production of the sentence may be the highest achievement the human race can presently boast of, complexity seems a small price to pay for approaching the truth.

Current Status of S-O-R Behaviorism

Whether S-R Behaviorism and S-O-R Behaviorism are alive and well today depends upon whom you ask. Palermo (1978, p. 20) states that both approaches to describing and/or explaining language have made two assumptions that are in error. First, both approaches have ignored the physiology and genetics of the language user, and secondly, both are generalizing from the findings of studies conducted on lower animals to explain human functioning. Palermo indicates that he tried using both of these approaches when they first became popular and found them entirely too narrow in scope. He does report the work of Staats (1971) as being an improvement over that of Mowrer and Skinner; Staats has tried to combine both classical and operant conditioning to explain language learning. Palermo apparently does not believe anyone has added much to Osgood's work; Palermo cites the work of Whitehurst and Vasta (1975) as being interested in S-O-R mediation but not making any new contributions. The assertion that Whitehurst and Vasta add nothing new to mediation theory is a superb tribute to the fact that Osgood's model still stands relatively intact.

It is Maclay (1973) who adds a healing touch to the disagreements. He states that no one looking at the major question, e.g., how do children develop their language, really debates the fact that empirical proof will surely appear to settle the arguments. Even before that day, both linguists and psychologists will (and presently are) cross boundary lines into each other's "territory." As this happens, it will become progressively more difficult to take a stand without someone from ones own camp finding a flaw or, better yet, a better explanation for ones data from a supposed opposing camp. But the tendency to attempt to create a controversy where perhaps none really exists is too strong for many to resist. For example, Kess (1976) gives Osgood credit for his model and finds it generally more adequate than that of either Mowrer or Skinner, but Kess still cannot resist going further with his comments until he finds himself saying that language is essentially a gestalt process where the total meaning of a sentence is more than the sum of its parts. Such a contention would please no S-R or S-O-R Behaviorist since Behaviorism has always found it presumptuous that anyone would claim to be able to identify the composition of a "part." To claim that the whole is more than the sum of its parts would seem to be the greatest presumption of all.

The evidence is fairly clear today that the development of additional S-R or S-O-R Behavioristic theories has come to a halt. Perhaps Osgood believed he had already said enough, or perhaps there simply was not enough reinforcement made available to cause him to pursue his own model. In any case, the basic model presented in 1963 was never significantly expanded in published form.

As for M. D. S. Braine's model dealing with contextual generalization, it seems to have gone the unexpanded route of Osgood's semantic generalization model. Long gone are the heated interchanges with Bever, Fodor, and Weksel and other Transformational Grammarians such as G. A. Miller. But is Behaviorism dead? We shall see.

References

Anderson, S., and Beh, W. (1968). "The Reorganization of Verbal Memory in Childhood." *Journal of Verbal Learning and Verbal Behavior, 7,* 1049—1053.

Bever, T., Fodor, J., and Weksel, W. (1965a). "On the Acquisition of Syntax: A Critique of 'Contextual Generalization.'" *Psychological Review, 72,* 467—482.

Bever, T. Fodor, J., and Weksel, W. (1965b). "Is Linguistics Empirical?" *Psychological Review, 72,* 493—500.

Bloom, L. (February, 1970). *Semantic Features of Language Acquisition.* Paper presented on the Conference on Research in the Language of the Mentally Retarded, University of Kansas.

Braine, M. D. S. (1963). "On Learning the Grammatical Order of Words." *Psychological Review, 70,* 323—348.

Braine, M. D. S. (1965). "On the Basis of Phrase Structure: A Reply to Bever, Fodor, and Weksel." *Psychological Review, 72,* 483-492.

Braine, M. D. S. (1971). "On Two Types of Models of the Internalization of Grammar." In D. Slobin (Ed.), *The Ontogenesis of Grammar* (153—168). New York: Academic Press.

Brown, R., and Berko, J. (1960). "Word Association and the Acquisition of Grammar." *Child Development, 31,* 1—14.

Carroll, L. (1906). *Alice's Adventures in Wonderland.* New York: Macmillan.

Chomsky, N. (1957). *Syntactic Structures.* The Hague: Mouton.

Chomsky, N. (1959). "Review of Skinner's *Verbal Behavior.*" *Language, 35,* 26—58.

Dale, P. S. (1976). *Language Development.* New York: Holt.

Ervin-Tripp, S. (1961). "Changes with Age in the Verbal Determinants of Word Association." *American Journal of Psychology, 74,* 361—372.

Ferster, C., and Skinner, B. F. (1957). *Schedules of Reinforcement.* New York: Appleton, Century, and Crofts.

Fillmore, C. (1968). "The Case of Case." In E. Bach and R. Hams (Eds.), *Universals in Linguistic Theory* (1—88). New York: Holt.

Hebb, D. O. (1949). *The Organization of Behavior: A Neurophysiological Theory.* New York: Wiley.

Hulse, S., Egeth, H., and Deese, J. (1980). *The Psychology of Learning* (5th ed.). St. Louis, Missouri: McGraw-Hill.

Kess, J. (1976). *Psycholinguistics.* New York: Academic Press.

Lambert, W., and Jakobovits, L. (1963). *The Case for Semantic Satiation.* Montreal: McGill University (mimeo).

Luria, A. (1959). "The Directive Function of Speech in Development and Dissolution. Part I: Development of the Directive Function of Speech in Early Childhood." *Word, 15,* 341—352.

Maclay, H. (1973). "Linguistics and Psycholinguistics." In B. Kachru (Ed.), *Issues in Linguistics* (569—587). Urbana: University of Illinois Press.

McCawley, J. D. (1968). "The Role of Semantics in a Grammar." In E. Bach and R. Hams (Eds.), *Universals in Linguistic Theory* (124—169). New York: Holt.

Miller, G. A., and Selfridge, J. (1950). "Verbal Context and the Recall of Meaningful Material." *American Journal of Psychology, 63,* 176—185.

Mowrer, O. H. (1954). "The Psychologist Looks at Language." *The American Psychologist, 9,* 660—694.

Mowrer, O. H. (1960). *Learning Theory and the Symbolic Process.* New York: Wiley.

Osgood, C. E. (1957). "A Behavioristic Analysis of Perception and Meaning as Cognitive Phenomena." *Symposium on Cognition, University of Colorado* (1955). Cambridge, Massachusetts: Harvard University Press.

Osgood, C. E. (1963a). "On Understanding and Creating Sentences." *American Psychologist, 18*, 735—751.

Osgood, C. E. (1963b). "Psycholinguistics." In S. Koch (Ed.), *Psychology: The Study of a Science* (244—316). New York: McGraw-Hill.

Osgood, C. E., Suci, G., and Tannenbaum, P. (1957). *The Measurement of Meaning.* Urbana: University of Illinois Press.

Palermo, D. (1978). *Psychology of Language.* Dallas, Texas: Scott.

Riley, L., and Fite, G. (1974). "Syntagmatic versus Paradigmatic Paired-Associate Acquisition." *Journal of Experimental Psychology, 103*, 375—376.

Skinner, B. F. (1957). *Verbal Behavior.* New York: Appleton, Century, and Crofts.

Spence, K. W. (1937). "The Differential Response in Animals to Stimuli Varying Within a Single Dimension." *Psychological Review, 44*, 430—444.

Staats, A. (1971). "Linguistic-Mentalistic Theory versus Explanatory S-R Learning Theory of Language Development." In S. Slobin (Ed.), *The Ontogenesis of Grammar: Some Facts and Several Theories* (41—62). New York: Academic Press.

Whitehurst, G., and Vasta, R. (1975). "Is Language Acquired Through Imitation?" *Journal of Psycholinguistic Research, 4*, 37—60.

– 6 –

NORMAL SYNTACTIC DEVELOPMENT

The actual course of how children's sounds and words and finally sentences develop has had many and varied interpretations. There are still vast areas where either the facts are missing or where the facts contradict each other. This is to be expected in a field as relatively new as this one, but there is another specific reason which is worth our attention. It lies in the heart of the scientific process itself. It is the issue of sufficiency/adequacy of observation. Most studies lack sufficiency because they are looking at surface structure functioning; many lack adequacy because of the limited number of children who compose the study's sample size. Many of the classic studies run by Roger Brown in the 1960s dealt with as few as two or three children (Brown, Fraser and Bellugi, 1964; Brown, 1968). Albeit it is possible to run studies on small groups of subjects, as B. F. Skinner (1959) has contended for many good reasons, it is usually wiser to use as many subjects as one can find when the issue confronting the researcher involves discussing variation around a main trend as well as the main trend itself. Any discussion of normal syntactic development would seem to necessarily lead us to a discussion of both variation and main trends.

Phonology

Of all the areas within normal syntactic development where we find the least disagreement, we have phonology. Phonology is the study of the sound system which is used in the reception and expression of oral surface structures. The physical mechanisms producing these sounds include the lips, teeth, tongue, nasal passages, vocal cords, lungs, and various bone structures in the head. With the exception of the vocal cords, all other physical mechanisms have primary functions aside from their secondary functions of producing speech. It is primarily in the development of vocal cord functioning that the human race's sound-producing equipment varies from that of the lower animals. Although tonal quality (timbre, resonance, and nasality) is partially learned and is, therefore, subject to regional cultural conditioning, it is still heavily determined by the genetically-determined physical equipment of the speaker.

Each language in the world has both vowel and consonant sounds. According to Dale (1976, p. 201), there are in English 20 consonant sounds, 12 vowel sounds, and two "liquids/two glides"; all four of the latter two sound types are often listed as vowels. The "liquids" are "l" and "r"; the "glides" are "w" and "y." A quick check against the written English alphabet shows that there are apparently 10 more sounds (36 total sounds minus 26 letters in the alphabet) than there are specific alphabetic letters. This lack of an isomorphic (one to one) correspondence between a sound and its English alphabetic representation is a troublesome problem for children learning to read and write. A case can be made for the logic of keeping the number of alphabetic letters low since they must be rote memorized and are generally more abstract in nature than are the speech sounds. The definitions of which sounds serve as consonants, vowels, and liquids/glides vary from language to language and even within a given language across time. The number of sounds and corresponding letters used in any language is a product of historical tradition coupled with the needs of the culture at any given moment. Very frequently used sounds and words become "streamlined" so as to reduce the tedium and redundancy of their "features" in daily communication. This last point, by the way, is predicted and discussed by O. H. Mowrer (1954) in his concept of "inertia" (see Chapter 4).

Clark and Clark (1977, pp. 177-207) discuss the levels of phonological analysis available to us. The most basic level is at the "allophonic" strata. If you slowly say the letter "l," it is apparent the total letter is a compilation of several smaller sounds. Each component qualifies. The number of allophones must be greater than the number of major sounds ("phonemes"). Measurement and analysis of the sound system on the allophonic level is quite difficult since allophones are especially sensitive to dialectical patterns in varying geographic areas and various forms of mispronunciation or omission caused by a host of personal factors such as momentary fatigue, eagerness to communicate, or affects of alcohol or drugs—just to name a very few. A certain number of allophones must exist within any given space of time if a phoneme is to be perceived; however, the necessary number of allophones may very well vary depending upon the amount and quality of contextual sound cues one has surrounding the to-be-recognized phoneme. For example, an "l" phoneme in the word "alive" may be missing a large number of allophonic components with no consequent misunderstanding of the phoneme itself as long as we are saying "alive and well." The amount of allophonic distortion or removal becomes increasingly critical as the context cues become less effective. In cases where context cues are missing or minimal, the person doing the listening may still understand badly distorted phoneme sounds if the listener is capable of imposing his or her own experiential background upon the situation. There is, of course, a limit.

Clark and Clark (1977, pp. 177-207) make a useful distinction between "phonetic" and "phonemic" development. The former is the descriptive system which portrays the language as it was actually presented. It is an uncomplicated form of shorthand coding and is not meant to be abstract or theoretical. The International Phonetic Alphabet is accepted as having the appropriate symbol representations capable of very adequate description of any known language. Many sounds in the IPA are not present in all languages at any given time. English, for example, has 36 phonetic units it can use to describe all possible adult-produced English utterances. That leaves us with 19 sounds unused and yet listed in the IPA. By their definition, each phonetic symbol is a "distinctive feature" since it causes a change in meaning in a word if the phoneme is changed; changing allophones does not necessarily cause meaning changes. Phonemic development is an abstract, rule-oriented process. A phonemic analysis attempts to establish the essence of a sound independent of the language in which a given sound occurs. A phonemic analysis looks for the very "truth" of a sound despite the sound's context or the experiences of the individual using the sound. A phonemic analysis attempts to define the specific rules which make the sound what it is in its pure form. A phonemic analysis is, therefore, more than a descriptive system despite the fact that it can serve its own descriptive needs. Phonemic and phonetic transcriptions are often confused for one another. The term "phonetic" is an adjective which describes the process being imposed upon the thing itself. The "thing itself," the phoneme, has various specific dimensions which include speed, timbre, pitch, nasality, and, of course, can be classified as serving the function of a consonant or a vowel or a liquid or a glide. A phonemic analysis is concerned about how suffixes and prefixes develop, are added to or taken from words, and how such additions/deletions affect word meaning and sound production. In short, as Clark and Clark (1977) put it, a phonemic analysis is literally concerned with what U. Neisser (1967) has referred to as an "analysis by synthesis." Perhaps it is something of an oversimplification, but an analysis by synthesis is generally thought of as a "gestalt-like" process where the sum is more than the additive result of simply combining the parts. This is a reasonable statement concerning the use of phonemes considering our previous discussion regarding the minimally disrupting effects of removing or distorting allophones.

Aside from the fact that the technology of both phonetic and phonemic analyses is presently very adequately established and is employed very efficiently both by linguists and computers, the question has arisen regarding the value of such analyses. One immediate answer, and it is a very good one, relates to the presence of many studies of a cross-cultural and/or cross-language nature in which the phonetic/phonemic analyses have produced very interesting and useful data which allows both discussion about the impact of past social forces and the promise of change through institutional, political, and economic impact. But the question is broader than all this; it concerns the essence of phonemics itself. Does the understanding of the sound system suffice to produce an explanation for the development of language? J. J. Katz (1964) cites the linguist Charles Bloomfield as having said that studying the nature and utility of the phoneme's essence is like studying a "fire in a wooden stove!" His point is well made; atomistic analysis of virtually everything in the Behavioral Sciences has most predictably raised cries of alarm concerning the loss of that something's essence. Trying to reassemble the whole from the parts has often left us short. The sentiments of Bloomfield were echoed by the Prague School of Linguistics prior to World War II in the writings of Trubetzkoy and Jakobson (Palermo, 1978, pp. 44–48). Jakobson and Halle (1956) popularized the idea that the phoneme is far too large to be a single unit. The phoneme is actually a set of "features" that must be identified by the user. Jakobson and Halle state that children compare features in pairs during the initial stages of phonemic growth. Features within the pairs act as perfect contrasting points and, therefore, serve to "anchor" each other in place. This may sound a bit unusual as a linguistic relationship, but we can see the general principle by realizing that we typically think in terms of word opposites when we see words such as "hot" (hot/cold), "slow" (slow/fast), "high" (high/low), etc. Jakobson and Halle, according to Dale (1976, pp. 215–216) list the basic contrasts as (1) oral vs. nasal, e.g., /b/vs./m/, (2) labial vs. dental, e.g., /p/vs./t/, and (3) stop vs. fricative, e.g., /p/vs./f/. All three contrasts develop simultaneously and then expands so as to incorporate all other features from the other phonemes. Ultimately, all the sounds the child will use are developed by this system. Since phonemes usually have more than one feature, we can see how in the above example /p/ can qualify both as a "labial" and as a "stop" simultaneously. The phoneme /p/ simply cannot be considered as a single unit. The general advantage of using Jakobson and Halle's approach lies in its greater in-depth look at changes occurring in word pronunciation (Palermo, 1978, p. 47). The system reads well enough. But, as Dale (1976, p. 217) points out, what the child knows about the sound system from a feature perspective and what the child is capable of producing are not necessarily isomorphic. Many children will protest your pronouncing "rabbit" as "wabbit" despite the fact they cannot say anything other than "wabbit" until after some maturing of certain specific mechanisms. The entire set of data has not come in on Jakobson and Halle's position, but at least few people would now claim that the phoneme is the "basic unit" of speech.

We know that consonant sounds are made with the lips, teeth, and tongue as the mouth is in the closed or nearly closed position. Vowels are made with the mouth in an open position and are produced by the vibrating of the vocal cords. The progression of sound development has been specified by Kaplan and Kaplan (1971). Their stages are as follows:

1. *Crying:* This form of sound production begins at birth and is generally produced in order to signal that a perceived personal need is not being met. Crying varies in intensity and duration as a function of the age of the child, immediacy of the unmet need, intensity of the unmet immediate need, and the amount of reinforcement such sound production is met with. Although crying is a biologically produced reflex, its expression seems subject to reinforcement contingencies produced in the culture.

2. *Prebabbling and cooing sounds:* By the end of the first month after birth, crying has generally been replaced as the child's major communication mode. Prebabbling occurs at this point. Prebabbling is defined as the production of partial speech sounds, or, more specifically, the production of allophonic sequences which do not comprise the production of fully operational phonemes. It is not infrequent that the prebabbling behavior may be heard by adults as being the utterance of full phonemes. This is generally, albeit not always, a delusion produced by the adult's normal tendency to close sounds in such a manner as to produce a gestalt whole.

Cooing behavior appears at the end of the second month and persists in abundance until the child begins to develop the "back vowel" sounds, which the cooing sounds appear to facilitate.

3. *Babbling:* This phase begins during the fifth or sixth month and is accompanied by the production of phonemically complete vowels and consonant sounds. The consonants develop from the back to the front of

the mouth; the vowels develop in the opposite direction. There seems to be a rather cherished myth that each child will develop all of the phonemic sounds used in all languages of the world during the period from six months to twelve months of age. The myth continues by saying that the use of selective reinforcement, e.g., from the parents or culture at large, causes the child to "drop out" the phoneme sounds that are not going to be used by an adult version. Wahler (1969) has contended such a "drop-out" procedure is a faulty reading of the actual sequence of events. Wahler contends that parents, e.g., mothers (who are usually more in contact with the child the first year than are the fathers), do not systematically and selectively reinforce the child, nor does the culture attempt to instruct the parents to achieve such ends. Albeit, Wahler's point is undoubtedly true regarding the fact that neither the parents nor the culture are systematic, the fact cannot be overlooked that both the parents and the culture "know" tacitly what sounds do and do not belong in the language. Parents and cultures are fully capable of shaping children toward progressively more accurate successive approximations of the language's sound system perhaps just as easily, if indeed not more so, as the parents and the culture shape successive approximations of either syntax or semantics. If we accept Wahler's argument against reinforcement's shaping the sound system, we supposedly would need to reject the idea that the child started from prebabbling and was shaped in successive approximations up to the point of a full-fledged adult phonemic system. After all, if we are to be consistent with Wahler's premise, an adult community and/or culture which cannot tell you what sounds not to use surely would have just as hard a time telling the child systematically what to use. If the adult community and/or culture is, therefore, removed from the picture, Wahler's position must reduce itself to the absurd contention that the child born into any specific language culture must genetically know what to develop. The selective reinforcement idea from either its position regarding selective "drop out" or from its position of successive build up is also rejected by Jakobson. The most reasonable solution to this apparent theoretical conflict lies in accepting a middle-of-the-road answer. Surely children make a genetically predetermined contribution to what sounds they will develop. At the same time, that same child is selectively reinforced for his/her production by parents and the culture; they learned to "hear" those sounds which provide a "good fit" to their expectations.

Generally during the first four months of babbling, vowels will outnumber consonant sounds at a ratio of 5:1. The quality and quantity of babbling is highly positively correlated to later IQ scores (at approximately age six years) for girls, but, for some unknown reason, is zero for boys. At one year of age both boys and girls tend to pause very briefly in their babbling and then do several things which are quite curious. First, they act as if redeveloping the entire babbling stage, but they do so in just a few days and, especially worthy of note, they do it in the reverse order of the way they originally did it! Consonant sounds are now rehearsed starting from the front of the mouth and are developed sequentially toward the back of the mouth. Vowels are rehearsed starting in the back of the mouth and are then sequentially developed toward the front. Second, the number of consonant sounds begins to rapidly outnumber the vowel sounds, this is typical for adults. The rehearsal acts as the "polishing" step to complete the already well-practiced babbling phase. Much of the babbling is accompanied by misarticulations due to adding or deleting allophones. Simple maturation of the speech organs and heavy doses of parental/cultural reinforcement correct these "errors."

4. *Patterned speech:* In this phase Kaplan and Kaplan say the child begins using his/her first true words. Curiously, the child uses very few phonemes to produce the first single words and appears to have lost some of the many phonemes at his/her control. This "loss" is an illusion; the phonemes are occasionally babbled independently of one-word creations. As the child expands his/her vocabulary, the phonemes left unused are gradually brought into play. There is no evidence that a specific set of phonemes is universally involved in the production of the first words; it apparently is mostly determined by the culture. This marks the crucial turning point in the separation of humans from the lower animals and paves the way for the development of syntax. However, disagreement exists over this latter point; Dale (1976, p. 206) believes that "segmental units" (consonants and vowels) develop during the babbling stage at the same time "supersegmental" units (stress, intonation, and rhythm) do. He believes semantic development may find its starting place in the supersegmental units. If McCawley (1968), Fillmore (1968), and Bloom (1970) are correct in their assumptions that syntax is first based upon initial, foregoing semantic development, Dale could reasonably assert that syntactic growth is begun during the babbling stage's development of supersegmentals. However, there is one small catch here; Dale, at present, cannot find the data to prove that semantic growth begins during and is dependent directly upon supersegmental unit development. If such proof can be found, we will need to push the initial stages of the development of syntax back some six months earlier than its generally accepted starting point at one year of age, which coincides with the production of the first word for children of normal intelligence and cognitive maturity. Dale may not necessarily

123

be as speculative as he first appears; he (Dale, 1976, p. 223) cites the work of Chomsky and Halle (1968) who said that development of a phonemic system is a parentally/culturally prescribed form of behavior calculated to meet the demands of social communication. Underlying each phonemic unit is a semantic unit which the child uses in personal processing before any phoneme or word is spoken.

The One-Word Phase

When the first word appears in Kaplan and Kaplan's (1971) "Patterned Speech" stage, the child is usually 12 months old. The first word is a hallmark event in the family. The child's "random babblings" prior to this point had gone somewhat unnoticed or had been classified as signs of better things to come. The first word usually takes the form of a noun, but it need not necessarily do so. Nouns are "open class," content words and communicate concrete meaning at this stage. There is nothing to necessarily stop a child from using a "closed class morpheme" (also known by the terms "pivot" and "functor"). The fact that children rarely use closed class morphemes as first words should prove to be a substantial embarrassment to M. D. S. Braine (1963a, 1965), who claimed children learned sentence frames first and then fitted the frames with the open class morphemes. Since Braine is not a mentalist/rationalist, he cannot claim that the child's performance does not necessarily reflect which is happening in the "child's mind." The first word acts not as just a single word but as a "holophrase." This means the child tries to express an entire set of thoughts through the use of the single word. For example, a word such as "Moma" can actually mean about anything the child cares to make it mean, but the probability is that the child is trying to tell anyone around him/her that a need is to be met. "Moma" does not necessarily mean that the child has a particular "female" in mind if the need is great enough. Many fathers (and unmarried males) have found it rather amusing and even occasionally mildly disturbing to realize that "Moma" is being pointed at them.

The number of single word utterances is larger than most observers might guess. Palermo (1978, p. 190) cites the general vocabulary of the child between 12 to 18 or 24 months to be approximately 200 to 500 words. Fortunately, not all of these are used as holophrases since some are functors. If all of them were used, the typical adult would have an unbelievably complex task understanding the child's intentions. According to Palermo (1978, p. 191), research on the one word sentence has been restricted. He cites the work of Bloom (1973) as well as that of

Greenfield and Smith (1976) to indicate the flavor of what little is available. Their research shows that children may be using the one word sentence in two ways. First, the single word stands as a "referential" unit; this means the word stands for whatever "specific" meaning the child wishes to communicate. But secondly, and perhaps much more importantly, the word has "combinational" meaning, which means the word is spoken to communicate a progression of ongoing events. For example, when the child says "Moma," s/he has action in mind which would surely read as "Moma (come, see, do, help, hold, etc.)," but the child is incapable of putting the second word into the necessary position. This combinational meaning explodes the assumption that the child in the one word phase is not at all concerned with the rules of developing syntax. This idea sounds reasonable since their older peers are still trying to complete sentences by making syntagmatic rather than paradigmatic word associations even at age seven or eight years (Riley & Fite, 1974). We are still forced to do a bit of "mind reading" in order to conclude that children in the holophrastic phase are thinking in terms of combinational meanings. Because of the very fact that they are using only one word per sentence, we cannot be certain that they are thinking in terms of two or more words per sentence. Palermo (1978, p. 193) makes a very interesting and subtle point after completing his review of Bloom (1970) as well as Greenfield and Smith (1976). He muses whether it is the context, and not the promise of other words yet to be associated with the single word sentence, which actually produces the illusion in the adult observer that surely the child is thinking far beyond what s/he says. It would indeed be easy to read combinational meaning into such a context. Palermo predicts that surely someone will pursue this issue; no one answered his call.

The Random Two-Word Phase

The title of this section is somewhat misleading because it implies that the stage of development following the one-word utterance phase is necessarily a stage of haphazard combinations. Palermo (1978, pp. 193—195) portrays this stage as starting at about 18 months of age and lasting for as long as half a year depending upon the individual child, the language's requirements, and the amount of reinforcement given. At least 70% of its utterances appear as organized syntactic units. The remaining 30% look like random combinations. Palermo cites the writings of Brown and Fraser (1964) and Brown, Fraser, and Bellugi (1964), among others, showing that the child at this period is prone to use a pivot word (closed class morpheme) and an open class word (noun or verb usually) when constructing the first two-word sentences. The order of the two words may be predicted to be about equally probably an "open-pivot" or a "pivot-open" or an "open-open" construction. An example of an "open-pivot" would be "Horsie down." The words may be reversed to produce the example of the "pivot-open" sentence. This should be quite interesting to those readers who accepted M. D. S. Braine's (1963a) theory of "contextual generalization" since he claimed that pivots were very crucial in the child's development of syntax. The fit to Braine's model may even be better than that when we consider the work of Brown et. al., cited immediately above, which shows that the words that are used are shortened and appear "telegraphic" in form. The case could be made that the child was using Braine's model while s/he successively approximated the adult models s/he has overheard. The fact that no inflectional endings or intonations are used in this phase discredits Braine's model.

The Ordered Two-Word Phase

As the heading "Random Two-Word Phase" used above was slightly misleading, so too is the present heading. Not all of the child's utterances in this phase are perfectly ordered—at least not in a fashion one could readily identify as an adult order. This phase is difficult to understand because it seems to challenge any theory presented so far regarding a sufficient description let alone a sufficient explanation. It is tempting to take Kess' (1976) point of view, which asks why so much has recently been said regarding such an admittedly short time period. The research conducted on this phase may have opened some very significant directions toward our understanding not only of this phase but of phases which follow it.

The controversy centers on the issue of what exactly is the strategy the child must adopt in order to put two words into a logically progressive adult sequence. McNeill and McNeill (1968) were perhaps the first to state that the child's strategy centers around his/her learning that the deep structure of any utterance is generally sufficient to communicate ones meaning to a listener. The child may then concentrate on the transformational rules which allow for the expression of greater and greater complexity of thought. This conclusion is partly based upon an analysis of Roger Brown's data collected on Adam, one of Brown's three most famous subjects (McNeill, 1966). But as Palermo (1978) points out, Bloom (1970) was quick to object to the sufficiency, and indeed the very accuracy, of McNeill's approach. As Bloom states it, the very first thing the child must do is to realize that the syntactic development of his/her words must match the order of events (actions) in the real world as adults perceive it. This is definitely not to say that the child must conceptually understand this, but at least the "tacit" intuition must exist if the child is to progress. We can see the inherent merit of Bloom's logic still further if we reconsider the point made in Chapter 4 of this book regarding the fact that TG had made little effort to do much with word meaning. It had said that meaning was somewhere "in" deep structure. You will also recall that Bloom (1970), McCawley (1968), and Fillmore (1968) and Bever, Fodor and Weksel (1965) contended that deep structure was presumptuous in its relative inattention to semantic development and too self-assurred in its attempt to hurry the business of the child's creation of rules in the transformational hierarchy. But the comments of Bloom and her colleagues in no sense solved our problem regarding how a child actually acquires and processes meanings. Bloom notes a curious event in that children entering this phase use not one but rather many strategies, e.g., some learn easily and continually practice sentences made of a subject and an object; others choose to concentrate on the verb-object sentence type, and still others prefer the subject-verb sentence as a starting point. R. Brown (1973) accepts Bloom's emphasis upon establishing meaning as part of syntactic development. He says that parents have little if any impact upon the child's syntactic development in this or preceding stages. One small exception to Brown's comment could be taken if we consider Palermo's (1978, p. 197) citation of the work of Nelson (1973). Nelson found parental reinforcement playing a significant role regarding the target at which the child's meaning pointed, e.g., children seemed to be part of one or another of two mutually exclusive groups. The first group was called the "referential group" because all communication seemed directed to points reflecting the child's interaction with objects but not with people. The "expressional" group oriented its comments in the direction of people to the exclusion of objects. At no point does Nelson state any disagreement with Bloom's comments on strategies or Brown's comments on the dismal failure of reinforcement to shape those strategies.

Roger Brown has done more research on the two-word sentence than anyone else. Although he was not the first to write on this topic (see Braine, 1963b), his research is accepted as being thorough on a longitudinal basis.

Brown's (1973) research used natural observation and experimentation. He and his colleagues, Fraser, Bellugi, and Cazden spent years watching the behaviors of three children: Adam, Eve, and Sarah. De-

127

spite this small number of subjects, the results produced remarkably similar findings for each child; the results are proposed as universals. Brown is aware that extensive research conducted with one subject is potentially quite beneficial just as long as the observation process continues across a very long period and is quite thorough.

According to Brown, children enter the two-word phase at a time of their own individual choosing; the same holds for entry into any phase which follows. The term "stage" or "phase" is rejected by Brown, since such implies strict time criteria for entry and departure. Brown rejects the concept that age is related to language development to any useful extent, albeit Brown is fully aware that such a relationship does yield a positive correlation in general to language growth. Brown prefers the language measure known as the "mean length of utterance" as his reference point. Brown (1973) presents a system for specific calculation of the "MLU," but for our purposes it will suffice to broadly define the MLU as the average number of morphemes used in any given utterance. A "morpheme" is here defined as the smallest meaningful unit existing within a word. For example, and somewhat oversimplified, the word "roots" effectively has two morphemic units: the word "root" and the "s." The "s" is not so obviously a "meaningful" unit to many non-linguists. Brown acknowledges this by specifically creating a second "class" or morphemes he calls "grammatical morphemes." Dale (1976, p. 30) lists the "grammatical morphemes" as follows:

1. The inflectional ending "ing" used as in "going," "coming," "jumping," etc.;

2. The "s" inflectional ending used in the third person regular singular verb tense, e.g., "walks," and as it is used in the third person irregular singular verb tense, e.g., the "s" on "has" vs. the "ve" on the plural "have";

3. The "ed" inflectional ending used in its regular form on past tense verbs as: "rooted," and as used in its irregular form in "came" (as in come, came, come);

4. The "s" inflectional ending which pluralizes nouns in their regular form: "trees" and in their irregular noun form such as in "sheep," which actually is derived from one sheep plus "s" to mean "sheeps" despite the fact we arbitrarily call it "sheep" in both the singular and the plural;

5. The prepositions "on" and "in" which follow development of "ing";

6. The possessive ending "s" as in "his," "hers," and "theirs";

7. The articles "the," "a," and "an";

8. The "be" verbs used as auxiliaries: "I am going.", "They are leaving, too.", and "She is helping us.";

9. The "be" verbs as copular verbs: "I am," "She is," and "We are";

10. The pronouns relating to the person or group of persons, e.g., "I", "he," "she," "they," "them," the possessive pronouns, e.g., "his," "her," "hers," "theirs," "their," the indefinite pronouns: "it," "its," and the demonstrative pronouns: "this," "that," "these," "those" (Palermo, 1978, p. 201).

Numbers 8 and 9 above pave the way for the eventual development of contractions: "I'm going.", "They're leaving.", but such contractions are never seen in the two-word stage. During the development of the three and four-word phases, contractions initially appear, but it is difficult for a child to acquire them even then because there simply are some statements which cannot be contracted. For example, if someone were to ask if a certain person was doing something (and assuming s/he was), it would be ungrammatical to respond by saying "He's" or "She's" instead of "He is" or "She is." Although this might seem to be a minor annoyance to an adult learning English as a second language, it surely is no minor inconvenience to the child who is trying to structure hypotheses regarding the language's structuring of contractions.

Brown indicates that none of the 10 items above will appear until the child is past the point of using just two simple, content words to make the two-word sentence. The "Subject object," "Subject verb," and "Verb object" sentence types depict what Brown refers to as Stage I language: the simple, two content word sentence. The 10 items above do not appear until Stage II language develops, and according to Brown but not according to Dale (1976, p. 30), the 10 items are completely developed before the child progresses to the next, not necessarily discrete stage in Brown's hierarchy. Dale contends the child's MLU should be about 4.00 before we see all the 10 items appear in fully functional form. It should be noted here that the 10 items seen above in no way implies that the order of the 10 is hierarchical. Two or more of the 10 may develop simultaneously; a child may begin one item, progress satisfactorily, drop its practice for a period of time in order to pursue a second item, and then return to the dropped item, which may have decreased in its frequency of accurate usage because the child has not practiced it for some time. The Stage I language has, according to Brown, a MLU equal to 1.75 with an upper maximum length of 5 morphemic units; Stage II has an MLU of 2.25 and an upper limit of 7 morphemic units (Palermo, 1978, p. 199). From these figures, it would be relatively easy to see how

129

both Brown and Dale may actually agree that a 4.00 MLU is necessary (Dale) and that Stage II language is the time for all 10 items to develop (Brown). It appears Dale was taking Brown's MLU statements as the only defining feature of a stage, whereas Brown's stages also are defined by a maximum number of morphemic units. But it is doubtful that Brown would actually debate the issue one way or the other since he and his colleagues have stressed the position that the stages are rather arbitrary conveniences.

What Brown is saying above can be stated succinctly as follows. First, in Stage I language, the child speaks "telegraphically," e.g., uses only the very most crucial words (open class only) to drive home a request or comment. This request or comment is going to be in the form of a "Subject object," "Verb object," or "Object Subject" sentence with about an equal probability of occurrence for each. Unlike the two word sentences produced in the Random Two-Word Phase, you are not going to frequently see the child pushing two holophrases together into one-sentence frame, which may deceive you into believing that you are actually listening to a true "Subject object," "Verb object," or "Subject object" sentence. During Brown's Stage II language, the child will acquire all ten grammatical morphemes and will do so in a fashion that seems independent of parental/cultural reinforcement patterns; the "rules" the child follows in completing this stage are apparently "known" only to the child, who, ironically, is neither cognitively nor linguistically able to state those rules. The growth in Brown's Stage II language gives the appearance of an "explosion" in the child's performance! Yet this explosion in no fashion means that all the language's subtle aspects have been mastered. It means that the possible number of interactions between the 10 grammatical morphemes and the child's stock of open class words is going to produce tremendous variety in the child's utterances. The possible number of two-word sentences of an ordered nature increases geometrically as the stockpile of open class words steadily increases. Brown has indicated that the development of the first two stages will generally occur between the ages of 18 to 24 months. It is no small coincidence that this time period is a perfect overlap of Jean Piaget's "Internalization of Sensorimotor Schemata" phase, which is the final step any child must complete prior to the successful ending of the Sensorimotor Stage. Following Sensorimotor cognition is the Preoperational stage, which Piaget describes as a time of "symbolic" communication (Piaget, 1952). Brown is aware of cognitive development's contributions to the language growth process. He echoes Bloom's (1970) conclusions that the child must be seen "holistically": the separate aspects of cognitive growth, parental/cultural reinforcement patterns, and genetics are separate only because the researchers studying them prefer to keep them as such so as to more easily study their separate complexities. In reality, the variables are highly interactive. Dale (1976, p. 31) makes this same point when he states that one of our most cherished myths about language development is suspect; the correlation between the chronological age of a child and that child's progression through stages of language development in Brown's model is only in the high +.60s. On the other hand, when the MLU is substituted for chronological age, the correlation jumps to a very satisfactory +.92. The correlation between the rank order in which children proceed through Brown's stages is in the +.80s to +.90s. In the preceding correlations, chronological age simply does not allow prediction of "holistic" language competence to the same extent as MLU. MLU is more closely holistic than is chronological age.

When does the child enter a stage where three words are spoken in adult order? Brown (1973) says that a child enters this phase when the child is perfectly ready to do so, and not before. By the time the child does start producing three-word sentences, the possible number of word combinations is larger than most adults have the capacity to imagine.

As we read Brown's position through the completion of his first two stages, it should strike us that there seems to be consistency in how children neatly use only open class words in Stage I and then add a select number of "grammatical morphemes" (closed class morphemes) in Stage II language. As Palermo (1978, p. 199) points out, it is all too neat and tidy to perfectly reflect the reality of the situation. Palermo believes that Brown would withdraw some of his position regarding Stage I language by now saying that the actual definition of what appears in Stage I should be defined as follows (where P stands for Pivot class word and O stands for Open class word):

S → O-O (as in subject-object, or infrequently, object-subject), or
S → P-O (as in "More milk"), or
S → O-P (as in "Milk allgone"), but never
S → P-P (as in "More allgone").

Dale (1976, p. 22) agrees with Palermo's testing of the possible sentence types, but he does not comment that he believes that Brown would, if he could, change the original composition of Stage I language. Palermo's prediction about Brown's actions is probably accurate. The pivot words Palermo has frequently seen in Stage I language include "more," "my," "here," and even "it." Pivots of lesser use occur later, i.e., "the," "of," "and," and "with"; these are more in the spirit of Brown's listing of the grammatical morpheme items in Stage II language as seen above. The reader should consider Palermo and Dale's remarks as positive criticisms; at no point did either author suggest that Brown's model was fundamentally in doubt. Brown's model stands perfectly acceptable today—as it did upon its original appearance.

Beyond Two Words

In one sense it is difficult to decide what is actually meant by the title of this section. Laypeople, and some experts, no doubt, would say that we are ready to discuss sentences having three or more words. We may ask whether the person making such a comment has any ideas regarding how such a transition is made from the discussion of ordered two-word sentences to full-fledged three-word sentences. We do know that Brown (1973) has said that the Stage III language period apparently begins at or about 24 months of age. According to Palermo (1978, p. 199), the MLU figure should be about 2.75 at this point, and the maximum length of utterance should be in the vicinity of nine morphemes. By this point in our discussion, the reader should be well aware that a morpheme does not necessarily mean a single word, since endings such as "ing," "ed," "s," etc., all qualify under Brown's (1973) use of the term "grammatical morpheme." Still, 2.75 is the MLU, and no one would accept the statement that the three-word sentence could not possibly appear at the very beginning of Stage III language. The 2.75 MLU is an average; two sentences such as "Mary hit Paul." and "I am." would yield a MLU as low as 2.50. But if the MLU is 2.75, we are obviously not going to see only three-word sentences; many will be two-word or perhaps even one-word sentences if such sentences meet the child's communication needs and the child is simply not ready to communicate a certain set of meanings via the use of a specific type of three-word sentence. Not all three-word sentences are equally complex and, therefore, some three-word sentences require a greater level of competence to produce. The semantic underpinnings may vary despite the fact that two or more sentences hold the same number of words.

Even in the three-word sentence, we will see many occassions where the use of language is highly egocentric. The child seems to know what s/he wants to say but has not the ability to actually say it. As a general rule, the less the child produces means that the amount of work produced by the listener in order to understand the child must be increased. If the child can produce only three or four words to express a thought, the words chosen within such a short sentence need to be as meaningful as possible. If the listener clearly realizes that the meaning of the child's sentence is not being conveyed as the child would most clearly like to present it, the listener may focus upon each individual word with increased intensity so as not to "miss" the meaning. But such a focusing procedure may actually lead to some increased degree of miscommunication if the listener actually spends too long on the first word or two while trying to determine specific intent on the child's part. The result is a breakdown in communication. In sum then, we can see the sentence's being lengthened actually does not necessarily mean an increase in communication ease; it may actually lead to a compounding of egocentricity, which in turn will possibly lead to a breakdown in the conveyance of the child's message. Fortunately, the child's cognitive growth is such that s/he "realizes" that s/he needs to convey meaning while considering the viewpoint of the listener. But there is no easy way for the child to grasp the listener's viewpoint if the listener is operating at a substantially higher cognitive level than the child. When a child addresses a child having the same level of cognitive motivation, we see the phenomenon of the "collective monology" as discussed by Jean Piaget. In it, the child speaks to a second child about issues the second child does not understand, but yet the second child does not seem to understand that s/he does not understand. The second child, in turn, responds to the first child, who likewise does not understand and fails to realize that s/he really does not understand. Such behaviors are extremely common during the three through five-word sentence periods. But, as Palermo (1978, p. 202) strongly implies, it is not the egocentricities that attract us to the belief that the child will eventually develop adult language. It is the obviously rapidly increasing semantic awareness on the child's part that seems to force order upon the ever-increasing sentence length. Parental/cultural reinforcements play an increasingly larger role as the child begins to slowly realize that it takes less effort to portray one's meaning accurately the first time. The saving grace for both the child and adult is the belief that the listener can respond accurately to even a poorly communicated message. After all, the listener is rarely totally void of some degree of experience related to that which the speaker so poorly attempts to present.

In order to achieve a better understanding of the period at the end of the two word utterance and beyond, we turn our attention to the writings of Bellugi (1965) and supplement her work with an occasional comment from Brown (1968). Bellugi has made a specific attempt to cite MLUs for a range of ages and to trace the progression of certain sentence forms in that range. Despite the relatively small age range and the limited attention to just a few factors in language, we can see how rapidly language does develop and how certain key word forms can literally cause startling increases in sentence production. Bellugi divides her study into three MLU stages: Stage One, which occurs at 24 months of age, has 1.8 to 2.00 morphemes as the MLU; Stage Two occurs at 29 months of age and has an MLU of 2.3 to 2.9; Stage Three occurs at 34 months of age and has an MLU of 3.4 to 3.6.

In Stage One, the sentence is composed of a noun and a verb. It should be apparent here that she is starting Stage One with Brown's old position rather than with what was discussed previously above where we saw at 18 months that the sentence could actually be a Pivot (P) — Open (O), or O-P, or an O-O construction. Bellugi contends that negatives are available at this stage but that they are "tacked onto" the sentences beginning or end, i.e., "Milk no!" or "No milk." Bloom (1970) says the child even at this stage does not merely put the negative into the sentence at just any position. "Milk no!" may most likely mean the child has had all the milk s/he wants, whereas "No milk" most likely means the child has run out of milk and wants more. Bellugi claims children can and do ask questions at this stage, but the questions are the type one would see if only the question transformation rule (T question) were applied in Transformational grammar. The reader may wish to refer back to Chapter 3 to review the use of the T question rule. The T question transformation rule allows the child to use intonation at the beginning or end of a sentence to signal the statement is a question. Adults use the same procedure, but are not limited to just the one procedure. Questions which would require a "wh" word to introduce them, e.g., "Where kitty?" or "what that?", do not exist at this stage. Questions which require the use of an auxiliary verb, e.g., "Is he there?", "Are you?", or "Did she?", are beyond the child's productive ability at this stage. It is possible, however, for the child to add the negative to the type of question which may be formed in Stage One so as to produce a statement such as "Milk no?" or "No milk?". The latter question will be easily recognized as "adult" at least in its frequency of use by adults if not in its linguistic complexity. Dale (1976, p. 105) states there are only two kinds of questions; one is the "wh" type, and the other is the "yes or no" type. Bellugi's work agrees that the "wh" type is slower in developing than is the "yes-no" type, but she seems to subdivide the "yes-no" type in a manner Dale does not explicitly do. For example, Dale gives the impression that "yes-no" questions use auxiliaries at all times. Many "yes-no" questions do use auxiliaries, but by no means do all. For example, "No milk?" is a question where the auxiliary is missing, it is a "yes-no" question, and we would be on soft ground to state that the child is implicitly using an auxiliary, e.g., the child is thinking but cannot produce a sentence such as "Is there no milk?" Nevertheless, we can easily

134

accept Dale's idea that the amount of information received in answer to a "wh" question is surely greater than that received for a "yes-no" question under most normal communication conditions. The child must evolve the language model past the use of simple "yes-no" questions if s/he is to easily adapt to the demands of the adult language community. Dale makes the excellent point that the child's ability to develop "wh" questions is probably less a linguistic issue than it is a semantic/cognitive one. For example, the answer to "Did Mike walk?" is either "Yes" or "No." The question "What is her name?" is requiring something other than a "Yes" or "No" and makes it harder to answer. Yet, from a transformational grammar point of view, the question "Did Mike walk?" requires several more transformations than does "What is her name?". It would be reasonable to assume the linguistic requirements of any question interact with the question's cognitive demands. This should be a very rich area for future study.

In Bellugi's Stage Two, the child can demonstrate basic knowledge of all the parts of speech, albeit this knowledge is occasionally quite "intuitive" in nature. "Yes-no" questions will remain much the same as in Stage One with the exception that now the questions will be somewhat longer and will reflect a cognitive/experiential evolution in the child's thinking. There still is no use of auxiliary verbs as an adult would use them, but some auxiliary verbs do appear in a fixed, rote-like position. The child uses the auxiliary in conjunction with a negative contraction, i.e., "don't" or "can't," but this does not mean the child believes s/he is using two separate words because sentences still will not occur where the auxiliary and negative appear separately. Not until Stage Three when the auxiliary truly appears as such in function can the child split the auxiliary from the negative. Therefore, we must conclude that the child does not have the auxiliary as such "conceptually" in Stage Two. Likewise, pronouns will take a considerable period of time past Stage Two to fully develop, e.g., "it" will not be used correctly until after age six years (Chipman & deDandel, 1974). The one thing, aside from the use of all the parts of speech, which makes this stage stand as a separate stage is that for the first time the child is capable of using "wh" words to introduce questions, but this does not mean the child is using "wh" questions. This seems at first to be a contradiction in meaning, but it is readily explained through the following examples:

1. When "wh" words are used simply to introduce a question, we could hear a statement such as "Why he go store?" or "Where Bill go?" or "Who she?" The "wh" word floats loosely at the sentence's beginning. The negative introduction of "Why not he not go?" becomes common. The child has an intuitive grasp of the fact that using only intona-

tion to produce a question, as was done in Stage One, now no longer is the most efficient way to signal a question. In many ways, this type of "wh" word could be left off the question, and we would still know that it was a question.

2. The "true wh" question, on the other hand, cannot allow us the option of dropping off the "wh" word if we are to understand the question. The "wh" word is simply not "tacked onto" the front of a sentence so as to merely catch our attention. The use of the "wh" in its truly adult form requires that the auxiliary verb be used in its adult form, and this is not possible for a child to do in Stage Two. The use of negatives in "wh" questions not only affects the "wh" word itself but is interactive with the auxiliary verb, too. With the auxiliary missing, the negative and the "wh" word must merely be tacked onto the front of the sentence itself as discussed immediately above.

In Bellugi's Stage Three, which occurs around the age of 34 months, a number of significant "breakthroughs" occur. First and most importantly, the auxiliary verb appears in its "true" form; it is not produced from rote, and it can be used separately from the negative in the same sentence, unlike in Stage Two where not only cannot the auxiliary and negative appear separately in one sentence but even contractions such as "isn't," "can't," "don't," etc. appear to mean something apart from the words upon which they are based (Palermo, 1978, p. 206).

This means that questions such as "Is he here?" or "Are you there?" or "Will they come?" become possible for the first time. Chomsky would say that the child is "creating" sentences in which the auxiliary verb actually fits where it should from an adult perspective. Bellugi would agree. If the "wh" word is now removed, it sounds as if something of great, integral significance has been taken from the sentence. The "wh" word is now highly interactive with the auxiliary verb, which is also highly interactive with the negatives in a given sentence. "Is he not here?" or "Are you not there?" or "Why do they not come?" become possible for the first time. With the addition of the past tense already at the child's disposal, such sentences as "Was he here?" or "When were they here?" become much more probable. Without the auxiliary verb, the child could never easily move words from position to position within the sentence without creating possible semantic problems. The use of "He is where?" by placing stress on the word "where" in order to create a question (as was common practice in Stages One and Two) falls woefully short of the efficient use of "Where is he?" The latter is more prone to receive reinforcement from the parent/culture complex. For Bellugi, this child's emergence into Stage Three means that the child will in very short order be able to understand, but not necessarily produce, every

136

one of the parent/culture's adult transformational rules; Menyuk (1969) fully agrees. Developing the auxiliary definitely plays a very key role in the development of such complex understandings.

Before leaving the "wh" question, it is interesting to review Palermo's (1978, p. 209) summary of Ervin-Tripp's (1970) research. Ervin-Tripp agrees that the "wh" question is more difficult for the child to process than is the "yes-no" question. But she goes one significant step further by having traced the development of the "wh" question as its various "wh" words appear. Without specifying dates for each type of word, she puts the order from first to last as follows: (1) "What," (2) "Where," (3) "What do," (4) "Whose," (5) "Who," (6) "Why," (7) "Where from," (8) "How," and finally (9) "When." According to Ervin-Tripp, this order reflects the changing cognitive processing strategies the child employed during the period Bellugi would generally describe as Stage Three language. It is interesting to speculate upon the contents of the list. The last "wh" word to develop is "when," and it is generally conceded that time is one of the very hardest concepts that a child must conquer in the concrete world. Palermo (1978, p. 209) cautions us against assuming that the "wh" questions will appear in their perfect adult form even when used in Bellugi's Stage Three language. As he puts it, to hear the child ask "What you did read?" is not unusual even in Stage Three. Cognitive changes coupled with reinforced practice create the adult form of the "wh" question in its perfect form. Brown (1973) leans far more heavily toward the influence of the cognitive changes than toward the reinforced practice. If Brown is correct, adult expectations for improved "wh" questions from their children will simply have to wait for the passage of time.

Kess (1976, p. 71) stated that following the development of an MLU level of 3.5 all furthur progress is essentially little more than polishing the finished product. Dale (1976, p. 112), on the other hand, states that although the child does then have all the basic units s/he needs to meet many personal needs, the 3.5 to 4.00 MLU stage is less a time of polishing than a time to create truly complex sentences. Palermo and Molfese (1972) echo Dale's point when they say that it is true that much syntactic development does occur rapidly before chronological age five years, but a great deal will continue to occur after that point, too. Palermo and Molfese stopped short of saying that more goes on after five or that at least as much goes on after age five years. According to Dale (1976, pp. 112–114), complex sentence development ater 3.5 to 4.00 MLU shows the child attempting to both formulate and test hypotheses regarding the formation of the language's rules. Sentences Dale cites in support of this contention are as follows (among others):

1. "I think it's the wrong way.", where "it's" clearly shows an attempt to use both a pronoun and a "be" verb (its) in the contraction "it's."

2. "Watch me draw circles.", where the child clearly indicates the use of the pronoun as a subject where the subject is actually understood to exist but is not actually seen.

3. "Whoever did this will pay for it.", where two sentences are combined into one, e.g., "Someone did this." and "Someone will pay for this."

But among the complexities of longer sentences, Dale likewise sees the hypothesis regarding the construction of some complex sentences failing to immediately produce complexity on an adult level. For example, we have the following:

1. "I show you what I got.", where the auxiliary verb "will" is completely missing from its needed place immediately following "I," the subject of the sentence.

2. "I tell you where is it.", where "will" is again missing as the necessary auxiliary and "is it" should be reversed.

These "errors" are not necessarily errors within the child's hypothesis. To the contrary, these statements may be perfectly correct fits to the child's constructed model of the language as best that model exists considering the child's cognitive stage. The following sentences presented by Dale illustrates the point nicely:

1. "That a box they put it in.", where the copular verb "is" remains missing and the article "a" should be replaced by the article "the."

2. "I show you the place we went.", where the auxiliary verb "will" is missing from its rightful place behind the subject "I"; unlike the sentences above where "will" is also missing, this sentence shows a past tense verb "went" referring to a past act. The past tense is more difficult for a child to understand than is the present, and, therefore, a past tense verb reflects a higher level of cognitive development than does the present tense verb, e.g., as the present tense verb idea is portrayed in the two preceding sentences above where "will" was omitted.

It is likewise true that a child may be fully capable of saying "He was hurt, and I took him home." and yet still be incapable of saying "I took him home because he was hurt." or "Because he was hurt, I took him home."—until, of course, the necessary cognitive prerequisites become operative. It is again worth reciting the research of Brown (1973) at this point. No parental/cultural reinforcement paradigm can produce changes in the child's language hypotheses unless the child is cogni-

138

tively ready to change hypotheses. The child seems to know intuitively at this complex sentence creation stage that s/he is using an error-filled model and simply does not appreciate being "ridiculed" by whom the child perceives as the more knowledgeable adult language user.

Perhaps the most classic example of following an hypothesis despite its apparent illogic exists in the form of creating past tense verbs using "ed." As we previously have seen in Brown's (1973) listing of the "grammatical morphemes," the past tense "ed" is available at Stage II language (at this point where two words comprise a nicely ordered sentence). As Dale (1976, p. 35) points out, however, the child is reluctant to leave well enough alone for long. Verbs in the irregular past tense such as "came," "saw," "went," and "did," just to name a few, were used quite consistently in what apparently was a "rote-memorized" form in Stage II language. As the child's cognitive development progresses, the "ed" appears as if it were part of an hypothesis regarding making present tense verbs become past tense ones. "Went" now becomes "wented," "did" becomes "didded," and "saw" becomes "sawed." This process offers us a "Catch 22"; it is excellent to see the child forming what is not an unuseful hypothesis, but the most frequently used verbs, according to Dale (1976, p. 35), are irregular verbs to start with. The hypothesis superbly fits regular verbs, but they are fewer in usage than the irregulars. Apparently the child must form the hypothesis, use it in daily practice, and accept the parental/cultural editing rules which then force the child to go back to the starting point in Stage II language so as to rote memorize again the irregular past tense forms of the verbs. Beyond the simple two word sentence lies an area requiring perhaps the most difficult semantic maneuvering of all; that area contains indirect objects and passive sentence constructions.

C. S. Chomsky (1969) has possibly made the most definitive statement regarding the development of the indirect object's position in the child's language. She indicates that the problem is one of both cognitive maturity and well-practiced habits. In the sentence "I told him when to leave." it is apparent to children as young as five or six years of age that "him" is the person who was told when to leave. After all, "him" appears to be the closest actor to the infinitive "to leave." In this case, the infinitive refers to the actor which has the least minimal distance from it. This sentence functions as an example of the "minimal distance principle" (MDP). But in certain sentences, the indirect object is inferred. "I asked what was wanted." has the indirect object physically missing. It is probably either "him" or "her," but it could just as easily be "them." Any of these pronouns could easily fit before the word "what" and would be understood by many five- and six-year-olds. Since the MDP knows no exceptions to the rules, it tries to convince the young listener that "I" must be the pronoun being addressed by "what was needed." At this point, the semantic correlates begin to conflict. The child who produces such a sentence may have no problem with the sentence if s/he actually is "talking to him/herself." For example, the child could be musing, "Now, let's see. I asked what was needed, and then ..." But, on the other hand, if the child is not talking to him/herself, who does the MDP suggest that s/he is addressing? There is no one. This is precisely Chomsky's point; when the MDP is violated, children under five or six years cannot cognitively process it correctly. "Ask" or "asked" becomes "tell" because the latter simply makes "better sense." Of course, an obvious way to avoid this problem is never to leave the indirect object out in the first place; many children prefer such a strategy if they are aware that the sentence does not seem quite right and yet they cannot quite say what is not right about it. Many children never notice the problem. Most children will grasp indirect objects by age eight or nine. Indirect objects are less frequently misinterpreted when the person or thing being defined as the indirect object is in front of the child. But even the presence of physical cues is not always enough. For example, Chomsky (1969) has demonstrated that children around five or six years of age have great difficulty making the physical cues match the meaning of an utterance. Given a blindfolded doll, each child in her study was asked if the doll was "easy to see" or "hard to see." Children under five to six years of age responded by saying frequently that the doll was "hard to see." With the indirect object put into its rightful place, the confusion on the child's part is substantially reduced: "Is the doll easy for *you* to see?" or "Is the doll hard for *you* to see?" This poses no mystery for anyone who is relatively well-versed in the writings of Jean Piaget; taking the visual perspective of another is usually considered to be a Formal Operations task. Formal operations are generally conceded to begin in early adolescence. It will be approximately nine years of age before the child can understand that the correct answer is that the doll is "easy to see." Palermo (1978, p. 215) states that Chomsky's research also shows that children at five and six years of age have no trouble understanding "He knew John would win the race.", but they cannot understand "John knew he would win the race." Children at five to six years of age cannot understand that in the second sentence "he" can refer both to John and to someone else. At about seven s/he will understand the use of personal pronouns in such a context. Donaldson (1970) according to Palermo (1978, p. 207) has shown that children at five to six years can understand "The trees are green.", but not "The trees are not yellow." Palermo states that deVilliers and Flusberg (1975) have challenged Donaldson's view by showing two-, three-, and four-year-olds can perform Donaldson's tasks if the children are properly taught. Palermo fails to add that careful inspection of deVilliers and Flusberg's work produces the inescapable conclusion that these very young children were doing little more than memorizing specific instances; the children showed no evidence of understanding what they were doing, e.g., they held no concept of the principle involved. Therefore, Donaldson's work stands. The type of task required by Donaldson falls well into the concrete cognitive operations of Jean Piaget. Concrete operations do not usually appear until after the child is seven years old. deVilliers and Flusberg's research points out one very interesting thing. If the nouns in the sentence are highly familiar, the child can more readily understand the nature of what something is not. For example, "A cow is not a bicycle." is easier to grasp than "A cow is not a kangaroo." (assuming the children do not live in Australia). This offers no conflict for Donaldson's position; it augments it. Familiarity with the terms may produce easier processing during Concrete Operations, but familiarity alone is hardly sufficient to allow the child to understand that if A is equal to B then A is not simultaneously non-B. Palermo (1978, p. 207) cites the research of McNeill and McNeill (1968) in support of his contention that semantics and syntax definitely are interactive and especially confusing to the child when negatives are involved.

The work of Dan Slobin (1966) ranks among the earliest writings on the nature of passive sentence understanding. First, a passive sentence may either be reversable, which means its content nouns may interchange positions leaving us with a grammatical sentence of different meaning. It is equally difficult to understand "Mary loves Paul." or "Paul loves Mary." Nonreversable sentences, on the other hand, pose fewer problems unless we do not know the meanings of the separate words. "The cow jumped over the moon." is a nonreversable sentence since cows can jump over moons, but there is little chance that a moon will jump over a cow. As Slobin points out, "The moon was jumped by the cow." is easier to understand as being grammatically/semantically correct than is "The cow was jumped by the moon." But what is a child to do if s/he hears "Mary was loved by Paul."? Does it mean the same thing as "Paul was loved by Mary."? This question requires far more effort than even the nonpassive reversable. But not all reversable sentences are equally hard to process; some come dangerously close to being only as hard as nonreversables. For example, "Mary was beaten by Paul." is a reversable passive. Is it possible to hear "Paul was beaten by Mary."? The child knows that "Paul was beaten by Mary." is less likely than "Mary was beaten by Paul." If the act of "beating" refers to socially acceptable acts of competition (tennis, baseball, running, etc.), the child is faced with a reversable relationship where the two possibilities may be equal. This raises confusion. The passive nonreversable will be easier for the child to understand and produce than is the passive reversable sentence unless, of course, the semantic elements of all words in the reversable sentence are meaningless to the child. Processing sentences for a child, according to Slobin (1966), is an act of checking content for truth or falsity. His research has produced the following three general conclusions; all three show the interaction between syntax and semantics:

1. Sentences containing negatives take longer to process than do comparable sentences missing the negatives.

2. Statements which are false require more processing time than do sentences which are true.

3. A statement which is portrayed as a lie but which is actually true requires more processing time than does a statement which is an apparent lie and, in reality, is just that—a lie.

It would be reasonable to assume here that if the preceding three conclusions hold for active sentences, imposing a passive sentence construction upon the three conclusions would result in yet longer processing time than for the active sentences but would in no manner change the content of the three conclusions above. In all of Slobin's comments, it is apparent that the child seems to be using some type of "hypothesis-generating" strategy in order to process negatives in passive and active sentences. But we also can easily see the hypotheses run away in some cases. For example, around age three or four, the child ceases to produce sentences which are essentially "reversed nonreversables passives," e.g., "Hunter was shot by bird!" But as that problem passes, we see the reversable passive suddenly appear as if the child is reconsidering the construction. The child labors to revise one hypothesis, e.g., the inadequate and ungrammatical reversing of a nonreversable passive. Palermo (1978, p. 120) cites Turner and Rummerveit (1967), who state that the passive sentence comes at least 60 percent under the child's control by age eight years. "Control" was defined as both comprehension and production. Palermo (1978, pp. 211–212) cites Bever, who says the child by age four years has the semantic skills to understand and produce noun-verb-noun sentences which seem to defy all attempts at rearrangement. As Bever sees it the child apparently wishes to believe the noun-verb-noun sentence is sufficient for all occasions. As Palermo notes, however, not all of Bever's research or conclusions on this issue have been accepted as fact.

The time is right for us to ask if anyone has decided why we see what we see above. Brown (1973) has attempted to draw some general conclusions; they are as follows:

1. Whatever is happening is definitely not due to the child's attempt to simply repeat what s/he has heard or was simply reinforced for saying. The data simply shows far too many consistencies to make a reinforcement/learning theory approach stand as the correct answer.

2. Easier linguistic units are learned before and with greater rapidity than are more complex linguistic units. The correlation between speed of learning and unit complexity is in the +.80s. Any unit which contains more information than does another linguistic unit is judged as more complex.

3. Semantic development and syntactical development occur in a complicated, interactive pattern. Each facilitates and, in some ways, mutually determines the growth of the other. This interaction is based upon cognitive development, perceptual set, and reinforcement parameters in that order of importance. Dale (1976, p. 31) would ask Brown to add one additional variable: "perceptual saliency" of the "amount of information conveyed." However, since "perceptual saliency" is hardly easily defined in operational terms, we would be better advised to leave it.

As Dale (1976, p. 128) puts it, the child at age five or six years structurally is using sentences which are adult-like in all aspects except for length and some culturally-determined vocabulary terms which add the "adult" flavor. In Brown's three conclusions about the development of syntax, he seems to be saying that he really cannot explain in anything other than general trends how the child moves so rapidly to Dale's position of granted syntactic competence by age six years. It is even harder to explain why the vast majority of development is completed by five or six years and yet some aspects of the language, e.g., indirect objects and passives, "refuse" to make themselves "adult-like" until the child is eight or nine despite constant reinforcement prior to that point.

David McNeill (1970) has provided us with data which depicts the normal development of syntax, semantics, and the interaction between syntax and semantics. The data is descriptive and useful.

We see syntax seems to be described graphically as it has been verbally portrayed in all the preceding pages. The growth is labeled "negatively accelerated" because it increases at a decreasing rate of speed. We see from the syntax graph that the child learns word order at an astonishingly quick rate of speed. As seen so frequently in the review of the literature above, the growth of syntax reaches its peak around five or six years of age; such units as indirect objects and passive sentences are

143

completed after that age period and are apparently a small enough issue to McNeill's data not to cause a ripple in the curve shape, albeit we should note that the curve shape does not reach an "asymptote" but rather keeps rising at an almost unnoticeable rate. We will address the development of semantics in the next chapter. We note here merely that McNeill sees its growth as essentially linear, which means semantic growth is the gradual adding of more and more elements until the child has "acquired" the total needed meaningful units to classify that something being learned as a "meaningful whole." For just this moment, we will let McNeill's graph rest as is. Its fate, however, suffers conceptually if we use an approach to semantics other than Behaviorism.

Interaction effects are not produced by simply adding the behaviors from two or more variables and then calculating the "average" behavior. For example, finding the point of syntactic competence for a six-year-old and then adding it to the point of semantic competence does not produce a point exactly midway between the two points. We can see this in the figure. The point that is derived seems to have a life of its own. Such indeed is the case, albeit this is a poetic way to describe a very

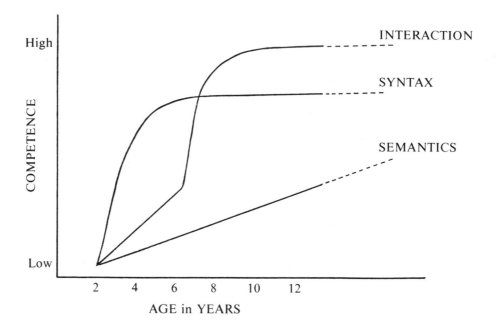

FIGURE 6.1: Growth in semantics, syntax, and the interaction of syntax and semantics as a function of age in years (McNeill, 1970).

complex product of a specific statistical process. The interaction effect reflects the separate effects of the two "pure" factors (syntax and semantics) when the two factors are not considered separately. It produces an effect we may label as "the real language" as we would see it if we could produce it at its best. In McNeill's study, only two pure factors exist: syntax and semantics. The interaction effect is made from the interplay of these two factors. The interaction reflects what we hear the child say and what we see the child write as age increases. The sudden increase in the interaction's growth at age six is especially mystifying.

If we look below age six years at the interaction, we see that the factor of syntax is noticeably more advanced than is the interaction effect, whereas the factor of semantic growth is much less well advanced. The child knows more about syntax than we would assume. At the same time, s/he knows less about semantics; in short, some words in the child's vocabulary are there only because the syntactic structures have probabilistically dictated their presence despite the fact the words are not understood. This dual illusion continues after age eight years of age, but now the illusion is that the child knows more syntax than s/he actually does and that the child knows more semantics than s/he does. Even between ages six and eight years, we can see that a partial illusion continues to exist. The interaction effect's curve actually overlaps/crosses the syntax graph at one point, but the semantics curve never reaches anywhere nearly as high as the syntax or interaction graphs. From these graphs on syntax and semantics, we can immediately conclude that children do not have to understand all they say before they say it. Semantics then, although quite beneficial as is seen from the interaction effect, is not the sole prerequisite for syntactic development. This is as it should be since common observation shows that children (as well as adults) may produce sophisticated sentences which are void of meaning.

But the really interesting area is again between six and eight years of age. Syntax is more advanced than semantics. The interaction effect begins a sudden positively accelerated rise around age six years; it surpasses the pure factor of syntax knowledge by the time the child is eight years old. We recall that Chomsky (1969) had discussed the problems children have with indirect objects and passive sentences at even ages six and seven and how by age eight years or so those problems are basically gone. We recall how Donaldson (1970) discussed the fact that children up to even six years of age have an inability to understand that because something is blue necessarily also means it is not red, green, or yellow, etc. We recall his implications made it seem that this problem was not one that could be "taught away." Something else caused it to change. The research of Turner and Rummerveit (1967) shows us that children will not be able to understand or produce passive sentences until they are at least eight years old. The research of Berlin (1975) as reported by Palermo (1978, p. 212) concludes that children cannot grasp the meaning of passive sentences until the child is at least seven years old, or, as Berlin puts it, until the child has the cognitive prerequisites, e.g., as in Piaget's stage of Concrete Operations. In short, something stands as the prerequisite for a number of significant changes in many facets of the child's language develoment between six and eight years of age. What that something is leads directly to a thorough discussion of Jean Piaget's cognitive developmental model, which appears in the next chapter.

Modeling Behaviors

Let us, for the moment, grant Brown's (1973) conclusion that children do not learn their syntax directly from parental/cultural attempts to deliver reinforcement. Let us also grant Brown credit for being one of the first to note that children "seem" to be developing hypotheses about how the language should appear. But now let us ask the question about whom or what it is the children are using to draw hypotheses. If we overlook the environment, we place ourselves into the position of saying simply that genetics produce the language in some kind of a self-sealed system. At no point does Brown push us to this extreme. But what does he give us to use when he seemingly casts aside classical and operant conditioning as the basis of language development? Frankly, he seems to leave us with the admonition that he really does not know what to leave with us. Perhaps what he could have left us is a relatively new field of study within the area of applied behavioral analysis; the subfield is known as "modeling" (Millenson & Leslie, 1969, pp. 359–360). Modeling occurs when one person has observed and can now more or less duplicate the behaviors of another person or group of persons as specific tasks are performed. E. C. Tolman (1932) described this kind of observational learning as stimulus-stimulus (S-S) conditioning because it required not a single act of duplication nor any immediate reinforcement on the part of the learner and teacher respectively. S-S learning allows us to learn by imitation, which is another name for the modeling process. Such a form of learning allows us to short-cut the use of the trial and error process seen in operant conditioning and allows us to place ourselves into an environmental setting where conditioning may demand our attention. Such learning allows us to avoid engaging in acts which can harm us, e.g., we see the results of driving a car into a brick wall and choose not to do it ourselves; we do not need to directly experience the same painful experience directly to know that it is not something we will choose later to avoid. Likewise, we can imitate behaviors which will produce positive reinforcements when we decide to eventually act. As Millenson and Leslie (1969, p. 359) put it, S-S learning describes complex processes involved in the learning of complicated sequences of behavior; neither classical nor operant behavioral rules can account for the speed in which these sequences are learned. With the preceding as our launch point, what happens if we assume that S-S learning rather than classical conditioning or operant conditioning or any combination thereof is the basis for syntactic development? Could it account for the complexity and speed of development so frequently seen throughout this chapter?

Millenson and Leslie (1969, p. 364) state that modeling is the basis of the rapid learning of language in children—as well as such processes as the learning of slang by adults, the development of verbal mannerisms, and the adoption of accents. Millenson and Leslie (1969, p. 365) cite the research of Harris and Hassemer (1972) to depict the effects of modeling upon children's production of various lengthed sentences. These authors used children of such age ranges (second and fourth graders) that their research findings, although highly acceptable in their own right, hardly are appropriate as the basis of any conclusion such as Millenson and Leslie (1969, p. 364) have made. It is difficult to clearly interpret Millenson and Leslie's thinking here. Are they defining language solely as speech and, therefore, wish to believe that modeling seen in a seven-year-old is just a more complex process than is the modeling used by 10—12-month-old children? It is interesting to note that Millenson and Leslie (1969) offer only a bit more than one-half a page to cover the issue of modeling in human language. Dale (1976) provides no support for the area of modeling in any form; he does not even mention the topic in his book. Likewise, Palermo (1978) does not mention the topic. We are left with the conclusion based upon a review of recent work in the field that modeling, per se, has had few serious advocates, and apparently those who have advocated it, leave us with more than a lingering suspicion that they are dealing only with speech and only with older children. Modeling may fit into the picture of speech production quite easily, but it seems doomed as a serious attempt to explain normal syntactic development. We can hear Brown (1973) stating again and again that the basic principles of operant and classical conditioning are not, in and of themselves, sufficient to produce an explanation for language acquisition. It can now be added that modeling is not of itself, nor when

used in combination with classical and/or operant conditioning, sufficient to explain language development.

Fraser, Bellugi and Brown (1963) had spoken long before Millenson
and Leslie (1969) drew their erroneous conclusions regarding modeling;
the Fraser, Bellugi, and Brown data showed that children can imitate
(model) adults, but the data also showed much of the modeling to be
specific to the particular task the children were memorizing. The data
showed, more importantly, that imitation was easier than comprehension. Production of new sentences was the most difficult of all. This last
finding should come as no surprise since the research by Brown (1973)
and Palermo (1978) clearly indicated that the processes underlying production have a semantic core which must be developed prior to actual
sentence production. The semantic core as a prerequisite would not hold
for imitation since one can repeat meaningless sentences. Lovell and
Dixon (1967) have echoed Fraser, Bellugi and Brown's conclusions;
they used children between two and six years of age as well as mentally
retarded youngsters. The retardation did not in any way change the relationship; imitation (modeling) was easier than was comprehending,
which, in turn, was easier than sentence production. But from these
studies, the conclusion seems inescapable that imitation (modeling) cannot serve as the beginning language learner's "basic tool" since imitation
in no sense necessitates comprehension, which is easier and apparently
the basis for the most difficult process of all—production. Production is
literally two stages beyond imitation. Before we completely throw imitation into the "baby's bathwater," we should note that nowhere here is
the position taken that imitation has no value. On the contrary, it must
function if the child is to learn the phonemes s/he will use in the parents' language.

Palermo (1978, pp. 216-217) provides us with a set of conclusions
which gives us the position that modeling seems to play in an adequate
discussion of language development. His conclusions are as follows:

1. At first, any normal infant acts "prelinguistically." There are no
"rules or hypotheses" about the formation or function of the language.
Parental/cultural reinforcements produces repetitions of phenomes, but
some sounds seem to appear spontaneously and are equally capable of
disappearing just as spontaneously.

2. "Rule-like" or "hypothesis-like" behaviors appear very early after
the child's prelinguistic phase is completed. Not all the hypotheses or
rules are close to being adequate nor are they well-defined. Instead, they
seem to depict the child's efforts to find "content" (meaning) and to
convey that meaning to others. (Although imitation could occur for the

mere sake of imitation, the attempt to infuse meaning into an utterance would seem to limit the number of attempts the child makes in order to imitate purely for the sake of imitation.)

3. Children build upon an expanding cognitive structure which, in turn, both facilitates and is facilitated by the acquisition of language. Simple imitation in and of itself does not lead to cognitive growth since there is no profit from memorizing meaningless verbal material.

4. In virtually all significant aspects of syntactic development, the growth of semantics has played a significant role and usually has acted as an implicit prerequisite. (Modeling, per se, requires no semantics.) Putting semantics into such a secondary position in modeling is its rightful place only for modeling. Palermo (1978, pp. 216-217) cites Slobin (1973) as having stated that all children in the process of learning natural language seek the greatest structuring of meaning they possibly can. This means that the syntactic development reflects such structuring to the best of the child's ability. Slobin also states that at first children approach syntax through semantic reference points which are not "tuned" to process the more subtle aspects of adult semantics, e.g., pauses, repetitions, elongations, and voice pitch. Such cues develop after the more basic components of semantics develop, e.g., the class to which a specific set of meanings belongs and the limits as to how far the boundaries of such a class may be extended. Slobin considers this process universal. Equally universal, again according to Slobin, is the child's tendency to ignore the ordering of words if s/he believes that the meaning is clear; this is apparently a receptive rather than expressive phenomenon. As a final point, Slobin expresses an interesting fact; children pay far greater attention to suffixes than to prefixes when they first begin developing language. Suffixes such as "s," "ed," and "ing" convey meaning regarding the time frame in which action occurred and also tells us how many objects or persons were involved.

Empirical Fit to the Classic Theories

As the current literature is placing its emphasis upon a semantic-based, cognitive approach to the development of syntax, it becomes all too simple to line up each of the major language theories discussed in all of the preceding chapters and then ask the advocates of each theory to show how each theory accounts for the development of meaning as the prerequisite for syntactic growth. Before the reader continues in this chapter, s/he is encouraged to take pen in hand and jot down exactly how s/he would answer that question from the viewpoints of Transformational grammar, e.g., Chomsky's model, S-R Behaviorism, e.g., Mowrer's model and B. F. Skinner's "model," and finally from the viewpoint of S-O-R Behaviorism, e.g., M. D. S. Braine's "contextual generalization" model and C. E. Osgood's probabilistic model.

First, we can recall that Chomsky's Transformational grammar model included (1) a "deep structure," which for all practical purposes was composed of a simple, present tense declarative sentence type, (2) varying numbers of transformational rules (with the exact number being determined by any specific culture's needs from the language), and (3) the surface structure, which was the overt expression (oral or written) of the product produced by the interaction of the deep structure and the transformational rules. Meaning was, according to Chomsky, somewhere in the deep structure, but he had little to say about it. In all too many ways, Chomsky makes it seem as if semantics was a separate issue apart from syntax. Once meaning entered into the deep structure processing, it seemed to be modified by the transformational rules until the desired changes in meaning occurred. It was effectively McCawley (1968), Fillmore (1968), and especially Bloom (1970), who proposed "Case grammar" in order to address this shortcoming of Transformational grammar. Case grammar looked specifically at the "deep structure" of children's one-and two-word utterances. It was apparent to the advocates of Case grammar that the semantic variable had to be considered before one took up the issue of how syntax actually developed. Bloom (1970), for example, stressed the concept of the "psychological reality" of the child's grammar. She meant only one thing by that; she wanted to explore the meaning structure of the child's world as the child himself/herself saw that structure. Bloom, McCawley and Fillmore engaged in an impossible task of trying to guess the nature of how an infant perceives reality and how that reality affects the growth of the very thing the infant lacks in order to introspectively explain his/her mental processing as an infant/adult-like language. Case grammar asked its followers to perhaps become a rare breed of researcher who is equally capable of being mentalistic/rationalistic and empirical at the same moment. The behavior of infants is not the "right stuff" many empiricists enjoy analyzing since such behavior simply refuses to adjust itself to the cooperation needed to promulgate pure experimental design. Transformational grammar in the meantime seemed perfectly content to let Case grammar do its work and build the groundwork for the development of a truly semantically based model of language. In the

150

meantime, Transformational grammar carried on in the usual Chomskian tradition it had started with. At present, Case grammar has not determined the semantic underpinnings of syntactic development. How far away such a discovery is remains a good question. Case grammar has set itself a two-fold goal; it wants to (1) understand the semantic core as a prerequisite to syntax, and (2) it wants to write a grammar describing that core. Until the first is done, the second is merely wishful thinking — or, at its worst, bogus erudition.

From the S-R Behavioristic point of view, we can readily recall that all of O. H. Mowrer's (1954) "The Psychologist Looks at Language" was dedicated to the sole purpose of explaining the nature of the conditioning of meaning. His contribution in that regard was an excellent one, but at no point did he even so much as hint at the possibility of qualitative cognitive changes, e.g., those presented many years before Mowrer's work by the famous Swiss intellectual Jean Piaget. Little can be added to or taken from Mowrer's detailed discussions of the "first-order conditioning," "second-order conditioning," "attenuation," "predication," and "inertia" processes. No one seems to have readdressed these issues since his publication. But we can easily recall that his work did not attempt to merge semantics into syntactic structures; he seemed content to pursue the transfer of meaning from word to word within the sentence, and then the only sentence type he dealt with was the simple, present tense declarative sentence, "Tom is a thief." We were eager to agree with him at the close of his article when he said he believed he had not addressed all of the issues in language development. He very obviously had not, but at least he seemed to have sensed the importance of semantics intuitively.

When we check B. F. Skinner's work on "language development," we immediately recall that Skinner did not in any manner believe that there was a special field known as language development in the first place. All roads lead us directly to the position that behavior of any kind is still just behavior. If behavior exists, it can be plotted; if it does not exist, there are no plots. Semantics develop through gradual shaping and successive approximation procedures. Syntax develops the same way. No discussion of the interaction of semantics and syntax seems necessary since, after all, it is all just behavior, and as we know, behavior is behavior is behavior. We find no discussion of "psychological reality" as we do in Bloom's (1970) work. What we do find is solid, easily observable, and graphable facts pertaining strictly to surface structure features of the language. Anyone familiar with Skinner's work knows well that he is definitely anti-theory and claims neither to be a theorist nor to have his own theory.

Regarding M. D. S. Braine's "contextual generalization" model, we find little interest in semantics as such. Braine builds a good, well-documented case through a series of studies, but, like virtually everyone seen in this section so far (with the exception of Bloom, McCawley, and Fillmore), he seems to have great difficulty bringing the model down to fit beginning first language. In fact, the closest he can come age-wise is with nursery school children. Braine's belief that language development is "perceptual" and not "cognitive" seems not to be supported in any sense as we reread the evidence presented in the present chapter; Brown (1973) Palermo (1978), and Dale (1976) have repeatedly shown that the process is squarely based upon cognitive issues. We are left with the rather embarrassing conclusion that either Braine has invented a model which does not describe the acquisition of language as the present chapter shows the normal progression of development to occur, or probably more rightly, Braine has erred in saying the process is "perceptual" and not "cognitive." Evidence in the present chapter would indicate language development to be well underway by approximately 10 to 12 months of age if we are using the one-word phase as our "starting point." Children may indeed generalize from context when they enter the "ordered two-word phase," but it is difficult to see the process evidenced when we look at the "random two-word phase."

As was noted in the present chapter, much of Brown's early work emphasized the fact that children used content words as the basis of first attempts at language production. Closed class morphemes, which Braine had based his entire model upon, were not identified as part of Brown's emphasis regarding critical language contributors. This is devastating to Braine's position insofar as that position would run in accounting for language development through the first word through the three-word phase. We can recall that Brown would somewhat soften his position today if he read Palermo (1978). Palermo and most other researchers are finding that the open word (O) plus open word (O) sentence is too narrow and must be replaced by the idea that the following three types of sentences are possible for beginners:

O + O → S
P (pivot or "closed class" morpheme) + O → S,
O + P → S, but
P + P cannot → S

This essentially gives Braine a new lease on his model's life today, but it surely does not mean that his model can stand as is as long as he continues putting stress upon just pivots. After all, "P + P → S" speaks for itself. As we recall from reading the present chapter, Brown's (1973) work clearly shows many of the closed class morphemes, e.g., "s," "ed," "ing," etc., coming into play early in the child's ordered two-word phase. This is good for Braine's model, but it still is damaging to Braine's model if that model is extended to earlier stages of Brown's model.

For C. E. Osgood semantics is fundamental to the understanding of syntactic growth. His entire model is based upon the idea that as each word is received by the child a simultaneous dual processing occurs upon the word on both a vertical and a horizontal level. Vertical processing places the word into a class with words of similar meaning. Horizontal processing occurs as the word is associated across classes to form a S-R association. For example, the word "The" vertically is processed by putting "The" into a class that includes other articles such as "a" and "an"; horizontal processing occurs as "The" acts as the stimulus to form an association with a proper cross-class response such as an adjective ("The red ..."), an adverb ("The very ..."), or a noun ("The sun ..."). The horizontal response class chosen is dependent upon the probabilities within the context. Semantics is the heart of Osgood's model since what a word means to the child determines processing both at the vertical and horizontal levels. A word with meaning that is acceptable to the child but not the adult community will not assist the production of adult syntactic patterns. The probability of adult production is increased as more and more words preceding any word in a phrase are processed correctly. His model stands as a mixture of M. D. S. Braine's ideas on contextual generalization, B. F. Skinner's ideas on operant reinforcement, and a refutation of Noam Chomsky. Osgood provides a model which is as sophisticated as any. No reviews were ever negatively critical of the model. The sophistication of the model was obvious; it was also presented in such a fashion as to let the professional public know that it was in no manner to be considered as a "final answer." This latter point was, as you will recall, the "flash point" for Chomsky's criticisms of Skinner's *Verbal Behavior*; Skinner was accused, all too justly, of preposing a "final answer" to the problem of language acquisition (Chomsky, 1959).

But something seems to be missing despite the fact Osgood's model does discuss the crucial position of semantics in the building of syntax. What seems to be missing is concensus over the very definition of semantics he used. It was a behavioral definition, and it claimed that semantics is a product of conditioning (either classical or operant or both in interaction). There is no discussion of how semantics may be affected by cognitive change. There was no discussion about the work of Jean Piaget or any other developmental cognitivist. The message seen in

Brown's (1973) work, Palermo's (1978) writings, and Dale's (1976) position is simply that semantics is a prerequisite for adequate syntactic development; semantics is based upon cognitive development. Semantic development is very much based upon a genetic unfolding of the capacity to categorize and process information in very different ways as chronological age increases.

Where then do we stand regarding the fate of grand theory building within the field of syntax development? Must we necessarily reject any theory if it simply fails to cover all aspects of syntactic development. In the late 1950s, the 1960s, and well into the 1970s, debates about adequacy, both philosophically and technically, raged on all levels among the varied disciplines of anthropology, sociology, linguistics, philosophy, psychology, and the physical sciences. There seemed more at stake than "cracking the secret" of syntax acquisition. There was the major question of what modifications could be tolerated within the timeworn and cherished scientific method before that method could stand no more modification without literally changing its form into something new. Chomsky (1957) had proposed a syntactic model of immense complexity based upon a disregard for the empirical scientific method. J. J. Katz (1964) had defended Chomsky's approach by proposing a defense of mentalism/rationalism. The S-R and S-O-R Behaviorists slashed back by defending the scientific method as practiced at its laboratory best and built an impressive collection of observed behavior patterns.

By the early 1970s, and definitely continuing today, a very slow awakening has led some, but not all, theorists to realize it would be presumptuous to continue defending any single classic theory to the total exclusion of another. The data coming in from various studies simply refused to fit into just one single model; it, at times, supported one part of a model so strongly that one could be led only to bitter disappointment by later seeing how poorly the same model handled other data. Slowly, most of the combatants lowered their shields, looked at the variety of incoming data, and realized that debating the "sufficiency" of any model was perfunctory. Data secured from thorough computer-assisted library searches is being pieced together to view the "whole." At present, few shields are being lifted. Bowerman (1974) said the existing classic models shared one major fault: each was far too powerful to handle the earliest attempts the child makes at language production. By "powerful," Bowerman apparently meant that each model was attacking the problem as if the child did not start using "a model" until two years of age. The unknown processes which underlie development from birth to age two years still lie untouched by the models. If an adequate model is to be prepared and if semantic development does precede syntactic growth, the resultant model must find a way to operationalize Bloom's (1970) search for the "psychological reality" in meaning for the infant. This is a very tall order and perhaps one in excess of present-day reasoning with or without computer assistance. "Too soon; too soon!" echoes all about us as we wade ever deeper into a growing flood of facts. The challenge and excitement are equally imposing.

References

Bellugi, U. (1965). "The Development of Interrogative Structures in Children's Speech." In K. Riegel (Ed.), *The Development of Language Functions* (103—108). Ann Arbor, Michigan: Center for Human Growth and Development, University of Michigan, Report No. 8.

Berlin, H. (1975). *Studies in the Cognitive Basis of Language Development.* New York: New York, Academic Press.

Bever, T., Fodor, J., and Weksel, W. (1965). "On the Acquisition of Syntax: A Critique of 'Contexual Generalization.'" *Psychological Review, 72,* 467–482.

Bloom, L. (1970). *Semantic Features in Language Acquisition.* Paper presented at the Conference on Research in the Language of the Mentally Retarded, University of Kansas.

Bloom, L. (1973). *One Word at a Time: The Use of Single Word Utterances Before Syntax.* The Hague: Mouton

Bowerman, L. (1974). "Talking, Understanding, and Thinking." In R. Schiefelhusch and L. Loyd (Eds.), *Languge Perspectives: Acquisition, Retardation, and Instruction* (285—311). Baltimore, Maryland: University Park Press.

Braine, M. D. S. (1963a). "On Learning the Grammatical Order of Words." *Psychological Review, 70,* 323–348.

Braine, M. D. S. (1963b). "The Ontogeny of Phrase Structure: The First Phase." *Language, 39,* 1–13.

Braine, M. D. S. (1965). "On the Basis of Phrase Structure: A Reply to Bever, Fodor, and Weksel." *Psychological Review, 72,* 483–492.

Brown, R. (1968). "The Development of Wh Questions in Child Speech." *Journal of Verbal Learning and Verbal Behavior, 7,* 279–290.

Brown, R. (1973). *A First Language: The Early Stages.* Cambridge, Massachusetts: Harvard Press.

Brown, R., and Fraser, C. (1964). "The Acquisition of Syntax." In U. Bellugi and R. Brown (Eds.), *The Acquisition of Language. Monograph of the Society for Research in Child Development, 29* (1), 43–79.

Brown, R., Fraser, C., and Bellugi, U. (1964). "Explorations in Grammar Evaluation." In U. Bellugi and R. Brown (Eds.), *The Acquisition of Language. Monograph of the Society for Research in Child Development, 29* (1), 79–92

Chipman, H. and deDandel, C. (1974). "Developmental Study of the Comprehension and Production of the Pronoun 'It.'" *Journal of Psycholinguistic Research, 3,* 91–99.

Chomsky, C. S. (1969). *The Acquisition of Syntax in Children from Three to Ten.* Cambridge, Massachusetts: MIT Press.

Chomsky, N. (1957). *Syntactic Structures.* The Hague: Mouton.

Chomsky, N. (1959). "Review of Skinner's *Verbal Behavior.*" *Language, 35* (1), 26—58.

Chomsky, N., and Halle, M. (1968). *The Sound Pattern of English.* New York: Harper and Row.

Clark, H., and Clark, E. (1977). *Psychology and Language.* New York: Harcourt, Brace, and Jovanovich, Inc.

Dale, P. S. (1976). *Language Development* (2nd ed.). New York: Holt.

deVilliers, J. and Flusberg, H. (1975). "Some Facts One Simply Cannot Deny." *Journal of Child Language, 2,* 279—286.

Donaldson, M. (1970). "Developmental Aspects of Performance with Negatives." In G. d'Arcais and W. Lavelt (Eds.), *Advances in Psycholinguistics* (397—410). Amsterdam: North Holland Publishing Co.

Ervin-Tripp, S. (1970). "Discourse Agreement: How Children Answer Questions." In J. R. Hayes (Ed.), *Cognition and the Development of Language* (79—108). New York: Wiley.

Fillmore, C. J. (1968). "The Case for Case." In E. Bach and R. Hams (Eds.), *Universals in Linguistic Theory* (1—88). New York: Holt.

Fraser, C., Bellugi, U., and Brown, R. (1963). "Control of Grammar in Imitation, Comprehension, and Production." *Journal of Verbal Learning and Verbal Behavior, 2,* 121—135.

Greenfield, P., and Smith, J. (1976). *The Structure of Early Communication in Language Development.* New York: Academic Press.

Harris, M., and Hassemer, W. (1972). "Some Factors Affecting the Complexity of Children's Sentences: The Effects of Modeling, Age, Sex, and Bilingualism." *Journal of Experimental Child Psychology, 13,* 447—455.

Jakobson, R., and Halle, M. (1956). *Fundamentals of Language.* The Hague: Mouton.

Kaplan, E., and Kaplan, G. (1971). "The Prelinguistic Child." In J. Elliot (Ed.), *Human Development and Cognitive Processes* (359—381). New York: Holt.

Katz, J. J. (1964). "Mentalism in Linguistics." *Language, 40,* 124—137.

Kess, J. (1976). *Psycholinguistics.* New York: Academic Press.

Lovell, K., and Dixon, E. (1967). "The Growth of the Control of Grammar in Imitation, Comprehension, and Production." *Journal of Child Psychology and Psychiatry, 8,* 31—39.

McCawley, J. (1968). "The Role of Semantics in a Grammar." In E. Bach and R. Hams (Eds.), *Universals in Linguistic Theory* (124—169). New York: Holt.

McNeill, D. (1966). "The Creation of Language by Children." In J. Lyons and R. Wales (Eds.), *Psycholinguistic Papers* (99—132). Edinburgh: Edinburgh University Press.

McNeill, D. (1970). "The Development of Language." In P. Mussen (Ed.), *Carmichael's Manual of Child Psychology* (3rd ed.) (1061—1161). New York: Wiley.

McNeill, D. and McNeill, N. (1968). "What Does a Child Mean When He Says 'No?'" In E. Zale (Ed.), *Language and Language Behavior* (51—62). New York: Appleton.

Menyuk, P. (1969). *Sentences Children Use.* Cambridge, Massachusetts: MIT Press.

Millenson, J. and Leslie, J. (1969). *Principles of Behavioral Analysis* (2nd ed.). New York: Macmillan.

Miller, G. and McNeill, D. (1968). "Psycholinguistics." In G. Lindzey and E. Aronson (Eds.), *The Handbook of Social Psychology, Vol. 3* (666—794). Reading, Massachusetts: Addison-Wesley.

Mowrer, O. H. (1954). "The Psychologist Looks at Language." *American Psychologist, 9,* 660—694.

Neisser, U. (1967). *Cognitive Psychology.* New York: Appleton, Century, and Crofts.

Nelson, E. (1973). "Structure and Strategy in Learning to Talk." *Monographs of the Society for Research in Child Development, 38* (1—2), 1—135.

Osgood, C. E. (1963). "On Understanding and Creating Sentences." *American Psychologist, 18,* 735—751.

Palermo, D. (1978). *Psychology of Language.* Dallas, Texas: Scott.

156

Palermo, D. and Molfese, D. (1972). "Language Acquisition from Age Five Onward." *Psychological Bulletin, 28,* 409—428.

Piaget, J. (1952). *The Origins of Intelligence in Children.* New York: International Universities Press.

Riley, L. and Fite, G. (1974). "Syntagmatic versus Paradigmatic Paired-Associate Acquisition." *Journal of Experimental Psychology, 103,* 375—376.

Skinner, B. F. (1957). *Verbal Behavior.* New York: Appleton, Century, and Crofts.

Skinner, B. F. (1959). "A Case History in Scientific Method." In S. Koch (Ed.), *Psychology: A Study of a Science, Volume 2* (359—379). New York: McGraw-Hill.

Slobin, D. (1966). "Grammatical Transformations and Sentence Comprehension in Childhood and Adulthood." *Journal of Verbal Learning and Verbal Behavior,* 5, 219—227.

Slobin, D. (1973). "Cognitive Prerequisites for the Development of Grammar." In C. Ferguson and D. Slobin (Eds.), *Studies in Child Language Development* (175—208). New York: Holt.

Tolman, E. C. (1932). *Purposive Behavior in Animals and Man.* New York: Appleton, Century, and Crofts.

Turner, E. and Rummerveit, R. (1967). "The Acquisition of Sentence Voice and Reversibility." *Child Development, 38,* 649—660.

Wahler, R. (1969). "Infant Social Development: Some Experimental Analyses of an Infant-Mother Interaction During the First Year of Life." *Journal of Experimental Child Psychology, 7,* 101—113.

– 7 –

SEMANTICS

Defining "Semantics"

After reflecting upon the concluding remarks in the previous chapter, which dealt with syntactic development, we must come to grips with semantics. Saying that semantics is the field of study which deals with the meaning of words is not really a very meaningful way of dealing with the term semantics. Such a "definition," if we may flatter it by calling it such, is circular. When a child asks for the definition of "triangle," we show the child a picture of "a triangle," and then hope that all the child's future questions about triangles have been answered by our definition. We are reinforced by the fact that possibly the child will not ask us to again define triangle as long as the example is confronted by no exceptions. It all appears so simple. We provide the experience; the child rote memorizes it. But here precisely lies the heart of the issue common to all areas in semantic study. If someone has been shown only a very limited number of examples which define a term, how does s/he recognize other examples within some range of examples? Surely it is naive of us to assume that each example from the entire range of examples must be perceived before we can say that we have grasped the "sense" of the thing in question.

For the sake of argument, we will assume from the start that the reality of "things" and "events" is not solely based upon our perceptions of those "things" and "events." Those "things" and "events" exist, we will assume, independently or our perceptions but yet are enriched or are detracted from in complexity by the very act of perceiving. We are both assisted and impaired by our own sensory and cognitive limits as humans as we seek to define "essence."

Present Research Interest in Semantics

If one counts the work of Ebbinghaus (1885) in his writing of *Memory* as being one of the earliest formal attempts to specifically define syntax, then semantic research efforts would date at least some 65 plus years later if the appearance of O. H. Mowrer's (1954) "The Psychologist Looks at Language" is used as the benchmark. Research in semantics seemed to have waned several times between Mowrer's classic work and the present data. Dale (1972, p. 131) states that interest in semantic research had reached a plateau during the early 1970s no matter which theoretical perspective was being looked at. Although it could be contended and easily defended that Dale overstated the case, there is little doubt that the substance of his point was accurate. The "Referent Theory" approach (to be discussed below) had never conducted research. The "Behavior Theory" approach (which will also be discussed below) had a following in the early 1970s, but many of its supporters had tired of reconducting classical/operant experiments, which did little more than confirm Mowrer's and Skinner's positions. Many had given up attempts to beat C. E. Osgood at his own game regarding the "semantic differential technique" and "semantic generalization." In the mode of a Behavioral approach, concept formation/concept attainment studies were still being conducted in the early 1970s, but their efforts would soon be overshadowed by major descriptive "breakthroughs" coming from experimental cognitive psychology. By the early 1970s the work of Jean Piaget, Vygotsky, and Luria had begun to make serious penetration of what had up to that point been a Behavioral Theory's "closed shop" in the United States; this "new" movement was steeped in a philosophical approach quite comfortably fitting those scholars of the rationalistic/mentalistic bent, e.g., Transformational grammarian's, but it sat badly with Behaviorists. By the early 1970s, Developmental Theory was "off the ground" but frantically flapping its fledgling wings to avoid crashing in United States scientific circles. Definitely in the Developmental Camp stood the work of McCawley (1968), Fillmore (1968), and Bloom (1970) on Case grammar; Roger Brown's efforts through the 1960s and early 1970s had foreshadowed much of their writings. It is important here that we note two things: (1) McCawley's, Fillmore's, Bloom's, and Brown's works all qualified as Developmental Theory (and were discussed in great length in the preceding chapter), and (2) their work was not rationalistic/mentalistic from the start and then later subjected to empirical testing as was definitely that of Jean Piaget, definitely that of Vygotsky, and to a much lesser extent that of Luria. It is the

159

writings of these three latter authors that will occupy our considerations in the present chapter.

By the mid 1970s, Dale (1976, p. 165) had changed his earlier position. Interests were literally on the verge of an explosion. Semantic growth became truly the "hottest" area of all in language development today not simply because it is a fascinating, rigorous discipline in and of itself, but because it may be the key to eventual understanding of syntax as well. We now turn our attention to the three major semantic theories as we prepare to see exactly where we stand today.

The Classic Theories

Referent Theory

Dale (1976, pp. 167-170) cites this particular theory of semantic growth as being the one with the least logical foundation in science. This approach assumes that the meaning attached to any word is somehow not simply "attached" but is inherent in the word itself. From this position, a child could understand the term "triangle" if the child merely would consider what s/he innately knew about triangles. In all too many ways, this approach reflects the classic Platonic approach to the "discovery" or "revelation" of knowledge. Plato assumed, apparently through the influence of Socrates, that all knowledge existed inside the person and that "teaching" was actually a process of awakening the person to this storehouse of knowledge. The method to produce this awakening was known as the "dialectic" technique (Plato, 1937). The technique stressed the use of questioning the person until the "truth" was revealed. Knowledge of geometric shapes and principles were already known by even the simplest of "uneducated" people; the dialectic proved it so—at least as Plato saw it.

If the reader accepts the logic against Referent Theory and wonders how anyone could have proposed such an idea in the first place, stop to think about the use of language as it applies to "magic" and religious functions of modern society. Anyone who has read the concluding chapters of *Rosemary's Baby* (Levin, 1967) can surely see that language is apparently assumed to have an element of innateness or else why would the plot of the book prove to be popular? We need not deal in demonology to see examples of "magic" terms in virtually every form of religion that has existed. Anyone who has read the *Exorcist* (Blatty, 1971) can see a classic conflict between innate word meanings in demonology used as weapons against innate word meaning in orthodox religions.

160

The Referent Theory appeared to have suffered fatal wounds as early as the first two decades of the 20th century at the hands of Sir Bertrand Russell (Dale, 1972, p. 133). Russell neatly turned the argument around to defeat Referent Theory. The original argument against it was related to how such a theory could show that things or events somehow send or transfer their "thingness" or "eventness" to the word so as to make the word hold innate meaning. Russell asked how a single term could have multiple referents and still exist as a term with "innate" meaning. Words such as "it," "you," "he or she," "they," for example, are classified as indefinite pronouns for a very good reason. They definitely do not refer to any one person or thing.

As a result of these issues, the reader would be painfully hard pressed to find anyone today who as a scientist would "jump upon his/her sword" to defend the Referent Theory. Yet without its proposal the next theory we consider is less rich in appearance.

Behavioral Theory

From a precise reading of history, one may conclude that this theory is actually not as old as the third theory—Developmental Theory—which we will consider below. However, Behavioral Theory, unlike Developmental Theory in the United States, was popular in the United States much earlier than was Developmental Theory, which still is being "discovered" by some here in this country. Even though both Behavioral Theory and Developmental Theory rejected the Referent Theory, the philosophical tenor of the times was such in the United States as to make Behavioral Theory at least appear at first to be the more adamantly opposed. Therefore, we attend to the "stronger voice" first, but we should keep in mind that its strength is an illusion also created by geographic proximity since Developmental Theory was a European product. If we watch our steps closely, we may just see a logical progression from Behavioral Theory directly into Developmental Theory itself.

This particular approach to an analysis of meaning has two subparts. One is defined as a strict S-R approach to the learning of definitions for various terms, and the second is a S-O-R approach, which allows at least some discussion of the contribution made by the "active mind" of the language user. Both approaches stress the contributing forces of an active environment, and both approaches are strictly empirical in nature. There is a progressive move from the S-R Behavioristic approach toward the S-O-R approach as we trace the movement from the 1950s into the present period. The transition is subtle and not necessarily smoothly continuous, but it is nonetheless quite evident upon close inspection of the research appearing under the general title of "Behavioral Theory."

Not too surprisingly, the work of O. H. Mowrer (1954) in "The Psychologist Looks at Language" qualifies far more easily as an essay on semantic acquisition than it does one on syntactic growth. Mowrer's position, as you will recall, stressed the use of I. P. Pavlov's "first signal system" in classical conditioning. Some form of a concrete experience (the UCS) was to be preceded by some neutral signal (a word, which he defined as a CS), and that combination of CS + UCS was to be repeated until the "meaning" of the UCS was transferred ("predicated") to the CS. The entire model has already been presented in Chapter 4 of this book; the reader is encouraged to reread that chapter at this point.

There was little doubt then, as there seems little serious doubt now, that Mowrer made a significant contribution, but the question arose then, and remains now, as to how far could the model go in claiming that all meaning was derived in just the fashion so diagramed in the model. For example, could a child of 2 years grasp the meaning of the CS "metaphysics" through his/her experiencing of the UCS that denotes the experience of metaphysics? Metaphysics means literally "beyond the physical," so where is the experience?

We note in all of this absolutely no reference to any active, cognitive contribution on the part of the language user. There are no "classes" or "categories" of events or things into which varying but similar experiences can be "sorted" or "arranged." This is not meant as a criticism of Mowrer's system; it is a reflection of the fact that the times were such that terms such as "class" and "category" and "sort" had no meaning. His model is straight forward, lean, and adequate to at least a point. After all, he was using Pavlov's principles, and those principles as related to classical conditioning have never suffered even a modest challenge.

Mowrer's (1954) article was followed three years later by two attempts to clarify semantic development, but neither of the two made any particular reference to the work Mowrer had done. We are already familiar with the first of these attempts; it was B. F. Skinner's work dealing with operant conditioning as applied to verbal behavior (Skinner, 1957). The message was the same for semantic growth as it was for syntactic growth. The language learner learned through operant conditioning that certain words were "acceptable" when used in certain contexts and were unacceptable when used in others. Repeated practice with the same word used in varying contexts ultimately led to a set of definitional "markers" or "features" which became the word's meaning. The same schedules of reinforcement applied to the analysis of semantics as syn-

162

tax, albeit the reader sees less apparent concern over the growth of semantics in Skinner's work. As we saw in the previous chapter, it could be true that semantics is the basis of syntactic development, but one would never come to that conclusion through reading Skinner's book *Verbal Behavior*. As in Mowrer's case, Skinner leads us also to believe that all word meaning is left to the dictates of the environment. There are no "classes" or "categories" of meaning within the Skinnerian framework. Every word's meaning is dictated by the reinforcement one has received for using that word; it is, therefore, quite conceivable that a meaning for a word in one culture may be entirely different from that for the same word in a different culture. There is no emphasis, or mention for that matter, upon cognitive processing or developmental stages. It would be tempting to say that Skinner's writings had virtually no impact upon semantic theory if it were not for the salutation C. E. Osgood gives Skinner in Osgood's "On Understanding and Creating Sentences" (Osgood, 1963), which we thoroughly reviewed in Chapter 5 above. You will recall that Osgood's model is definitely a semantic-based model even as he directly addresses syntactic growth. Osgood acknowledges the contribution Skinner made in causing us to think only in terms of observables and no more. Osgood then develops his theory of semantics (as presented in Chapter 5) and shows us that observables can be analyzed at many levels.

What was not mentioned in Chapter 5 was the model Osgood had proposed earlier which did not directly address semantics' contribution to syntactic growth but rather looked at a side of semantics which is less precise than that of "objective" meaning. The model was known as the "semantic differential technique" and appeared the same year, 1957, as Skinner's *Verbal Behavior*.

Osgood, Suci and Tannenbaum (1957) designed the "semantic differential technique" (SDT) to measure three dimensions of meaning. Those dimensions were (1) evaluation, which seems to develop earliest in children, (2) activity, and (3) potency. Evaluation refers to the "goodness/badness" elements in a term. Activity refers to the speed of movement in a term, and potency refers to the strength/weakness elements in a given term. Each dimension is usually measured using bipolar adjectives placed at opposite ends of a seven-point scale. Using evaluation, for example, the word "excellent" might appear at position one on a continuum with position number seven being defined as "failure." Position number four would mark a point of absolute neutrality between the bipolar adjectives. If you were presented with a term such as "triangle" and were asked to rate it somewhere on the seven-point scale, you would perhaps have some difficulty making a decision but might be heartened by the midpoint (position four) meaning neutrality. Perhaps you would choose the fourth position if you were to see as much "excellence" as you did "failure" in triangles. But then some people would not agree with you for reasons dictated by their own experiences. This sense of disagreement is what prompted Osgood's (1964) article "Semantic Differential Technique in the Comparative Study of Cultures." As Osgood's study indicates, a single term may have almost as many meanings as there are cultures to consider the term. But even at this, the three basic dimensions of meaning from the SDT's viewpoint appear consistently in all cultures. The technique has not undergone revision or restructuring since its beginnings in 1957, and as with its copartner the semantic generalization model, it has suffered virtually no significant criticism.

Following the year 1957, we can trace a movement in Behavioral Theory which indicates the strict S-R approaches of Mowrer and Skinner had fewer followers than did the S-O-R models of C. E. Osgood. The movement was subtle, but it was also quite real. Let us now pursue history.

In 1958, Roger Brown was more oriented toward a learning theory approach to semantic growth. In that year, he asked whether children started with very specific meanings for words or if the meanings were quite general. Most adult observers had predicted the former to be true because so many of children's labeling processes appeared so very specific. However, it was found that the second idea was more the case. Adults tend to use very specific terms which children adopt as their own. The cognitive functioning of the child is not mature; the meaning of any term can reflect only the level of present cognitive maturity. As the child grows older, many meanings will grow to be as specific as the terms used. We can see at that time Brown was not hinting at any kind of a developmental/cognitive process; it is all very direct imitation (learning the specific term) and then reinforced practice as we seek to progressively sharpen our definitions. His position changed in the mid-1970s as he joined the Developmental Theory approach and left Behavioral Theory behind (Brown, 1973).

Ervin and Foster (1960) essentially agreed with Brown's position and clarified it further. They pointed out that each term has two dimensions. The first is "denotation," which refers to specific "markers" of meaning, and the second is "connotation," which refers to the more generalized meaning of a term as well as its judgmental and emotional overtones. For example, the term "book" has a very specific set of markers which will tell you that the term is used both as a noun and as a verb. These markers are conventionally "housed" in a dictionary, and we let that dictionary stand as society's position regarding specific meanings. These markers are subject to change; we see such changes in each new edition of a dictionary. Ervin and Foster conclude that children tend to denote less well than do adults and that children are far more prone to connote than are adults. For example, children seem to believe that if something reflects happiness that it will undoubtedly also be "good" and "beautiful." If something is strong, it must be large and heavy. Katz and Fodor (1963) echoed the findings of Ervin and Foster (1960) with the added assertion that children's connotative processes seem to be woefully lacking. For example, a "bachelor's wife" was quite an acceptable phrase to many of their childhood subjects.

John Carroll (1964) set the tone of works to come in the Behavioral Theory approach as he wrote his "Words, Meanings, and Concepts." His position was aimed at practitioners as well as theoreticians. According to Carroll, if one knew the meanings of a word then one understood that word "conceptually" as well. At first glance, this seems to be a casual enough statement, but its implications are very significant. To possess a concept, one needs to possess the "features" (physical attributes) of that concept. One does not hold a concept unless all features are present in ones thinking. Therefore, since there are no such things as partial concepts, one must have total meaning if one says one holds a concept. Speaking this way forces us to quickly build "classes" or "categories" into which one deposits ones experiences (partial meanings) until an entire concept is developed. There are, therefore, no partial concepts by the strict definition of the term "concept." Such thinking actively opposes other Behaviorists surrounding Carroll. Those Behaviorists proclaiming to be strict experimentalists were most offended. To understand the offense, we must first understand what the experimental Behaviorists meant by the term "concept." Our reference for the explanation is Hulse, Egeth and Deese's (1980) *Psychology of Learning* as seen on pages 213—220. The term "feature" is consistently used to mean physical attribute. There are five types of concepts seen by Hulse, Egeth and Deese, unlike John Carroll, who apparently sees only one type.

First, and most simple, the "affirmative" concept is defined by having one and only one feature. For example, the verbal statement describing this concept reads as "All blue things are features of this concept." If one were presented with a display board showing many variously colored geometric shapes, pointing consistently to "blue" things of all shapes would lead to a behavioral experimenter's saying the concept had been formed. By this token, infrahumans could also form concepts.

Second, and more difficult than the affirmative, is the "conjunctive" concept type. This type requires two or more features to be simultaneously present in order to call something a concept. For example, we could require that a thing be both "blue" and "triangular" to qualify as an example we will reinforce. This would mean that blue circles are negative examples, as are blue squares, yellow triangles, etc. Only blue triangles are reinforcable. The degree of complexity may be geometrically increased by adding one additional feature at a time to make the concept require three, four, five, or more features before it is a positive example of the concept.

The third concept type is referred to as the "inclusive disjunctive" and is more difficult than either of the preceding concept types. It requires "either/or" decisions. For example, anything that is blue may be a positive feature, anything that is triangular may be a positive feature, and, of course, anything that is a blue triangle is a positive example. A red triangle is now just as positive as is a green triangle; a blue square qualifies as positive with the same ease as does a blue circle or a blue triangle. Suddenly so many things are possible as positive features that the person doing the choosing of features may become highly confused.

The fourth concept type is known as the "conditional." It states the case as "If one specific feature is present, then a second specific feature must also be present, but if the second one is present by itself, then it does qualify as a positive feature whether the first feature is present or not." An easy to understand example of this would exist if you were told that "If it is a blue geometric shape, then it must be a triangle also, but if it just appears that you are seeing just a triangle, you may disregard its color and still receive reinforcement for selecting." Blue squares no longer are positive examples of the concept; yellow triangles do qualify, whereas blue circles do not. Red triangles do qualify. On a more day-to-day basis, a statement such as "If you wish to work in the library, you must be quiet, but if you wish to be quiet, you may go wherever you wish"; or "If it is a hawk, it must be able to dive rapidly from the clouds, but all things that dive rapidly from the clouds need not necessarily be hawks." This is more difficult than the inclusive disjunctive.

The fifth concept type is the most abstract of all and forces our cognitive abilities to be mightily exercised. It is referred to as the "biconditional" concept type and reads as follows: "If it is blue, then it must be a triangle, and if it is a triangle, then it must be blue." There are relatively few examples of this in our daily life, but here is one: "If the surgeon's knife is carbon steel, then the incision will be clean, and if the incision is to be clean, the surgeon's knife must be carbon steel (and only carbon steel)." The major drawback in studying this concept type, especially if you are asking your subjects only to point at correct examples of the concept instead of verbalizing them, is that the subject actually only has to point to the example which has the two required features and can ignore the "if, then" relationship between the two features. This makes it no more difficult than the conjunctive concept type discussed above. For example, pointing to a "blue triangle" when using the rule "If it is blue, then it must be a triangle, and if it is a triangle, then it must be blue" results in similar action when one is under the rule "All blue triangles are positive."

This behavioral approach to the defining of concepts had led to considerable research since it lends itself to the easy preparation of materials and to the easy, empirical analysis of results. It is, of course, an associationistic approach. "Categories" and "classes" are not discussed.

Carroll seems interested only in the conjunctive concept type since he says that a concept is defined by the sum total of all its meanings (features). How do we know what a tree is? We merely add up all the features. Carroll then offers a surprise. Despite experiences determining what a concept is, there is a "mystical" entity called "the conceptual invariant." It is a cultural universal and yet is not dependent upon experience. Indeed, it defies experience. For example, all cultures have a "God" of one form or another even if the culture has no words to describe that concept's features. For a Behaviorist, Carroll suddenly seems to have put experience second to a nativist, genetic reality of some sort. We can see Jean Piaget smiling.

Carroll sees concepts as having denotation and connotation; denotation splits into two subparts, "genus" and "differentia." "Genus" refers to the general grouping into which a meaning is placed. "Breaking down" of the superordinate grouping into its subordinate parts is called the "differentia." If he had added the idea that the genus/differentia were directly affected by the age of the language processer, he would have been the first and only Behavioral theoretician to anticipate the writings of the Developmental theorist Jean Piaget. He did not. Instead, he directs his final comments to us who teach. He suggests using the deductive approach to teaching concepts as opposed to an inductive one. Deduction sets forth a concept and then asks students to find examples of it. Induction presents the examples and forces the students to discover the concept.

Johnson (1967) had shown that the context and the position within a sentence marking a word's appearance are potent determiners of word meaning. This conclusion goes beyond Aristotle's three principles of associations. Goss (1961) had already challenged the idea that concepts were based upon any type of simple asociative process. He proposed an active role for verbal mediation in concept formation, which no doubt, is a position someone such as John Carroll could respect. However, in

167

1961, Kaplan had written that the processes of forming concepts did not depend upon verbalization, but some kind of symbolic process was needed. Both Kaplan and his co-worker Werner believe that someone must discuss the use of images in conceptual processes. Both authors saw symbolization as especially dependent upon the image process and believe that symbolization is essentially more than a linear summation of separate sensations. In this sense then, we see some overlap with John Carroll's thinking, but the emphasis upon symbolization's being as capable of building concepts as is verbalization is definitely not the usual mechanism for Carroll. Katz and Fodor (1963) were among the first to severely chastise the Behaviorists for their apparent "error" in assuming that the semantic component could be separated from the syntactic one for any kind of analysis. It might be tempting for the reader to assume that this was the first actual direct shot leveled at Behavioral Theory by the Developmental Theory Camp, but this would be a serious error on the reader's part. The reason is simple: Katz and Fodor believed that the study of semantics was nothing but a linguistic problem and did not fit into the domain of a psychological concern. Bolinger (1965) was perhaps the first to reject as "meaningful" the concept of "semantic marker" or "feature." Behavioral Theory in general had accepted the concept of semantic marker to denote specifically the genus and differentia of a thing or event. John Carroll's (1964) definitions of "genus" and "differentia" are typical of many that had preceded. Bolinger saw genus and differentia as essentially not going far enough. He preferred to see meaning as more: the dictionary is not just a storehouse of old, conventional markers, but society's best attempt to compress and "freeze" action. He stops short of discussing "classes" and "categories," but one does not have to labor long to see the implications of what he says would easily lead us to them.

Clark and Clark (1977, pp. 409–410) give us the best reason for the decline in interest in the Behavioral Theory in the late 1960s. They cite the work of Bierwisch (1970) to illustrate how much the field of semantic development had expanded past the more convenient, but far less adequate, definitions/limitations placed upon the field by the Behaviorists. Bierwisch's position cites five interacting dimensions that any concept must be considered from if we are truly looking at semantics:

1. *Anomaly*: How and why do we know that a concept is used incorrectly in a given context?

2. *Self-contradiction*: How and why do we realize that various features of an elaborated definition are not out of harmony with other parts (words or phrases) within the same or connected sentences?

3. *Ambiguity*: What are the parameters which determine confusability regarding word meaning in or out of the context of a sentence or set of sentences?

4. *Synonyms/antonyms*: How and why do we realize that concepts are similar or essentially opposite? After all, a synonym is not an exact replacement of any term, and an antonym is not absolutely opposed to the meaning of the first concept. For example, "quick" is often used as a synonym for "fast," but "quick" is a reference to a fairly short burst of action, whereas "fast" is more often seen as a dimension of speed sustained across a long period. "Fast" and "slow" are antonyms, but they are not totally dissimilar opposites since both refer to speed.

5. *Entailment* (also known by the Piagetian term "inclusion"): How is it that one can understand that the sentence "Few Behaviorists undertake Developmental Theory in semantics." means exactly the same thing as "Some Behaviorists understand Developmental Theory in semantic research."? (This process is occasionally, but not frequently, referred to with the term "reciprocity" as well as the two terms above.) It should be apparent to the reader that such dimensions as Bierwisch lays out are hardly the stuff of Behaviorists.

G. A. Miller (1962) had left the Behavioral Theory Camp in order to pursue issues beyond the scope of Behaviorism. His article summarizes seven basic points; the reader cannot help but see the power of his ideas and how these ideas direct us toward a Developmental Theory. Let us review all seven.

First, Miller says that not all the physical features within any given language are necessarily significant in the understanding and/or production of that language, and not all the significant features which produce understanding/production of any language are necessarily physical. We can readily agree with the first part of this statement if only we think of the spelling patterns in English. For example, the word, "through" could perhaps just as easily be spelled "thru"—as indeed it is occasionally. But yet, "thru" qualifies as a misspelling when we seek the traditional, conventional wisdom of those around us. But the latter half of Miller's statement is not so readily apparent. Significant features of language are "not physical." Before accusing Miller of engaging in mysticism, let us think of a sentence which reads "He read the book and found it_." This pause at the end of this sentence begs for some type of predicate adjective, i.e., "good," "well-written," "poor," etc. How long we wait for an answer which would fill in the blank depends upon how interested we were in the topic in the first place. A sentence which reads "He found the book, and then he read it." offers no ambiguity and causes no pausing on our part as we await the "punch line." The reason for the pausing in the processing of the first sentence is clearly based upon the "presence" of something which is non-physical.

Second, the meaning of any word does not equal the thing to which the word itself refers, or, in other words, labels are arbitrary "tags" assigned to real events, places, or things. The events, places, or things exist independently of the labels and do not dictate dimensions upon those labels, i.e., the length of the word "ant" is not such simply because it refers to a very small insect.

Third, the meaning of any sentence is not the sum of exactly all the meanings of each word within that sentence. This stands easily to reason since each word in any sentence is by itself capable of many different meanings. Only perhaps one or two possible meanings of any given term are appropriate within any single sentence. But as Miller sees it, the curious issue here is not in the fact that context determines word usage/meaning, but rather it is how the combining of words in any sentence allows us to know what to keep.

Fourth, syntax controls the interaction of meanings within any given sentence. This point seems readily acceptable and is witnessed daily in the course of common events. For example, to say "Paul hit Mary." or to say "Mary hit Paul." conveys very different meanings. Miller would find few Behaviorists who would disagree with this point.

Fifth, the number of words, meanings, and sentences that can be generated is limitless. Again, Miller would probably find few, if any, Behaviorists taking exception with this position.

Sixth, the language and the user of that language are separate entities. This point would appear most easily understood if we consider the vast number of languages in the world. It would be irrational to believe that a specific culture holds its language as carefully intact as it does because that language was a "genetic best fit" for that group of people.

Seventh, there is a biological (species specific) component in language production and comprehension. This point is extremely crucial to our understanding of Miller's position as he moves away from Behavioral Theory.

Behavioral Theory has not died, but Miller's work certainly left it wounded. It had been wounded even earlier but seemed too much in love with itself to notice. Ben Whorf (1956) had proposed the "Strong Whorfian Hypothesis," which said that words were essential to thought. Indeed, there could be no thought without words. When the data came in from various cultures showing this hypothesis was at least overstated, Whorf proposed the "Weak Whorfian Hypothesis," which said merely that words assisted in thought but were not essential to thought's existence. But something somehow was essential. Could it be a genetic unfolding process? If so, Whorf and his Behavioral peers did not acknowledge it.

Developmental Theory

Piaget's System. Unlike Behavioral Theory, Developmental Theory does not overlook qualitative cognitive change as a function of age. Developmental Theory also happily accepts classical and operant conditioning procedures and grants to those procedures a place of significance throughout the entire development sequence from birth through later life. In fact, the only thing advocates of the Developmental Theory do seem to almost reflexively reject is Referent Theory. Developmental Theory advocates do place heavy emphasis upon knowledge of neurophysiology, cognitive processing, attempts of an organism toward producing organization patterns into which experiences may be classed/categorized, and a sense of purpose for life which supercedes simply being classically/operantly conditioned. Developmental theorists are philosophically in harmony with Behaviorists in that both believe behavior is determined by some set of causal principles; humans are restricted to those principles and are not "free" to violate them. Behavioral Theory is simply unwilling to spend its research time pursuing internal parameters to the extent that Developmental Theory chooses to. Some Developmental theorists seem virtually consumed with internal concerns, e.g., Jean Piaget, but this concern has come not at the expense of trying to argue away the importance of the environment's associative conditioning principles. The question asked by the Developmental theorists concerns the sufficiency of Behavioral Theory, whose experimental rigor and statistical analysis techniques are unchallengably productive in their own right.

If the reader assumes that Developmental Theory is actually newer than Behavioral Theory, s/he is both incorrect and correct simultaneously. Being incorrect results from not dating Dèvelopmental theory at least back to the writings of Jean Piaget in his book *Language and Thought of the Child* (1924); being correct results from believing that few scholars accepted his position until at least the late 1960s and early 1970s. The writings of Vygotsky and perhaps to some extent, those of Luria suffered the fate Piaget's works experienced: general acceptance and acknowledgement in their home countries earlier in this century followed by a tortuously painful period of rejection and then acceptance in this country in the late 1960s. The writings of Piaget appear in summary form in many books today. However, few of those books seem particularly interested in the heart of his position on language development. Our focus and reference for many of the following pages is taken from *Language and Thought of the Child* itself. The reader is invited to read this work for its intellectual contribution to philosophy as well as Developmental Theory despite the book's seemingly frequent attempts to disregard literary style and smoothness. It is, as are many of Piaget's books and articles, prone to use a specific term in different ways without advanced warning, but the clarity and power of the ideas are such as to have received the critical acclaim of scholars world-wide. Let us now turn our attention to Piaget's contributions. We begin with the model he presents of cognitive growth, which according to him, is a necessary precursor to growth in language. For our purposes, let us assume that all age levels are "typical" or "average." Piaget is far less interested in exact ages than he is in descriptions of what happens in these stages. Virtually all but the most severely mentally retarded of children will pass through these cognitive stages, according to Piaget. Ages will vary in each stage according to the child's native ability and the level of stimulation his/her environment provides as the "raw data" for that ability.

Piaget begins by breaking the age range between birth and 12 to 13 years into three major stages. They are, from first to last, the Sensorimotor Stage, the Preoperational Stage, and the Concrete Stage. The age range for each stage respectively is birth to two years, two to seven years, and from seven to twelve or thirteen years. Each stage except for the Concrete has its own substages, which have their own age ranges.

The Sensorimotor Stage is broken into six substages. The first is known as the "Exercising of Readymade Sensorimotor Schemata" and runs only from birth to around one month of age. The child in this substage is occupied with his/her own reflexes and body. The environment makes so small an impression that almost any family structure will suffice to meet the child's needs. To say the child "cognizes" at this substage is a gross exaggeration. The child is aware of his/her reflexes, but in no sense purposefully produces those reflexes by self-stimulating actions. The child is figuratively an observer of a "fireworks display" of uncontrollable reaction; the display remains in only short-term memory (30 seconds duration or less) and then is lost from consciousness. Classical and operant conditioning are fully functioning starting at even this early substage, but Piaget prefers to see those forms of conditioning as occurring at some level other than on a cognitive one.

From one month to about four or five months, the substage is known as the "Primary Circular Reactions" substage. We grant "Primary" as meaning "first," and here it means the first of apparently several "circular" periods of reacting. In this use of the term, the child may reach out

172

to touch, look, listen, move, or turn his/her head in order to detect a smell, but never understand the connection between the action taken and the perception of the stimulus toward which attention is being directed. The child pushes a small toy off the edge of the bed and, yet fails to understand that the toy has fallen to the floor. The child can act upon things as a causal agent, but the same child is baffled by that thing's reaction. S/he initiates the first part of the circle; the reaction completes it in mechanical fashion as the child fails to see any connection.

From the end of the "Primary Circular Reactions" substage to the child's eighth or ninth month the child is in the "Secondary Circular Reactions" substage. This substage is the logical second step in the sequence of learning "cause-effect" relations. As we saw in the preceding substage, the child has learned something about "cause" but has no real understanding such as an adult would have. In the present substage, the "effect" is first seen. The child now acts upon and realizes the possibility, but not the probability, of a reaction. Toys dropped over the edge of the bed are now actively pursued by direct searching behaviors in the area where it should most likely have landed. "Cause-effect" is definitely not understood on the conceptual level. Indeed, Piaget's entire model states that there are no concepts until the child is at least six or seven years old. It is apparent that Piaget would not agree with John Carroll's (1964) position that words, meanings, and concepts are all one in the same and are learned solely by conditioning.

From approximately the ninth through the twelfth months, the child exists in what Piaget refers to as the "Coordination of Secondary Schemata" phase. This substage is characterized by the child's increasing knowledge concerning cause-effect. The child also makes a major breakthrough in regard to interacting with the environment by learning to successfully crawl, creep, and finally walk. Although Piaget has never placed as great a stress upon the impact of the environment as he has upon the contributions of simple maturity, he admits the ability to crawl, creep, and walk puts the child into a much more advantageous position from which to sample things, events, and personal relations. Piaget's point is easily understandable; if the child is to mature cognitively, then the amount of "raw material" to be processed by the child's innate tendency to structure and organize must be kept flowing at an optimal level. Too much stimulation, however, causes a cognitive overload, which can produce just as serious a set of negative results as can too little stimulation. We can see the influence of the German philosopher Immanuel Kant upon Piaget insofar as it was Kant who steadfastly believed that the universe was organized and that all living creatures sought to understand and simultaneously become harmonious with that organization (Durant, 1926, pp. 276–325). The child's "coordination" of "secondary schemata" refers to the child's attempt to put his/her world into some type of organized whole which s/he can predict and feel generally safe in. The child is not yet at the age level which will allow him/her to seek novelty; there is too much to do here at this point in merely grasping the cause-effect relations seen from the new physical perspectives that crawling, creeping, and walking can provide. The child remains heavily dependent upon the parents to "cushion the blows" when testing of cause-effect has proven rather disastrous. But there is something in this substage which goes even beyond the importance of crawling, creeping, and walking; it is the child's newly developed capacity to engage in imitative learning (S-S learning). For the first time, s/he can observe an action/reaction and can learn from that observation. Combined with the child's ability to crawl, creep, and walk, we have now a creature who actively processes data in a much more efficient manner than has been done previously. Imitation saves time, energy, occasionally hurts less, and frequently is as rewarding as actual direct participation. Imitation is that special "stuff" of adult interactions which makes a society progress. The child's initial attempts at imitation are quite crude; the child cannot take an adult perspective. During the period from the end of the twelfth month to the middle of the eighteenth, the child is in a substage known as "Tertiary Circular Reactions." "Tertiary" means "third," and a bit of reviewing in the preceding paragraphs shows us that we already have two "circular reactions" substages. This substage is geared to polishing knowledge of cause-effect. The child now is actively involved in the "runabout" phase. Running may seem of little significance to an adult until one looks at it from the viewpoint of amount of information gathered. Running forces faster, more efficient use of one's cognitive abilities as compared to crawling, creeping, or walking. Piaget says that the second most characteristic event in this substage is the child's "seeking of novelty." That which is "safe" and "familiar" begins to be replaced to some extent by that which is a bit daring and perhaps a bit dangerous, as well. The child is literally testing the limits of the organizational processes.

We have seen the term "schemata" several times above and have let it go undefined. As we approach the next substage, we are pressed for a definition. This does produce a small problem since it is virtually impossible to find a place where Piaget has defined the term and has stayed strictly within the term's definitional boundaries. For our purposes, the term "schemata" is best defined as a pattern into which images or representations of those images have been organized to the very best of the person's cognitive ability. Cognition employs schemata as its content following the processing of incoming sensations. Schemata are not ends in and of themselves; they are an intermediate step between the sensory input and the thoughts which will be the ultimate product of the cognition. Perhaps the best example of this comes from our knowledge (Hebb, 1949) that a child enters life with only the ability to see "figure-ground" relations. Very rapidly, the child "learns" to fill in detail and to recognize shapes.

This sixth stage runs from the eighteenth through the twenty-fourth month. It is known as the "Internalization of Sensorimotor Schemata" substage. During this period, the infant imitates almost constantly, and novelty remains a high priority in the child's life. But more importantly, the child begins to prepare to become a "symbolizer." Specific prerequisites to becoming such are acquired during this substage, but symbolization itself comes in the next major stage itself. The prerequisites appear basically through maturation. As in all of Piaget's phases, the environment does make it possible for maturation to occur at its own rate, but the environment cannot increase that rate to any significant extent. The child will develop the prerequisites to symbolization as soon as the child is ready to do so. Symbol prerequisites are as follows:

1. The child must understand that objects have "permanence." The child must understand that objects, people, and events are still real even if s/he is not there to experience them.

2. The child must understand that the "speaker and the audience" are separate. The child must be aware of the need to use some communication system which his/her audience consensually validates as "acceptable."

3. There must be enough cognitive maturity to allow the creating of symbols.

4. The child must actually develop the elements of the symbol; this is a technological issue. What is a symbol? What form will a symbol take under which circumstances and for how long? Here we find ourselves guessing. Since symbols are "hypothetical constructs," they cannot be seen directly, nor may they be manipulated as independent variables.

Assuming all has developed well in the child's first two years of life, we now press into the major stage which runs from the end of the second year to the period of about six or seven years of age. This period is known as the "Preoperational Thought" stage and is subdivided into (1) the "Preconceptual" substage from the end of the second year to the end of the fourth and (2) the "Intuitive" substage, which begins where the first substage quits and ends at the period of the sixth or seventh year in most children. The hallmark of the entire Preoperational period is that the child will have no concepts, as Piaget defines the term.

Peroperational thought is what it says it is—thinking that occurs before the child can deal with propositions operationally. This means the child will spend these years attempting to develop whatever additional cognitive prerequisites are necessary to allow the luxury of later adult thought patterns. Preconceptual thought is characterized by egocentric thinking which generalizes far beyond its data at one moment and then turns upon itself in a manner to ruthlessly restrict itself when the process of generalization might just be appropriate. Classes are indefinite. Which items or events belong in which category seem to vary from moment to moment as the environment changes. Of special interest is the process known as "transductive reasoning." In this the child reasons from one specific instance to a second one with no concern about possible environmental changes which could change the applicability and accuracy of the transfer. One bird is the very same as a second one because the child cannot understand there is a second one. It is merely the first one in two places!

There is another characteristic of this stage which makes it significant. For the first time, the child will use "images" as the content of thought. This is not to say that all thought is image-oriented, but at least the child begins the process. An image is not a perfect copy of the thing or event being perceived; an "icon" is a perfect copy, and Piaget has no place for icons in his model. An image is a more or less crude representation of what has been perceived. it is affected by one's past experiences, cognitive ability, intellectual potential, and motivations at the time of the perception. Images are produced in order to free oneself from the "here and now" of experience. A horse can be recalled starting in this phase because the image can be retrieved from storage. Prior to this phase, no such retrieval was possible, albeit a child could produce the word "horse" as a conditioned response when presented with the picture of or actual presence of a horse. Whatever meaning is attached to the actual horse is also attached to the image. Images are relatively easy to retrieve; actual physical models of the things for which images stand are often impossible to find without great effort. Using the image produces an economical short-cut to experiences as they have been impressed upon us by experience. One small problem arises rapidly; the storage capacity of any human cognitive system is apparently finite. Images must exist in some size/shape and number; all of this should, technically speaking, cost us "space" within the storage system. It is at this point in Piaget's model that we first see the use of the term "symbol." A symbol is not an image; an image is the "raw data" of a symbol, which is apparently more reduced, compacted in size than is the image itself. Some believe that a word is a good example of a symbol because a word is usually cognitively quite compact and is not infrequently attached to an image which seemingly "fills the mind" after the symbol has triggered its retrieval. Piaget, however, definitely does not use "symbol" to mean "words." Words for Piaget are "signs" and are more sophisticated than are symbols. But despite their compactness, symbols are more difficult to process than are images at this phase level since the symbols are two steps removed from the concrete physical reality of things whereas the images are only one step removed. No child is eager, at least at this cognitive level, to venture too far away from the immediate present in his/her thinking. Nevertheless, the child now has the initial ability to begin the image/symbol processing, which will allow the beginning efforts to take place toward the building of concepts. There are no true classes or categories here in this stage; things/events are sorted on the basis of having one single dimension in common while yet all other dimensions are disharmonious matches. Frogs, chickens, and foxes may find themselves as images in the same classification area in the child's thinking because of the fact they all share at least one dimension—two eyes. Rational consideration of "better fits" are beyond the child's capacity at this point.

We need to introduce several new Piagetian terms at this point. "Intention," "extension," and "inclusion" are all related in Piagetian parlance to concept formation. In order to form any concept, Piaget believes all three processes must be at work. By that definition, there are no "partial concepts," and words, despite Carroll's (1964) position, are not concepts. By "intention" Piaget means there is a process which puts information into classes (or categories). By "extension" Piaget means that there are restrictions to those classes which cannot be violated without forcing the cognizing person to switch to a related class. "Inclusion" depicts the process which allows us to put objects/events within a class into a hierarchy from most to least complex, smallest to largest, lightest to heaviest, etc. Since there are usually many dimensions upon which an object/event may be put into a hierarchy, inclusion is considered exceptionally more difficult than either intention or extension. Intention and extension are "yoked"—that is, each depends upon the other to make its existence possible, but neither is dependent upon the presence of inclusion. Inclusion is dependent upon the processes of intention and extension; without either there absolutely cannot be inclusion. The child in this preconceptual period deals ineffectively with intention and extension. Inclusion is completely beyond the child at this age. Not until the

Intuitive Stage will intention and extension appear more like that of an adult. Inclusion will still not yet become available, however. It will not appear until Concrete Operations do at age six or seven years.

The Intuitive Thought Stage starts at age four years and will not be completed until the child is six or seven years old. During this period, the child will remain perceptually bound to the image/symbol relationship and will continue to be unable to form well-organized classes. Piaget's own term "Intuitive" would indicate the child is on the brink of concept formation. But since inclusion is not within the child's capacities, concepts do not exist in this stage. What does exist is the persistent effort a child shows as s/he attempts to organize the world as s/he sees it into classes. The Intuitive child still "centrates" upon stimuli in a fashion similar to that of Preconceptual children. By "centrate" Piaget means that the child focuses upon one or two details of a situation and stays with some hypothesis formed regarding those small details until the child receives enough discouragement to cause the dropping of the hypothesis in place of a second one. The centration process is not quite as narrowly defined as is the "transductive reasoning" seen in Preconceptual periods; the Intuitive child is aware that one single dimension is usually not sufficient to produce the desired results from a reasoning process. Nor is it really safe for us to say that the Preconceptual child never uses centration; indeed they do since transduction is merely a special, narrow subclassification under centration.

The evolution of thought within the Intuitive Stage is seen clearly in the child's attempts to understand numbers. One prerequisite for establishing the concept of number is that the child must learn something about "one to one correspondence" among two sets of objects. At four to five years of age, the child can see no one to one relationship if a set of five items spaced one inch apart is compared to a set of five identical objects placed three inches apart. At five to six years of age, the child intuitively seems to know that the two above-described sets are the same in number, but the same child will deny their set equality if you merely rearrange the objects in one set while also increasing the space distance between those objects. Not until six or seven years of age (the beginning of Concrete Operations) will the child understand the fact that reordering has no effect upon the set equality and that space distance is irrelevant yet deceptive at times. We see the same pattern developing in the child's attempt to establish order of objects by the dimension of size, e.g., ranking objects from tallest to shortest, lightest to heaviest, etc. From four to five years of age, the child seems to order on the basis of some single, usually irrelevant dimension. For example, let us assume we have six sticks that are each one-half inch in width but which vary in height from six to twelve inches. Let us also assume we painted a red line on each stick according to the rule that as each stick's height was objectively judged higher by you and me that we agreed to paint the red line at a lower point on that stick. For example, if a six-inch stick's red line was exactly midcenter around the stick, the 12-inch stick's line was virtually at its very bottom (as we shall call it here since obviously a stick has no top or bottom except by consentual agreement). If we gave the sticks to the four- to five-year-old, it would not be uncommon to see the child try to rank the order from tallest to shortest by using the red lines as the source of information. Even then, if one red line varied slightly from another, the child might use such deviations as the "stimulus of the moment" upon which to base a judgment. The child from five to six years has no such problem. S/he is not detracted by irrelevant detail, but if after s/he has successfully ranked our sticks from highest to lowest we then ask to see the child superimpose a second set of sticks to fit in rank order between the sticks in the first, ordered set, we will be told by the child that it cannot be done. The child from six to seven years on will have no problems interposing sets.

By six to seven years of age, the child is ready to enter Concrete Operational Thought. This period coincides with the beginnings of serious attempts at teaching reading, writing, and mathematics. Prior attempts to teach these skills have usually met with limited success. The child's attempts at forming concepts to this point have had one very common factor in all situations: the child has not enjoyed or been tolerant of much change in the environment if that change has also affected his/her perception of what a class is to be. As a result, confusion has been easy to come by, and frustration has occasionally occurred with little understanding of its cause on either the child's or the parents' parts. Prior to this point, the child could put on a toy sheriff's badge and believe s/he was the sheriff no matter how many other details of his/her dress and conduct betrayed the hoax; as the Concrete Operations stage begins, the betrayals of pretences become obvious. But something is gained which makes the loss very easy to overlook: the ability to perform "operations" appears.

Before entering Concrete Operations, the child must understand four "laws" of Nature. These laws are not taught as such. Each is known by anyone functioning at least at this Concrete Operations level, but actually stating the laws is again a different story. Maturation in combination with a sufficiently stimulating environment seems to produce the knowledge. Exactly what in the environment and exactly which physical processes are involved still stands as our "unknowns." In any case, the principles are as follows:

1. *Commutivity*: The elements within a set may be reorganized in any order without changing the set itself.

2. *Identity*: For each element in a set, removing an element from the set must be followed by replacing that element with the symbol "O" if the element's place is to be held and the set is to remain intact.

3. *Composition*: The elements of any set comprise individually and as a group proper subsets of the total set; likewise, the total set comprises a proper subset of itself.

4. *Reversability*: If part of the elements of a total set are removed, what is left in that set is the total set's original composition minus the specific amount that has been removed.

All of this calls for "decentration" on the child's part; to "decentrate" means to stop "centrating" and to start attending to more than one detail at a time. Most of us have practiced this for so many years in so many different contexts that we have forgotten we ever were without it.

The cognitive growth patterns at Concrete Operations are indeed spectacular. Not only does the child now have the four laws at his/her command, but inclusion rapidly develops as intention and extension are "polished." The result of completing inclusion is in the development of concepts in the Piagetian sense. For the first time, a child cannot only form intact classes but can use these classes accurately in hypothetical, but concrete, situations. By no means does this imply that the classes are in final form; many classes will be further differentiated/refined as the child has more experiences while in Concrete Operations and beyond. But the processes are intact which allow such differentiation as the child moves into Concrete Operations to a deepening degree. The child now holds all but the most adult-like of capacities: the ability to "operate on operations" and to form abstractions.

Piaget's last cognitive stage, Formal Operations, applies to age 12 or 13 years and above. It is not included here since our purpose is to show the interaction between thought and language; it is accepted generally that children have excellent grasps upon natural language long before age 12. Chapter 6 of this book substantiates that claim. It is necessary to say that Formal Operations allows abstract concepts (and, therefore, abstract language) to develop, thanks mainly to genetics. We must, however, turn our attention to Piaget's views of the earlier stages of language growth.

Piaget's model for language development goes hand-in-hand with his models of cognitive growth. For the Sensorimotor Stage, Piaget claims that the child is "presymbolic," e.g., the child has no images (and, therefore, no symbols) with which to achieve representation of the world. The words the child speaks are separate from the content of cognition, which uses the concrete, immediately here and now world as the data upon which to react. Words are used "reflexively"; they are the products of classical or operant conditioning and are produced automatically.

During Preoperational Thought, the child will be "symbolic" in his/ her language. This means that images will now be elicited when specific image-related words are used. The use of image-based symbols allows some freeing of oneself from the immediately present, concrete realities of meaning, but it does not allow as much freedom as we will see in the next stage. Images, after all, have concrete origins.

From the beginning of Concrete Operations and for the remainder of one's life, the language process is fundamentally "sign" in nature. By this, Piaget means that the child is capable of using words to refer to processes and events which do not have obvious image-based referents. The Concrete Operations child will be less capable by far of using this new language tool than will the adolescent. Granted, a child beginning Concrete Operations will be highly image-based, but there will now be an increasing number of support terms which have no concrete image base and essentially "hook" themselves by association to actual concrete symbols such as were used in Preoperational Thought. By this process of attaching a "sign" word to one or more "symbols," the child may practice using "signs" without losing complete touch with the concrete realities of Concrete Operations. Piaget sees an evolution from the predominant use of "symbols" during Preoperational Thought to the predominant use of "signs" as Concrete Operations appear and especially as Concrete Operations blends into Formal Operations at twelve or thirteen years of age. It would be unrealistic to assume that the child moving into Concrete Operations suddenly one night would leap up and begin spouting strings of the abstract "sign" words. Concrete Operations would not allow it; at the same time, that same child will not at 12 or 13 years of age suddenly become totally abstract, e.g., use nothing but "sign" terms. As Piaget claims, using "sign" terms is generally a process too infrequently engaged in even by those who are cognitively capable of using it. We may define Piaget's language system as follows:

PRESYMBOLIC (birth to two years): Environmental input as sights, sounds, words → reflexive reactions only.

SYMBOLIC (two to six or seven years): Environmental input as sights, sounds, or words → Images → Symbols (which are more compact and more complex than images) → Cognitive processing using these symbols → Symbols which are but one step removed from the Response Stage → Responses in the form of Words (which are very heavily dependent upon the "here and now" materialistic side of life).

SIGN (six or seven years and on): Two ways now become possible. The first is more probable in daily interaction. Environmental input as sights, sounds, and words → Images → Symbols (which are even more compact and more complex than those symbols used in the Symbolic Stage) → Cognitive processing of those symbols → Symbols (of immense complexity which are but one step removed from the Response Stage) → Responses in the form of words (which are rapidly evolving into being less and less dependent upon "here and now," materialistic reference points). Or, Environmental input in the form of Words → Cognitive processing of those words without the need for image/symbol conversions as intermediate steps between Environmental input and Cognitive processing → Responses in the form of Words that underwent Cognitive processing.

The reader should see two things in this second alternative in the Sign Stage. First, it is definitely not a simple reflexive model. Second, it does free the language producer from the use of images/symbols; this allows for the creation of abstract language terms (which generally have no images/symbols to represent them). This second alternative in Sign is more appealing to adolescents and adults since they have entered Formal Operations cognitively.

If meaning in the Sensorimotor Stage was fundamentally associative, e.g., classical and/or operant in nature as those forms of conditioning are interpreted by each of the six substages of that major stage, what is meaning in Preoperational, Concrete, and Formal Thought? It is a safe prediction that Piaget will claim that it is not merely associative. Meaning becomes the extent to which one can organize experience into classes, perform concrete or formal operations upon those classes, and evaluate the "goodness of fit" of one's meaning against that of others having had similar experiences. Therefore, meaning is not a static entity, but rather it changes as the person's cognitive abilities change with the person's increased maturity and level of experience. Just as simple classical and/or operant associations were made through experience in the Sensorimotor Stage, so will such associations be made through all other stages. But the difference between the Sensorimotor and all later stages is the decreasing dependency upon simple association that will rapidly emerge as the child moves up the cognitive hierarchy. Meaning literally becomes something more than the "sum of its parts" because the cognitive processes actively determine how the associative part will fit. Piaget is careful here not to underestimate the role of the environment; he simply wants the innate processes which allow for "cognitive unfolding" to also have an important place in our consideration of meaning's development. In fact, let us say that the "unfolding" has the very most important role. In the past, easily determining at which cognitive/language stage the child functions has been difficult. The vast majority of attempts still occur in clinic-like settings. However, some psychometric techniques have recently appeared and at least promise us speedier answers (Furth, 1970; Patterson & Milakofsky, 1980).

The reader must above all remember that Piaget's position states that cognitive growth precedes the development of language. Without evolution in cognition within each developing child, the language growth ceases. The cognitive stage determines how images, symbols, and signs will be expressed. The cognitive stages cannot be forced to mature; the language system, therefore, cannot be forced either. Albeit, language and thought (cognition) are not one entity: they are tightly interwoven processes.

As if this were not already a complicated enough model, Piaget adds another step by asking us to accept the fact that speech and language are distinct concepts. Speech is the outward manifestation of the inner language processes. But even here he manages to impress upon us the importance of the cognitive developmental stages. For example, the child in Sensorimotor Thought is said to be "presocial" in speech. The Preoperational child is said to be "egocentric," and the child starting in Concrete Operations is from that point on said to be "socialized." Speech, then, not only represents levels of social conformity but also reflects the cognitive evolution pattern as well. The "presocialized" child is just that—presocial; his/her speech patterns are at the very mercy of many bungling efforts to imitate adults. The "egocentric" child is more in harmony with society's dictates, but still there is much room for growth. The "egocentric" term includes the component terms "echolalia," "monolog," and "collective monolog" as well. Echolalia is not used here in the pathological sense usually featured, e.g., when we discuss the language pattern of autistic children who repeat the same phrase in sequence. Echolalia here refers to the normal, repetitive process that children engage in as they reinforce themselves for using certain types of speech patterns (could this be Skinner's "automatically self-reinforcing" concept which caused Chomsky to become so indignant over Skinner's "technical terms"?). Monolog refers to the "speeches" a child may often give apparently for his/her own personal benefit. Collective monolog refers to the amusing scene in which two or more children are simultaneously presenting monologs to one another without the slightest interest in whether the "audience" is understanding the presentation. It is irrelevant to ask if there is anyone who understands because "everyone" understands as long as the speaker understands his/her own monolog. Ironically, most children who engage in this behavior seem perfectly assured that the other children are listening intently to the presentations of the other speakers. What never seems to dawn upon the child who believes this is the impossibility of listening with equal intensity to two simultaneously presented messages.

During the "socialized" phase of speech development, the child will engage in the asking/answering of questions, will give and follow commands, will both give and receive criticism, and will actively seek to "adapt information." This last item is occasionally confused with Piaget's twin process terms which describe the process of cognitive evolution from its beginning in each child. We speak here of "assimilation" and "accommodation." By assimilation, Piaget refers to the process of bringing new facts (at least new to the perceiver) into the general field of interest as defined by the particular cognitive level's capacity to entertain such data. Once the data has been assimilated, it must be classified and stored neatly somewhere. This process is referred to as accommodation. Accommodation seeks to place all incoming information into either existing schemata or seeks to create new schemata to accommodate the input. Both assimilation and accommodation are affected by and mutually affect the cognitive evolution process each child will normally experience. The phrase "adapted information" is not a substitute for either assimilation or accommodation. "Adapting information" is a specific creation of Piaget's; it refers solely to speech functioning. We must note here that in no sense is Piaget particularly interested in speech itself; there are no discussions of phonology or predictions as to when a particular part of speech will first make its appearance. Piaget is interested in language, which for him is not defined in terms of surface structure dimensions.

Piaget's basic position on language development was developed in his writing from 1921 to 1932. From 1933 to 1940, his attention was devoted to "fleshing in" the basic model of cognition which had evolved piece by piece from his earlier writings. His later work was devoted to the study of specific concepts, e.g., time and space. As with his friend Albert Einstein, once the basic model had been prepared, it would take virtually the efforts of a lifetime to validate it empirically. Piaget's writings in *Language and Thought of the Child* are not presented as a psycholinguist would approach the topic. Piaget was rather the forerunner of Cognitive Psychology, and yet the credit for this field is usually granted (by those in the United States) to an United States product, E. C. Tolman. Tolman and Piaget were contemporaries, but Piaget's rationalistic methodology was not prone to receive easy acceptance in the United States' Behavioristic climate of the first four decades of this century. Vygotsky's writings won acceptance more slowly in the United States than did Piaget's. The latter's position was difficult for most American psychologists to understand. Once they understood the rationalistic/mentalistic approach Piaget used in model building, however, Vygotsky's position was better understood. In that sense, Vygotsky wrote Piaget's coattails into American circles.

Vygotsky's Position. L. S. Vygotsky lived from 1896 to 1934 and wrote in that short space of time a single book of moment to those interested in semantics; it was called *Thought and Language* and appeared in the United States in 1962. His position is especially in disagreement with Piaget's line of logic regarding the prerequisites for language development. It was Piaget who said that the development of cognition came slightly before there would be growth in the language processes; the latter was directly dependent upon the former. Vygotsky said that the processes of cognitive growth and language development occurred simultaneously with an ever increasing dependency of one upon the other. If the reader cross-references Vygotsky's stated age ranges for each language/cognition stage, s/he will see an amazing perfect fit to Piaget's contentions for the age ranges in his language and cognitive models.

From birth to two years of age, the child exists in Vygotsky's "Primitive Speech" stage. Thought and speech are distinctly separate there are no concepts here. Thought is based upon processes other than verbal ones, and speech is nonconceptual in its content. Although Vygotsky does not divide this stage into any substages, the agreement between his basic contentions and those of Piaget is virtually perfect. Piaget claims there are no concepts at this stage; he also claims that the use of language is in the form of classically conditioned stimuli or operant cues. Although Vygotsky does not discuss classical or operant conditioning, per se, it is clear that he believes the use of speech is purely reflexive at this first stage. We should note here that "speech" for Vygotsky is more than what it is for Piaget. Speech for Vygotsky is closer to Piaget's term language, but Vygotsky seems happier to simply call all verbal functioning simply "speech." For Vygotsky, what is produced by the child is what was being processed at various stages within that same child's language system. This would seem to put Vygotsky in closer harmony with, say, Skinner's S-R Behaviorism than it would Piaget's thinking, but Vygotsky is very definitely interested in internal mental processes that Skinner would not discuss under any circumstances.

From the end of the second year and until the end of the third, the child is in the "Naive Psychological" stage. During this time period, the child will begin to merge speech and thought so as to produce

Vygotsky's concept of the "unorganized heap." This means the organization process has begun, but that it is not consistent. To this extent, Piaget is saying the same thing. For both Piaget and Vygotsky, there are no concepts during this time period. For Vygotsky, the connection between the speech and thought processes are at best minimal at this stage. Depending upon the child's level of experience and cognitive capacity, the contact between the speech and thought functions vary; the correlation between amount of experience/cognitive capacity and amount of interaction between speech and thought is highly positively related for Vygotsky. We do not see Vygotsky discussing "Preconceptual" and "Intuitive" processes here as we saw in Piaget's writings, but the implications of his work seem to tell us he is in fundamental agreement with Piaget's description of the cognitive stages. The point of major disagreement between the two lies in Vygotsky's belief that language can directly interact at this stage with thought. If we held Vygotsky to his position that language is speech and if speech is words, then Vygotsky has clearly omitted Piaget's middle step: the image/symbol mediator. For Piaget, not until six or seven years will the child use the word directly in thought with no need to convert the word into an image first. Although Vygotsky is not opposed to the use of images in general, he sees no need to use them as mediating devices between the word and the thought about that word.

As the second stage in Vygotsky's model coincides with Piaget's Preconceptual Thought Stage, the next stage, Vygotsky's "Egocentric" stage is a perfect reflection of Piaget's Intuitive Stage. As with Piaget's this stage starts around the beginning of the fourth year and is not completed until the child enters Concrete Operations around the sixth or seventh year. The characteristic Vygotsky chiefly ascribes to this stage is that the child deals in "complexes." A "complex" is not a concept; it is virtually the same thing as the product Piaget sees coming from intuition, e.g., a fairly organized set of stimuli which yield to the child's ability to form intention/extension but cannot yet be subjected to the process of inclusion, which will not occur until the child is about six or seven years old. As in Piaget's use of the term "intuitive" to describe this stage, Vygotsky believes that the child almost grasps concept but is still just a few prerequisite skills short of the mark.

In the preceding stage, the overlap between speech and thought has steadily increased until about as much of the child's thought has a speech component as does not. This 50/50 split allows the vast majority, but by no means all, of thought to have a very substantial speech component. Piaget would still ask us to accept the need for the image as the mediator between the word and the thought; Vygotsky would not.

186

In the final stage, Piaget and Vygotsky fall into a harmonious relationship. At this final stage the child may use the word itself as the raw data for cognition; as Piaget finally grants it. For Vygotsky, this stage is little more than a continuation of a trend established during his second stage; that is, speech and thought have finally reached an almost total dependency upon one another. This stage, which starts at age six or seven years, is referred to by Vygotsky as "Ingrowth Speech." We see at this stage the beginning of "true concepts" to use Vygotsky's term. There is perhaps a small distinction between Piaget and Vygotsky on this matter not so much on the issue of this period's being the hallmark of concept formation but rather in Vygotsky's use of the term "true" to describe the concepts. For Piaget, a concept exists (is clearly defined by intention, extension, and inclusion), or it does not exist. For Piaget, the Vygotskian use of "true" is as senseless as discussing "a touch of pregnancy"; either you are or you are not. This is not to say Piaget believes concepts are unchangable as we collect more experiences related to those concepts, but the adding or subtracting of features from any concept is not going to change the fact that the concept is still intact. A concept for Piaget is like an internally well-ordered, highly flexible balloon that may have itself stretched, pulled, and pushed against a thousand ways without the concept itself being destroyed. In any case, Vygotsky and Piaget are in agreement that the words ("signs" now for Piaget) may directly interact with the cognitive processes. This pattern will last the remainder of one's life.

Semantic components for Vygotsky, as for Piaget, reflect how the child can process experiences through the various stages in the proposed model. Vygotsky, unlike Piaget, is a bit metaphysical in his discussion of the role of meaning. His position sounds very similar to those held by Fillmore (1968), McCawley (1968), Bloom (1970), and Brown (1973) as well as that of Palermo (1978). The essence of meaning does not lie in the word itself. This position, like that of Piaget, is at odds with Carroll's (1964) position that words, meanings, and concepts are essentially one in the same. Vygotsky really never defines the heart of this essence, and we might note here, neither have the Case grammarians to this day. One thing is quite apparent from reading Vygotsky's work: he does not believe semantics builds in a simple, linear accumulation of experiences within a passive organism. That puts him into opposition even with such advanced behavioral thought as was first proposed by Osgood in his "semantic generalization" model as we reviewed it in Chapter 5. For Vygotsky, meaning is that something that is known at a level which defies accurate interpretation. Vygotsky's position is that the meaning essence must develop before the words to describe that essence are developed in any meaningful way. This would put him in opposition to at least two modern writers, Clark and Clark (1977, p. 410), who paradoxically assert that people can know the meanings of words without knowing what the words refer to. Vygotsky seems to say that each word a person detects either will or will not result in that person's recall of a "category" of meanings which is related to that word. The category is not, however, simply a storage center for the accumulation of S-R associations (as it is for Osgood's "semantic generalization" model). This set of ideas has been greatly updated and clearly presented under new terminology in the modern-day writings of McCawley (1971, 1975) and Putnam (1975). The categorization process for Vygotsky is an active process which itself attempts to encircle action seen in the child's experiential world. Dale (1976, p. 175) captures this idea succinctly by reporting the observations of Bloom (1973). She observed that the word "car" to a nine-month-old meant the action of a vehicle moving, but it did not refer to an immobile automobile in any sense nor to any vehicle which the child was in whether or not that vehicle was moving. But Dale (1976, p. 175) cautions us against assuming that we can presently prove that the child generalizes first and then later draws specific subcategories. He clearly stated at the time of his writing that the data shows no clear trends in any direction let alone toward generalization. Despite this uncertainty, Dale (1976, p. 177) does assert that it is clear from his review of the' research that semantic categories and cognitive categories are not one in the same. Vygotsky would surely find this pleasing support for his own model.

Luria's Position. Much of Luria's work appeared in the United States at about the same time as that of Vygotsky's despite the fact Luria actively began his research efforts some 25 years after Vygotsky's death. The research bent of Luria's work is what makes his contribution significant. Vygotsky had done most of his model building via the method of rationalism/mentalism. Despite Luria's goal, as Oleron (1977, pp. 41—48) continually points out, these research efforts left a very great deal to be desired regarding the number of subjects used, the adequacy of pre- vs. post-comparisons of behavioral change, and the degree to which generalizations occur after very little data had been collected. Although it is not true, as Oleron asserts (1977, p. 47) that psychologists are not interested in studies conducted using very small numbers of subjects and that only physiologists are interested in such, Oleron's points are generally well taken if one makes even the most casual of reviews of Luria's work. As did Piaget, Luria attempted to keep his research efforts aimed toward the general goal of model building and not the description analysis of group behavior. Luria firmly believed that the use of language, which he defines simply as "words," preceded and enhanced the development of cognition. Piaget's position is just the reverse of this, and Vygotsky had proposed the simultaneous growth of language and cognition.

Perhaps the best way to understand Luria's position is to review the short summary of work that he and a co-worker, Yudovich, did in 1959 using two Russian twins, Yura and Liosha, as that summary is presented by Oleron (1977, pp. 43—44). The language development of these twins was severely retarded by normal standards for children of about five years of age. This was due, according to Luria, to the social reinforcement each twin gave the other as each communicated with basically only the other sibling and with the parents. Luria strongly believed language grew through the gradual development of S-R bonds. Practice caused the bonds to strengthen; lack of practice, of course, had the opposite effect. The twins in Luria and Yudovich's study had essentially developed their own patterns of egocentric speech which really had little "speech" involved at all. Ventures toward physically present objects, people, or events were often used in place of actual speech. If the event or object was one which had appeared in the past and was the topic of the moment, only the briefest and simplest of words were used to alert the co-twin to the topic. In short, much of the communication was nonverbal and, at best, it was quite brief; no details were added which were unnecessary. As Oleron's account has it, the co-twin Yura was the first to be given what today would be called an "enrichment" program in order to upgrade the child's language processes and, consequently, boost the level of cognitive processing. Luria had noted that the children seemed to follow few rules in playing games, and what rules they did follow seemed irrelevant to the nature of the game itself. Following the enrichment program, all this changed, at least for Yura. Oleron (1977, pp. 47—48) openly questions the adequacy of the conclusion by citing the above mentioned problem of the small number of subjects. Oleron does not question Luria's observations concerning the physical, minimally symbolic nature of the twins' communication (called "sympraxic" communication), but does openly wonder if any additional attempts at proving Luria's major contention, e.g., increasing language skills facilitates the growth of cognition, have actually supported him. Oleron cites the research of Wozniack (1972) as well as that of Miller, Shelton and Flavell (1970) as casting very serious doubt on Luria's basic conclusions that any attempt to upgrade language development is a causal factor in the improvement of cognitive processing. The latter study used over 150 subjects from three to five years of age and found no significant differences at any of these ages between the performances of those given verbal labels and those not given any. Findings such as these of Miller et al. are in support, however, of the position of Jean Piaget, e.g., language is little more than an encoding of actions produced by the non-language cognitive developmental processes; providing language in and of itself can produce no direct effect upon cognition but can make cognition at that specific stage of development function more efficiently at, and only at, that one stage (Rogers, 1975). The Miller et al. study puts Luria's position at odds with Vygotsky's assertions that language and thought develop simultaneously and indirectly strengthens either Vygotsky's or Piaget's claims to accuracy. One could, but apparently no one has to date, claim that Luria's own research on Yura and Liosha could be subject to harsh scrutiny as the study stands. If the children were approximately five years old, there is little doubt that the mental processing level was that of Intuitive Thought on the Piagetian hierarchy if the children were as developed as far as one might reasonably expect for that age. At the very best, Intuitive Thought is not known as a period of rigorous rule formation and heavy verbal interchange about the nature and conduct of such rules. According to Piaget, there are no concepts at this age level even at its peak of functioning. Consequently, definitions would easily appear "vague and ambiguous" as Luria had claimed were the definitions of Yura and Liosha.

Rogers (1975, pp. 173—183) cites some excerpts from Luria's (1959) writings which are generally held by most scientists to be the heart of the Lurian position. Luria cites case study after case study reporting how certain basic interruptions or facilitations of cognition can occur if the person augments his/her processing with verbal labels. As the age of the child decreases, the need for ever-increasing amounts of externally-produced verbal direction is decreased. According to Rogers (1975, p. 173), the child actually gradually develops two types of concepts, as Luria sees it, and both of them are definitely available to a greater or lesser degree before Piaget's Concrete Operations Stage. First, there are "spontaneous" concepts in which the child's background of experience is quite sufficient to allow us to conclude that the child has a concept despite the fact the child cannot verbally state that concept. If the label (name) is provided, the child then "knows" the concept as well as s/he probably ever will. For example, Luria contends that even a two-year-old knows what a cat, dog, and perhaps even a horse are. If Luria is correct, waiting until Concrete Operations can produce "inclusion" as well as polish the rough edges off "intention" and "extension" is nonsensical—despite Piaget's protests.

The second concept type, the "scientific," is defined by Luria to mean that a label (word) is first presented and then is followed by many examples and experiences which complete the concept formation process. The reader should recognize this idea to be the one very similar to that proposed in the United States in 1964 by John Carroll. Luria's recommendations regarding the "teaching" of this concept type is virtually identical to that of Carroll's (1964) model. But Carroll, unlike Luria, has already been seen as steadfastly avoiding the problems one faces when trying to split language and thought's arrival in the child's growth pattern.

There seems one almost totally undisputed fact that makes Luria's work significant whether or not one agrees that language can act causally to "speed up" cognition. There is more frequent speaking to oneself among younger children about social rules than there is among older ones. For example, we would find it perhaps at least unusual if we heard a seven-year-old saying to himself/herself aloud, "Now, we must never touch a hot stove like this, or we'll surely be burned." From a three- or a four-year-old, a hearty "Don't touch!" spoken by the child for his/her own benefit would not be so unusual; the child, according to Luria, is facilitating cognition by imposing "external" sanctions against himself/herself much as an adult would do for the same child when the child first learned not to touch the stove. No one seems to dispute this observation; the dispute is over the function of such behavior. Is it causal to, correlational with, or a consequence of cognitive processing? If this question appears to be remote from the reader's present world of experience and interest, just stop to contemplate the number of times you "externalized" instructions to yourself while performing perhaps a fairly complex motor task. Did your comments produce better performance, simply accompany the performance without any effect, or come after the performance was in all but the most automatically completable final stages when what you said aloud was irrelevant to the performance? There should be little surprise that Luria's position sounds in great part like J. B. Watson's early Behavioristic position that "thinking" was just "inner speech." Luria would find that highly acceptable as long as we added a lengthy discussion of cognition, which was a taboo subject for Watson, the Founder of American Behaviorism. Luria, unlike Watson, went further to demonstrate how external verbal commands could "jam," "overload," or "interfere" with well-practiced children and even brain-damaged adults. For example, when instructed to pick up an object which the very young child clearly recognizes, the presentation of contradictory requests can actually produce a total breakdown in the desired behavior despite the fact the child is perfectly capable of performing each set of instructions in sequence (Rogers, 1975, pp. 175–176). A child, say at two years, seems to lack the ability to store one set of instructions in memory until the first act is completed—if it is now completed at all. Since a two-year-old should be much more dependent upon outside direction to complete a task than would be an older child, Luria cheerfully predicts the greater amounts of interference when two sets of mutually harmonious commands are presented simultaneously. This finding stands experimental testing quite well, and in and of itself at least casts some favorable support toward his model at some point in that model.

There is one point which seems most curiously out of step in Luria's model, and that point simply refers to his conception of how S-R bonds work. He has stated throughout his model that S-R bonds are learned in the usual, slow, associative manner that most classical conditioning is learned. At least in that regard, the influence of his Russian predecessor, I. P. Pavlov, is abundantly evident. But Luria persists (Oleron, 1977, p. 42) in asking us to believe that S-R bonds can be processed in a manner Pavlov never discussed and, most probably, would never have accepted. Luria asks us to believe that one set of S-R bond connections may be substituted for another set in such a fashion as to produce instant behavioral suppression. For example, saying "Do this!" to a person and immediately following that with "Don't do that!" will produce a smooth flow of sequenced behaviors where the first one is stopped short as the negative command is produced. His best examples of this procedure are seen in articles occuring in the early 1960s (Luria, 1960, 1961). The question is actually one of how such an easy substitution can be accomplished. Luria does not explain the physiological correlates of this process, and to this date no one else has. Yet, it is apparent to even the most casual observer that such a process seems to be active in all but the youngest of children, who are incapable of sequencing behaviors appropriately as a response to sequentially presented adult instructions.

Resolution of Theoretical Contradictions

If we recall the course of events which characterized the debates over syntactic development, we can remember that there were no clear winners or losers as such. This is not to say that all sides of the debate left the court with equal numbers of points; we saw simply that there were enough shortcomings in all the major theories to leave a great deal of room for improvement and innovation. We saw that it was illogical to consider any single theory as being flexible enough to account for all the facts that have slowly emerged now that research has been actively pursuing the topic the theories have speculated about. Brown's (1973) work was especially instrumental in showing us many facts about normal childhood language development which simply refuse to fit any theory as the theories still stand. We clearly saw that the issue of syntactic analysis hinged specifically on our first understanding semantic development. We are now prepared to address two questions. First, do we presently have the capability and willingness to resolve the theoretical debates over semantic development, and, second, what exactly is happening in the field of semantic research which contributes to the understanding of the meanings children have and how those meanings determine and interact with syntactic development itself?

In answer to the first question, we have already resolved a small portion of our problem. We have outrightly rejected the Referent Theory and all it stands for; we are agreed that events, actions, and objects hold no specific semantic information of significance to us. This leaves us with only two major theories to consolidate, and, if we recall the conclusion of the debate on syntactic growth, we should not be at all surprised to see that part of the issue is going to be based upon which set of philosophical assumptions one wishes to accept. On the one hand, the Behavioral Theory Camp has asked us to spend our efforts discussing observables and to draw conclusions in a very conservative fashion upon only these observables. On the other hand, the Development approach has demanded that our interest be drawn away from the purely S-R bond associative ideas of the Behaviorists so we may see the evidence for the existence of stages and phases of qualitative change in the child's life. The Behaviorists have apparently ignored such stages/phases, per se, but they have noticed some changes in behavior at different age levels. These changes have been attributed to the summing-up of small, methodically reinforced bits of behavior forming into chains of more complex behaviors without any Behavioral Theory reference to stages or phases.

The evidence is far too overwhelming from the literally thousands of studies testing Piaget's model to deny that there are no stages or phases which each normal child eventually passes through. The evidence is also equally supportive of the idea that children (as well as adults) learn by S-R bond association (classical and operant conditioning) as well as at least S-S conditoning (observational or imitative learning). Must we think all in one set of terms for only one theory when it could at least rationally be argued that semantic processing occurs not just at the associative level but also at the cognitive level as well? Instead of forcing a conflict, could it not be proposed that the principles of classical and operant conditioning as well as S-S conditioning are alive and well at all stages of development and that those stages determine the direction toward which the child's attention will be directed as the conditioning processes occur? If such a merger is proposed, we could see a cognitive directional system dictating the type of associations which are being made during that system's functioning. The cognitive stage could then determine how associations will appear to us after such associations have been screened or filtered by the given cognitive stage, but in no sense would the actual principles of association be changed at any time. This is a very tall order for any fledgling science, and as of this moment no one has gone beyond being addicted to his/her theoretical biases. Regarding what is being done in the field of semantic research today, one could safely conclude that there is a virtual explosion of interest, speculation, and, unfortunately, a growing predisposition toward focusing more upon minute issues than upon holistic ones. Dale (1976, pp. 178—187) clearly shows us an apparent cognitive bent to research efforts. For example, the work of Clark (1973) and Nelson (1974) is cited (Dale, 1976, p. 178) to show that both authors are apparently Piagetian at heart since both seem to agree that the first thing the child learns is "meaning" before any labels are attached to the concept being learned. Palermo (1974) is cited as having shown that preschoolers use "less" and "more" interchangably until "something" seems to happen with remarkable speed. This "something" is apparently cognitive maturation.

The research of Riley and Fite (1974) has strong Piagetian leanings, albeit at the time of publication these leanings were not mentioned. Children change from syntagmatic to paradigmatic word association patterns during the same period they are making the transition into Concrete Operations. The shifting from syntagmatic to paradigmatic is not the cause of the cognitive change. It is surely the reverse that is true. Kess (1976, pp. 163-176) asks us to drift toward some type of a linguistic analysis of meaning rather than taking a developmental/cognitive approach. This would be a poor course of action since linguistics is better suited to present and discuss descriptive, symbolic models of the rules of syntax, not semantics.

When we see Palermo's (1978) work on semantic development, we also see the same interest in a linguistic-effort to explain meaning as we saw in Kess' writings. Palermo cites the writings of Chomsky (1971) showing that Chomsky's original lack of interest in semantics as seen in his 1957 *Syntactic Structures* had changed considerably. In 1971 he echoes the belief of Katz (1970) that meaning is probably attached at some point to deep structures. This is little more than a concession to the work of Fillmore (1968), McCawley (1968), and Bloom (1970), as

194

they presented strong evidence in favor of such an interpretation. But as Palermo interprets it, Chomsky's (1971) writings added a bit of a twist that McCawley, Fillmore, and Bloom were opposed to. That is, Chomsky decided to contend that the meaning factor was attached not only to deep structure but was also attached to the surface structure; there was no apparent connection between the meaning variable and the transformational rules themselves. This apparently still stands as Chomsky's position as well as that of Katz, and according to Palermo, it is a position that has few buyers. Palermo (1978, p. 41) indicates that spin-off research attempts following Chomsky's (1971) position have attempted to do one of two things. First, some scholars are attempting to "raise" the deep structure level toward the surface structure by creating as many new rules as possible to fit under deep structure. Second, some researchers are attempting to lower the surface structure toward the deep structure in order to minimize the distance between the two levels. The latter approach would seem most quickly doomed to end in something that will resemble an eventual Behaviorist-like statement. Palermo (1978, p. 41) says that many efforts in the linguistic approach to explaining meaning are running into a major stumbling block, which was voiced by Bever, Fodor and Garrett (1975) in review of the position taken by Katz and Fodor (1963); no one yet in a linguistic approach has accounted for the "psychological reality" of the semantic component. If the reader recalls, this very same comment was pointed out five years previously by Bloom (1970) as she asked for an explanation of the "psychological reality" of syntax and then proposed that it surely must lie in the semantic component's development. If Bloom (1970) has pushed "psychological reality" to the semantic level and if Bever, Fodor and Garrett (1975) have pushed it out of syntax, we may possibly be back to some of Piaget's basic contentions. Language in and of itself is merely a reflection of action. Considering the fact that we still do not understand the action level let alone the cognitive stages' actual "psychological reality," it is little wonder that Palermo (1978, p. 42) concludes his writings on semantics by saying that it is definitely a very timely research topic and one that, at least at the time of his writing, offered no serious answers or conclusions satisfactory to any scholar in the field.

Hulse, Egeth and Deese (1980, pp. 342—446) have prepared an excellent chapter regarding the status of meaning and meaning-related research which is admittedly separated in spirit and function from linguistically oriented research. We will use the highlights of their comments to enter a field of computer-design research which is directly based upon a cognitive approach to the problem, albeit the specific cognitive approach is definable more in terms of general-experimental design than in the more philosophically-worded Piagetian or Vygotskian approaches. A general-experimental design approach is prone to discuss "classes," "categories," and "classification schemes," but usually has little, if any, interest in the proposed qualitative changes in cognitive processing which Piaget and Vygotsky would assert come with age. Hulse, Egeth and Deese cite an impressive list of research studies in this general-experimental area, and we will make no attempt to review all of them. But a very clear trend easily surfaces in what we will see below. To this point, we have frequently spoken of "classes," "categories," and other cognitively oriented processes such as "operations." Also to this point, we have been very lax in discussing how classes, categories, and operations "appear" in at least the abstract sense. "Classes" and "categories" hold reference to research done in the field since 1970. "Operations," on the other hand, do not "appear" in any visual-descriptive sense at present; we have yet to really adequately determine exactly which behaviors go with which operations. This perhaps will furnish the careful reader with the heavy hint that we may fall short of an adequate explanation of meaning if we are being strictly Piagetian or Vygotskian about it, but let us not despair quite so soon. Hulse, Egeth and Deese give us much to consider on the level of "classes" and "categories."

Outright, Hulse, Egeth and Deese (1980, p. 364) reject Conrad's (1972) contention that any concept we choose exists somewhere in our central nervous system in a manner which makes the concept appear as a self-contained entity with all its defining features held inside a set of personal boundaries surrounding the heart of the concept itself. Visually, if such a system did exist, we would essentially see millions of self-contained vessels holding all the features necessary to define each vessel's central theme, the concept itself. This would produce exceedingly heavy demands upon any memory storage system and would drastically increase information processing time. The system would simply break down under its own mass. It would seem more logical to assume that a better way must exist. The first "better way" Hulse, Egeth and Deese discuss is a "network theory" proposed by Quillian and his associates (Quillian, 1968; Collins & Quillian, 1969, 1972; Collins & Loftus, 1975). Conceptually, the model is quite simple. Instead of each concept holding within its boundaries all of its features which make the concept what it is, classes of features are grouped starting at "the bottom" with the most frequently shared features and ending in a hierarchy with the least frequently shared features. For example, the set of features "four-legged animal" describes a multitude of creatures, whereas the set of features "with horns" does not. If someone asks us to distinguish between a "cow" and a "horse," the first set of features "four-legged animal" is attributed to both; we then move "up" the hierarchy of possible sets of similar-to-each features until we land upon "with horns," where obviously we see a distinction between the two concepts. We could, depending upon our past experiences and level of intelligence, make even finer distinctions between the two creatures if there were some need to do so, e.g., if reinforcement was present to do so. When we enter the hierarchy, we apparently must always come in at the very bottom and then start making decisions. At each meeting of a set of features (class or category), decisions must be made to either accept or reject whether a set of features describes the concept we seek to end our search with. Some searches will end quickly. "Is a bird a tree?" will be solved more rapidly than will "Is a cedar bush a tree?". But there is apparently an assumption behind this model and its functioning that is not specifically discussed by Hulse, Egeth and Deese. How do the feature sets (classes or categories) come to be in the first place? It would appear that the sets develop by mere association based squarely upon Aristotle's principle that similar stimuli are naturally associated in time and space. If this is the assumption, it is in direct contradiction to Piaget's position in which he believes S-S bond association is not the sole, nor necessarily most important, determinant of class formation. We must consider the developmental cognitive stages he proposes. But yet, at the same time, one of Piaget's own concepts fits quite nicely into Quillian's model. The concept of "transductive" reasoning, which typifies thought for Piaget from ages two to four years (through Preconceptual Thought, in other words) shows the child reasoning from the similarity of one specific set of features to a second specific set while ignoring all other possible sets. In that sense, a two-year-old could easily confuse a "cow" and a "horse" since they are both "four-legged animals." If the transductive child cannot "climb the hierarchy," as Quillian might put it, then a "cow" and a "horse" will be mistaken for one another until the child can climb that hierarchy. Just perhaps the Piagetian admonition against simple S-S association as the basis of class building can still be accepted if we perceive his position as being merely opposed to S-S bond association as the one and only process involved. Surely, the attentional directions of the child must play a very critical role in allowing S-S bonds to be built. If Piaget is seen as proposing "attentional direction processes," Quillian and Piaget's followers could easily use each other's position to strengthen their own.

As Hulse, Egeth and Deese (1980, p. 366) clearly state, there are many who do not accept the "network theory" proposed by Quillian. Meyer (1970; Meyer & Schvaneveldt, 1976) have proposed a "set theoretical" model which uses many of Quillian's ideas but goes one step further by overlaying Quillian's basic principles with the principles of prepositional logic. Albeit, this is a complex procedure and, frankly, one that goes into enough detail to make it too space consuming here to present the entire model, its basic construction may be conceptualized as an attempt to demonstrate how a word's meaning in one class is capable of becoming connected through various associative channels to a second or third class so as to speed prepositional thinking. For example, if you are told that "All men are mortal; Socrates is a man, and, therefore, he was mortal," it is fairly easy to see that the first preposition ("All men are mortal.") would require more time to process than would the latter two prepositions. In the first preposition, we must essentially check our meaning of "All men," which admittedly is a large number, to see if each is "mortal." The preposition "Socrates is a man." is a very particular preposition and requires only one "true or false" decision on our part. "Therefore, Socrates was mortal." also requires only one "true or false" decision and is labeled particularistic. This is, of course, something of an oversimplification; the more difficult part to understand deals with the manner in which the associative chains are made between classes which allow us to make prepositional statements in the first place. The most fundamental difference between Quillian's model and Meyer's is that the latter includes the "classes or categories" of the former and then goes one step further to add the prepositional logic. Meyer apparently assumes the classes (categories) are built through simple S-R association and, therefore, includes no discussion of qualitative changes in cognition as produced by age, e.g., the Piagetian system. As Hulse, Egeth and Deese (1980, pp. 367-368) point out, both Quillian's model and Meyer's have a flaw large enough to cause serious concern. Neither processes false statements efficiently. For example, in Meyer's model, if a person is told "All panthers wear gym shoes." and "All leopards wear gym shoes.", the processing time for each statement's producing the response "False!" should be equal since neither panthers nor leopards have anything in common with gym shoes to begin with. But such will not be the case; it will take longer to process the statement dealing with the leopards. Meyer's answer to this seeming paradox is that the number of features that fit into the class "leopards" is larger than the number fitting into the class "panthers." This is true; a panther actually is a leopard, but a leopard is not necessarily and more probably is not a panther. But, as Hulse, Egeth and Deese demonstrate, such logic on Meyer's part does not solve the problem because just as soon as the first feature of the class known as "All leopards" is checked against the class of features known as "gym shoes" we will see that at least one immediate contradiction applies. If one does not apply, then the term "All" need be pursued no further. Another paradox pointed out by Hulse, Egeth and Deese comes from a study by Landauer and Freedman (1968). Let us assume we are to judge the truth or falsity of "A canary is a fish." and "A canary is an ostrich." Since a canary is neither (but since it is a bird as is an ostrich), it should be predicted from Quillian's model that the falsity of "A canary is an ostrich." would be seen before "A canary is a fish." After all, a canary and an ostrich are in the same semantic class of "birds," checking one against the other should require little "movement," e.g., we do not need to move from class to class as we would from "canary" to "fish." But for some reason this prediction fails. It is just the opposite of what we should expect. There seems to be no explanation for this outcome save perhaps from the speculative viewpoint that the two features, "canary" and "ostrich" have enough similarities, i.e., feathers, two legs, a beak, etc., that the two are not as simply discriminated between as one might imagine. We are cautioned against drawing hasty conclusions here, because it apparently depends upon which words are being used; sometimes "special links" appear between some words in what would appear to be two or more unrelated classes. The example Hulse, Egeth and Deese provide is one in which we are to process the sentence "A canary is a banana." and "A canary is an apple." One might at first see no possible connection anywhere, but there is one; "canaries" and "bananas" are tied to the feature "yellow." Therefore, it takes longer to judge the falsity of "A canary is a banana." Smith, Shoben and Rips (1974) have according to Hulse, Egeth and Deese (1980, p. 369) produced a "feature comparison" model which incorporates Quillian's model as well as that of Meyer. This model starts by immediately comparing all features simultaneously between the two to-be-compared terms in order to first see if any similar features exist. If the answer is negative, then a conclusion to equate the two terms is false. Meyer's approach compares only two features at a time. If there are any features in common but not all are in common, Smith's model then and only then tests individual features two at a time as does Meyer's model. If all the features of one word are similar to all the features of the second, we have perfect identity; Smith's model "sees" this immediately. But Smith's model also has no mention of the qualitative age changes.

Whether we accept any of the computer models above or whether we stay within a Piagetian context or even attempt to mix the two systems, we are a great distance away from a linguistic model's attempts to solve our problem and are, hopefully, headed in a direction of greater understanding of what was above referred to as "psychological reality." That concern also existed in Hulse, Egeth and Deese's (1980, p. 374) writings since we see them asking us not to feel obligated to accept any of the computer models outlined above; as they see it, the field is still far too young for final answers.

There is one additional aspect of developing the computer models of meaning which we have yet to briefly discuss. The question of where "images" are to be placed in any meaning network has not yet been addressed. We will recall that Piaget's system did put emphasis upon the use of some kind of image functioning variable in the nature of semantic processing. Complicating the issue even further is the fact that the Piagetian model is not the only popular model of image functioning—as we now will see.

Paivio (1971) in *Imagery and Verbal Processes* states that we have overlooked a fundamental fact of brain physiology. The brain has two hemispheres, and each is equally complex, prone to process different information, capable of storage/retrieval of its own information, and perfectly capable of forming its own type of concepts with its own special information. For right-handed people, the "right brain" (right hemisphere) deals with images; the "left brain" deals with words. If information presses the listener/reader, the type of information determines which side is first activated. The picture of a triangle would, in a right-handed person, be processed first in the right hemisphere and would (before its entire processing was completed in that right side) then be sent to the left hemisphere for verbal labeling. As the left side does its processing on the data sent to it by the right, the right continues to finish its processing. The left side, in this particular example, logically finishes later than the right. The process is merely reverse if information presses as verbal first. The verbal would be cross-referenced to the image-processing right side.

The Paivio procedure fits under the title "the conceptual peg hypothesis." Both sides of the brain seek each other's information, code it in each side's special way, and store it in preparation for later retrieval. Both sides are forming concepts, and, most critically, both are equally complexly involved in forming their own concepts. Both sides function parallel to each other; the sides are rarely isomorphic (perfectly one to one) with each other unless the brain receives both a picture and its verbal label (name) precisely at the same time. This would indeed be a rare occurrence. Any gap in presentation time between the picture and the label would give one or the other of the hemispheres a head start. Any head start is significant; the brain's processing speed is clocked in milliseconds.

No one in this chapter has proposed a model of semantics based upon this dual-processing model Paivio proposes. However, it is necessary to note that Paivio also admitted that his model was a hypothesis. It has gained immense support since 1971. If ultimately universally accepted, it will require position statements as to how developmental stages occur in the hemispheres and how these occurrences determine concept formation at different ages.

Since Paivio's model was presented in 1971, new computer models of cognitive processing have been proposed by Anderson and Bower (1973) and by Anderson (1976). Anderson and Bower proposed HAM (human associative memory) and Anderson proposed an updated model of that basic program; the update was labeled ACT (Hulse, Egeth & Deese, 1980, pp. 387–391). Both models are capable of sampling stimuli, encoding that stimuli, storing it, and finally retrieving it upon demand. Most significantly, these authors assume that the basic unit of all language processing is the "proposition," which is defined as a declarative sentence's statement of a set of features which may be judged either as true or false by the perceiver. This actually does not exist in any concrete fashion; it lies under each issue one speaks about or listens to and is simply "understood" to exist by users of the language. Both verbal material and images as input are treated as propositions by HAM and ACT. The problem has not been so much in finding support for the verbal material's use of propositions as it has been for finding it using the images (Anderson, 1978). Paivio (1971) has stated in advance of seeing these, or any other, models that he rejects the basic idea behind the "proposition" since it ignores images.

Two additional issues regarding Paivio must be briefly addressed. First, no computer model to date has attempted to combine Piaget's developmental stages with Paivio's "split-brain" model. It is unknown if the two hemispheres' functions are evolving at the same rate of speed within the child. Such dual evolution would seem to affect semantics systematically. Second, the adequacy of any computer model of semantics must rely upon a discussion of memory. Paivio's model has disturbing implications for two of the field's classic theorists.

Research by Broadbent (1963) indicated once a stimulus has arrived at the retina a one to two seconds phase of "short-term memory" (STM) occurred in which an image appeared. A second phase of STM occurred which lasted approximately 28 seconds. During this phase, the image received a possible modification via neurophysiological processes beyond the sense organs. Broadbent contends that the STM process ended at this point: the STM phase loses the image and any memory of it. There is a possibility that the image from STM may enter what Broadbent defines as "long-term memory" (LTM), which depends upon verbal coding and a protein change somewhere in the storage centers of the brain. LTM remains permanently stored. LTM has a linguistic base;

STM has a "photoelectric" base. Adams (1967), another expert on memory storage functioning, has thrown his hat into Broadbent's ring instead of Paivio's. Adams proposes both a STM and LTM function with both having marked similarities to Broadbent's concepts.

Earlier we had posed two major questions to be eventually answered as we reviewed the existing research and models of semantic development. First, we asked if we had the capacity and willingness to resolve the theoretical debates over semantic development. From reviewing the current developments in the field, the answer seems somewhat mixed. Yes, apparently the willingness is there in full force; the field of semantic development is considered to be one of the very timely areas in language research. The awareness that syntax itself may rest squarely upon the shoulders of semantic development has caused renewed, serious attention to be directed toward semantics. The awareness that a cognitive substructure underlies transitions in children's meanings seems to be firmly established. Willingness, however, may only be a prerequisite since capability ultimately decides most issues. Even with the use of computers, we are not close to an answer. In fact, some might make the case that the use of the computer has actually slowed us in some ways because it means we are following a set of assumptions which may be incorrect but which are vital to the functioning of the computer programs. The issue of the need to determine the "psychological reality" of the semantic variable was first specifically addressed by Bloom in 1970. After almost two decades of relentness pursuit, the problem remains as it was when she addressed it the first time. All attempts made to this point have been purely descriptive, and many studies have had difficulty even doing that. The concept of "psychological reality" appears to be a wall no one has yet scaled, but that is not to say that we cannot do so eventually (Black & Chiat, 1981). The second major question in this chapter asked what the development of children's semantics looked like. We saw a very detailed discussion of the work of Piaget, Vygotsky, and Luria and then were confronted with several computer models which ignored developmental cognitive psychology. It can be seen in this that there is a larger issue than simply describing/explaining semantic growth. Will we approach the issue using a "bottom-up" or by using "top-down" attack? Experimental cognitive psychology, S-O-R Behaviorism, and S-R Behaviorism have insisted upon the former; developmental cognitive psychology and philosophy have insisted upon the latter with its assumptions of genetic contributions and belief that rationalism/mentalism is as good a tool as is experimental empiricism.

The question of semantic processing has also received renewed attention from those in the field of philosophy. Much of this interest is due to the long-standing realization that the nature of semantics is crucial to the understanding of logical reasoning. Donald Davidson's (1967) "Truth and Meaning" had started many thinking along the lines of using propositional logic combined with truth tables to judge the falsity of a given sentence's content. Mark Platts' (1979) *Ways of Meaning* continues in the Davidson tradition as both writers seek to answer the question of how one defines meaning in a natural setting. Research efforts from the field of linguistics show interest now in the field of "natural semantics," i.e., Klein's (1980) work on the nature of semantics in positive and comparative uses of adjectives.

As we will see in the next chapter, semantics plays a very troublesome role in children's learning to read. Attempts to "derive meaning from the printed page" have failed for a reason surely obvious now to us all. The meaning was never "in" the printed page to start with; it was inside the reader, who allows the printed material to act as conditioned stimuli in order to elicit conditioned responses from inside the reader. But if "inside the reader" equals "semantics," how will we yet understand reading or measure language?

References

Adams, J. A. (1967). *Human Memory.* New York: McGraw-Hill.

Anderson, J. (1978). "Arguments Concerning Representations for Mental Imagery." *Psychological Review, 85,* 249—277.

Anderson, J. (1976). *Language, Memory, and Thought.* Hillsdale, New Jersey: Erlbaum.

Anderson, J., and Bower, G. (1973). *Human Associative Memory.* Washington, D.C.: Winston and Sons.

Bever, T. G., Fodor, J. A., and Garrett, M. (1975). "The Psychological Reality of Semantic Representations." *Linguistic Inquiry, 6,* 515—531.

Bierwisch, M. (1970). "Semantics." In J. Lyons (Ed.), *New Horizons in Linguistics* (161—85). Baltimore: Penguin Books.

Black, M., and Chiat, S. (1981). "Psycholinguistics without Psychological Reality." *Linguistics, 19,* 37—61.

Blatty, W. (1971). *The Exorcist.* New York: Harper and Row.

Bloom, L. (February, 1970). *Semantic Features in Language Acquisition.* Paper presented to the Conference on Research in the Language of the Mentally Retarded, University of Kansas.

Bloom, L. (1973). *One Word at a Time.* The Hague: Mouton.

Bolinger, D. (1965). "The Atomization of Meaning." *Language, 41,* 555—573.

Broadbent, D. E. (1963). "Flow of Information within the Organism." *Journal of Verbal Learning and Verbal Behavior, 2,* 34—39.

Brown, R. (1958). "How Shall a Thing Be Called?" *Psychological Review, 65,* 14—21.

Brown, R. (1973). *A First Language: The Early Stages.* Cambridge, Massachusetts: Harvard University Press.

Carroll, J. (1964). "Words, Meanings, and Concepts." *Harvard Educational Review, 34,* 178–202.

Chomsky, N. (1957). *Syntactic Structures.* The Hague: Mouton.

Chomsky, N. (1971). "Deep Structure, Surface Structure, and Semantic Representation." In D. Steinberg and L. Jakobovits (Eds.), *Semantics: An Interdisciplinary Reader in Philosophy, Linguistics, and Psychology* (183–216). Cambridge: Cambridge University Press.

Clark, E. V. (1973). "What's in a Word? On the Child's Acquisition of Semantics in His First Language." In T. E. Moore (Ed.), *Cognitive Development and the Acquisition of Language* (65–110). New York: Academic Press.

Clark, H., and Clark, E. (1977). *Psychology and Language.* New York: Harcourt, Brace, Jovanovich.

Collins, A., and Loftus, E. (1975). "A Spreading-Activation Theory of Semantic Processing." *Psychological Review, 82,* 407–428.

Collins, A., and Quillian, M. (1969). "Retrieval Time from Semantic Memory." *Journal of Verbal Learning and Verbal Behavior, 8,* 240–247.

Collins, A., and Quillian, M. (1972). "Experiments in Semantic Memory and Language Comprehension." In L. Gregg (Ed.), *Cognition in Learning and Memory* (117–137). New York: Wiley.

Conrad, C. (1972). "Cognitive Economy in Semantic Memory." *Journal of Experimental Psychology, 92,* 149–154.

Dale, P. S. (1972). *Language Development.* Hinsdale, Illinois: Dryden.

Dale, P. S. (1976). *Language Development* (2nd ed.). New York: Holt, Rhinehart, and Winston.

Davidson, D. (1967). "Truth and Meaning." *Syntheses, 17,* 304–323.

Durant, W. (1926). *The Story of Philosophy.* New York: Simon and Schuster.

Ebbinghaus, H. (1913). *Memory* (Trans. H. A. Ruger & C. E. Busenius). New York: Teacher's College. (Original work *Über das Gedächtnis* Publ. 1885)

Ervin, S., and Foster, G. (1960). "The Development of Meaning in Children's Descriptive Terms." *Journal of Abnormal and Social Psychology, 61,* 271–275.

Fillmore, C. J. (1968). "The Case for Case." In E. Bach and R. T. Harms (Eds.), *Universals in Linguistic Theory* (1–88). New York: Holt.

Furth, H. (1970). *An Inventory of Piaget's Developmental Tasks.* Washington, D.C.: Catholic University, Department of Psychology, Center for Research in Thinking and Language.

Goss, A. (1961). "Verbal Mediating Responses and Concept Formation." *Psychologcial Review, 68*(4), 248–274.

Hebb, D. O. (1949). *The Organization of Behavior.* New York: Wiley.

Hulse, S., Egeth, H., and Deese, J. (1980). *The Psychology of Learning* (5th ed.). New York: McGraw.

Johnson, M. (1967). "Syntactic Position and Rated Meaning." In L. Jakobovits and M. Miron (Eds.), *Readings in the Psychology of Language* (472–479). Englewood Cliffs, New Jersey: Prentice-Hall.

Kaplan, B. (1961). "An Approach to the Problem of Symbolic Representation: Non-verbal and Verbal." *Journal of Communications, 11,* 52–62.

Katz, J. J. (1970). "Interpretive Semantics versus Generative Semantics." *Foundations of Language, 6,* 220–259.

Katz, J. J., and Fodor, J. (1963). "The Structure of a Semantic Theory." *Language, 39,* 170–210.

Kess, J. (1976). *Psycholinguistics.* New York: Academic Press.

Klein, E. (1980). "Semantics for Positive and Comparative Adjectives." *Linguistics and Philosophy, 4*(1), 1–45.

Landauer, T., and Freedman, J. (1968). "Information Retrieval from Long-Term Memory: Category Size and Recognition Time." *Journal of Verbal Learning and Verbal Behavior, 7,* 291–295.

Levin, I. (1967). *Rosemary's Baby.* New York: Random House.

Luria, A. R. (1959). "The Directional Function of Speech in Development and Dissolution." *Word, 15,* 341–352.

Luria, A. R. (1960). "Verbal Regulation of Behavior." In M. Brazier (Ed.), *The Central Nervous System and Behavior: Transactions of the Third Conference* (359–423). New York: J. Macy, Jr. Foundation.

Luria, A. R., (1961). *The Role of Speech in the Negation of Normal and Abnormal Behavior.* London: Pergamon.

Luria, A. R., and Yudovich, F. (1959). *Speech and the Development of Mental Processes in the Child.* London: Staples Press.

McCawley, J. D. (1968). "The Role of Semantics in a Grammar." In E. Bach and R. T. Harms (Eds.), *Universals in Linguistic Theory* (124–169). New York: Holt, Rhinehart, and Winston.

McCawley, J. D. (1971). "Prelexical Syntax." In R. J. O'Brien (Ed.), *Linguistics: Developments of the Sixties—Viewpoints of the Seventies. Monograph Series in Languages and Linguistics, 24,* 19–33.

McCawley, J. D. (March, 1975). *The Role of Lexicographic Information in Dictionary Definitions.* Paper presented at the Annual Conference of the International Linguistic Association, New York.

McNeill, D. (1970). *The Acquisition of Language: The Study of Developmental Pscholinguistics.* New York: Harper and Row.

Meyer, D. (1970). "On the Representation and Retrieval of Stored Information." *Cognitive Psychology, 1,* 242–300.

Meyer, D., and Schvaneveldt, R. (1976). "Meaning, Memory Structure, and Mental Processes." In C. N. Cofer (Ed.), *The Structure of Human Memory* (54–89). San Francisco: Freeman.

Miller, G. A. (1962). "Some Psychological Studies of Grammar." *American Psychologist, 17,* 748–762.

Miller, S. A., Shelton, J., and Flavell, J. A. (1970). "A Test of Luria's Hypotheses Concerning the Development of Verbal Self-Regulation." *Child Development, 41,* 651–665.

Mowrer, O. H. (1954). "The Psychologist Looks at Language." *American Journal of Psychology, 9,* 660–694.

Nelson, K. (1974). "Concept, Word, and Sentence: Interrelations in Acquisition and Development." *Psychological Review, 81,* 267–285.

Oleron, P. (1977). *Language and Mental Development.* New York: Wiley.

Osgood, C. E. (1963). "On Understanding and Creating Sentences." *American Psychologist, 18,* 735–751.

Osgood, C. E. (1964). "Semantic Differential Technique in the Comparative Study of Cultures." *American Anthropologist, 66,* 171–200.

Osgood, C., Suci, G., and Tannenbaum, P. (1957). *The Measurement of Meaning.* Urbana: University of Illinois Press.

Paivio, A. (1971). *Imagery and Verbal Processes.* New York: Holt.

Palermo, D. (1974). "Still More About the Acquisition of 'Less.'" *Developmental Psychology, 10,* 827–829.

Palermo, D. (1978). *Psychology of Language.* Dallas, Texas: Scott, Foresman, and Company.

Patterson, H. O., and Milakofsky, L. (1980). "A Paper-and-Pencil Inventory for the Assessment of Piaget's Tasks." *Applied Psychological Measurement, 4*(3), 341–353.

Piaget, J. (1924). *La Languge et la Pense chez l'Enfant.* Neuchatel: Delachaux.

Plato (1937). *The Dialogues.* Translated by B. Jowett. New York: Random House.

Platts, M. (1979). *Ways of Meaning.* New York: Routledge and Kegan Paul, Ltd.

Putnam, H. (1975). "The Meaning of 'Meaning.'" In *Mind, Language, and Reality* (215–271) (Philosophical Papers, Volume 2). Cambridge: Cambridge University Press.

Quillian, M. (1968). "Semantic Memory." In M. Minsky (Ed.), *Semantic Information Processing* (216–270). Cambridge, Massachusetts: MIT Press.

Riley, L., and Fite, G. (1974). "Syntagmatic versus Paradigmatic Paired-Associate Acquisition." *Journal of Experimental Psychology, 103*(2), 375–376.

Rogers, S. (1975). (Ed.). *Children and Language.* London: Oxford University Press.

Skinner, B. F. (1957). *Verbal Behavior.* New York: Appleton, Century, and Crofts.

Smith, E., Shoben, E., and Rips, L. (1974). "Structure and Process in Semantic Memory: A Featural Model for Semantic Decisions." *Psychological Review, 81,* 214–224.

Vygotsky, L. (1962). *Thought and Language.* Cambridge, Massachusetts: MIT Press.

Watson, J. B. (1913). "Psychology as the Behaviorist Views It." *Psychological Review, 20,* 158–177.

Whorf, B. L. (1956). "A Linguistic Consideration of Thinking in Primitive Communities" (circa 1936). In J. B. Carroll (Ed.), *Language, Thought and Reality: Selected Writings of Benjamin Lee Whorf* (65–86). Cambridge, MA: M.I.T. Press.

Wozniack, R. (1972). "Verbal Regulation of Motor Behavior: Soviet Research and Non-Soviet Replication." *Human Development, 15,* 13–57.

– 8 –

READING AND MEASUREMENT

Essence of the Problem

In the preceding chapter, considerable space was devoted to analyzing how meaning is learned. We saw that a simple S-R conditioning approach was not sufficient. Further, we saw that a cognitive approach such as that of Jean Piaget would question how much meaning can be acquired at various age levels since genetics sets limits on a child's ability to understand events. No known conditioning process can, according to Piaget and his followers, override this genetic restriction. In the preceding chapter, the position was formed which stated that semantic development is surely the basis of syntactic development rather than vice versa. This position is essentially in agreement with the thinking of Jean Piaget. The preceding chapter leads us to believe that the process of syntactic/semantic development has a strong "top-down" component. This means that genetics is busily assisting in normal language development and that conditioning theories must take a close look at these genetic processes. A "bottom-up" approach would stress conditioning rather than genetics and would ask us to spend our time reviewing classical and operant conditioning principles rather than speculating about genetics. The "top-down" approach is deductive; genetics is a given, and all else must fall under its domain. The "bottom-up" approach is inductive and asks us to assume no givens except, of course, for the belief that nothing is given. Induction is the method of science; deduction is the method of philosophy. Induction to deduction is probably a continuum, and so it probably is for the empiricism and rationalism issue. Such a continuum surely exists for the "top-down" and "bottom-up" issue. But how many theorists so far in this book have treated these issues as continua? On one hand, the S-R Behaviorists and the S-O-R Behaviorists have acted inductively (in a "bottom-up" manner) while those such as Chomsky and Piaget have approached us from a deductive ("top-down") angle. There seemed to be no middle ground. If one carefully studies the history of psychology, one sees these extremes as a general trend. The classic example of this was the "Founder of Experimental Psychology"—Wundt. His work is usually said to have started in 1879 at Leipzig, Germany; it was truely a "bottom-up" effort to scientifically determine how visual information became part of consciousness. What is rarely discussed is his work on that same issue, which also took place at Leipzig from 1874 to 1879. This work was "top-down" and, in its failure, caused Wundt to adopt the "bottom-up" approach. It, the "bottom-up," also failed.

The field of reading has reflected the same methodological/philosophical conflicts mentioned immediately above and throughout all of our discussion of the growth of syntax and semantics. Heilman, Blair and Rupley (1986, pp. 4–5) cite Geyer's 1972 statement to the effect there were already more than 80 theories of reading available. The 80, as Heilman, Blair and Rupley see it, can be categorized as "bottom-up" or "top-down." Few theories use the two approaches in some kind of combination. As these authors state it, the "bottom-up" approaches treat the reader as making no innate contribution to the task. The "top-down" approach places the reader in a key role as a person who actively structures materials. This structuring would seem to easily include genetic predisposition/cognitive phase. The "bottom-up" approach returns us to the same "blank tablet" assumption of the philosopher John Locke. It is Locke's philosophy that underlies the S-R position and is not completely antithetical to S-O-R Behavioral thought. Reading, therefore, is a reflection of the same debate we saw as the child learned to listen and to speak. However, in the study of reading there is perhaps a glimmer of hope. Reading is more concrete than are syntax or semantic development. Reading should be easier to measure. Perhaps by understanding reading, we may be able to return to syntax and semantics to ask questions there. First things must include defining the reading process.

From the S-R Behavioristic Approach

Dale (1976, p. 224) says that Charles Bloomfield in the early 1930s was among the first to bring our attention to the "grapheme/phoneme" relationship in the reading process. We condition children to think of a specific letter or set of letters each time a specific sound or set of sounds occurs. If the child successfully masters this, the process of reading, at least in its immature stage, can be a pleasant experience for the learner as well as the teacher. Bloomfield, who was also discussed in J. J. Katz's "Mentalism in Linguistics" (see Chapter 3), offers no special advice as to how to teach the grapheme/phoneme association. It is assumed that he would have accepted some type of classical or operant conditioning approach since both (especially the former) were available in workable form in 1933.

Sir James Pitman and St. John (1969) was quick to see that the grapheme/phoneme relationship was not always consistent (Dale, 1976, p. 226). One example is this: the word "through" can just as easily be spelled "thru" and remain pronounced the same. We see the latter on doors, but we do not see it frequently in the reading materials of children. As Pitman had noted this incongruity must be of concern to a beginning reader since there are so many examples of such grapheme/phoneme misfits. But, as Pitman noted, the incongruity is rarely so great as to make the association an impossible match. It is a misfit involving only a limited number of letters. Pitman proposed the "Initial Teaching Alphabet," which would start the child with a consistent grapheme/phoneme relationship and then allow the child to learn gradually the "exceptions to the rules" at a pace comfortable to the child. The child was to use the same alphabet for spelling as was used for reading. The teaching method was a simple conditioning approach. But, as with Bloomfield, the reading process was being defined with very tightly drawn limits as to what reading includes. Despite the efforts of Bloomfield and Pitman, concern arises. Dale (1976, p. 225) states there was little research defining the correlation between the ability to use oral language and the ability to learn to read. It is possible, therefore, that memorizing a grapheme/phoneme association pattern was not the answer to producing successful reading in the first place.

To the best of this writer's knowledge, O. H. Mowrer did not specifically extend his writings to the field of reading. We reviewed his position in Chapter 4. Nonetheless, his position fits, at least in part, nicely into reading procedures. The words in print are like the spoken words in that both are conditioned stimuli. Neither the spoken nor the written word carries meaning innately. Its meaning in either the oral or written form comes from the process of either (1) associating that word directly to an experience (thus producing "first-order conditioning") or (2) associating the word to an oral or written word which has previously acquired meaning by associating itself to an experience ("second-order conditioning"). If a child is to be a success at reading, the child must realize that s/he must see the words not simply as words but rather as stimuli which will elicit meaning from within the reader. The meaning is in no manner on the printed page itself, nor is it in the spoken word. If it were on the page itself, the reader's contribution would be minimal. This, by the way, makes the position of Heilman et al. noted above somewhat at odds with the S-R approach Mowrer proposes. Mowrer definitely believed meaning was in the reader/listener even though that person started as a "blank tablet." Heilman et al. (1986, pp. 4—5) state that the "bottom-up" approach concentrates upon the words themselves rather than the reader's contributions. The word is a stimulus for Mowrer and nothing else. If the child has no meaning to let the stimulus word elicit, then that stimulus word could just as easily be one of any number of other meaningless patterns. The word itself carries no message. In order to produce good readers, Mowrer would insist that we produce many experiences for our potential readers prior to our trying to associate words with those experiences. "Word-calling" is no more reading for Mowrer than for any other theorist. Where then is the "blank tablet"?

Operant conditioning lends itself well to the teaching of reading. When the reader has performed correctly, the teacher needs only to use one of the reinforcement schedules reviewed in Chapter 4 to produce the desired rate of learning and the consequent resistance to extinction desired. Skinner only briefly addressed reading in his *Verbal Behavior,* but one need not look too deeply between the lines to see he is asking for the use of operant conditioning in all aspects of the verbal behavior process. Even though Skinner's "textual responses" (reading) requires no genetic "top-down" contribution from the reader, we would be wrong to assume he believed the reader was a "blank tablet." Operant conditioning is an active, trial and error learning process. As in earlier chapters, the major question about Skinner's position centers on the amount of time operant conditioning would require to produce a mature reader. This problem has been circumvented by the writings of Staats and Staats (1962) and generally Staats (1964) as they promote the application of operant conditioning to the reading process. Few who carefully read these authors can readily dismiss the utility of their message. Children, as well as all other organisms of any age, learn more effectively if systematically reinforced. The question remains as to whether operant conditioning alone is sufficient. What conceivable reinforcer would cause a child to read a passage successfully where the child understood absolutely none of the words? The processes of using "shaping" and "successive approximations" is very time consuming and not infrequently frustrating no matter what the reinforcer is.

From the S-O-R Behavioristic Approach

The "contextual generalization model" of M. D. S. Braine (reviewed in Chapter 5) was never proposed as a model for reading. However, the "cloze procedure" in reading uses context generalization principles and predates Braine's own "contextual generalization" theory (Braine, 1963). You will recall Braine asked children to memorize a short, nonsense sentence and then tested for stimulus generalization to other nonsense sentences. Since the first sentence had, at least, been learned, some kind of "meaning" transferred/generalized to later sentences. Such is the process underlying the cloze procedure. If you can successfully learn to read "Tom is a thief.", you should be able to successfully generalize to "Mary is a thief.", "Tom is a poet.", etc. As in Braine's model, the cloze procedure stresses the successful use of and attention to small, pivot words such as, prepositions, articles, possessive nouns, word prefixes (such as pre, anti, etc.), and word endings (such as ize, ment, er, etc.). In fact, you could return to Chapter 5 and read Braine's list of "closed class morphemes" as if that list had originally been proposed by cloze procedure advocates. The cloze procedure would instruct the reader to watch how sentence frames have many common features, i.e., "_ is _ing to_" may define the frame of literally thousands of sentences. Now, if only the reader could memorize a handful of general frames and a limited number of closed class morphemes (pivot words), the reading process would become simpler than using simple operant conditioning in order to painfully shape the reading of each and every "new" sentence. That is the entire point of cloze: each sentence is definitely not "new" since there are but a few general sentence frames to start with. Braine had said there were about nine such frames in English; not so ironically, Noam Chomsky had said there were about nine transformational rules in English.

C. E. Osgood's (1963) "On Understanding and Creating Sentences" fits well as an advocate of the S-O-R approach to reading. His full model of "semantic generalization" is reviewed in Chapter 5. We need only note here that his model allowed for both "left to right" processing of words in a sentence and for vertical processing within each word. In general, as the reader sees the word "The" at the start of a sentence, the "convergent" (left to right) process instantly predicts what the next word will be. At the same time, the "divergent" (vertical) process recalls other words identical or closely similar in meaning to the word we are reading. This vertical processing then rushes to assist the convergent process in predicting the following word in the sentence. This dual-processing continues throughout the entire sentence. Osgood's model is capable of

211

accepting Skinner's operant conditioning as well as the cloze procedure. Osgood's model conceives of meaning as being far, far more than a "simple accumulation of habits" (as was proposed by Noble in 1952). By being open to other models, Osgood successfully does what Staats and Staats (1959) asked Behaviorists to do—listen to each other and share their knowledge. Osgood shares with Mowrer a concern for semantics as the basis of all aspects of language. A reader who carries no meaning into the reading process simply cannot profit from reading; indeed, they simply cannot read. We must note that both Braine and Osgood are far less "bottom-up" than are Mowrer and Skinner. Braine and Osgood are, of course, S-O-R Behaviorists; S-O-R recognizes some limited contribution from the learner's genetics, but S-O-R is still a very far cry from a "top-down" approach.

Recent research by Rayner as reported by Carroll (1986, p. 136) has some interesting implications for Osgood. Rayner showed that readers "see" what they are focused upon and up to seven through twelve letters ahead of that focus. The reader will recall that one of the oldest questions in psychology has been how much information is seen in a single focusing. But here Rayner added the "special part" of the data; meaning was restricted to the letter being focused upon and a range from only one to six letters ahead of that focus! If Osgood's "semantic generalization" model works as he proposes it, the convergent and divergent processes must be incredibly dynamic since range of meaningful letter perception is so restricted. This is despite Carroll's (1986, p. 136) statement that college students read at about 280 words per minute on the whole. This speed is dramatically lessened for complex materials and is somewhat increased for materials of less technical variety. However, Carroll (1986, p. 138) also adds that the "word superiority effect" (first proposed by Cattell in the late 19th century) had already shown that the perception of words (especially in context) is much faster than is the perception of letters (especially if they are out of context). Perhaps this takes some of the pressure off Osgood's model and lets it perform a bit more leisurely. Carroll also notes that the "word superiority effect" fails to function if the words are unfamiliar. This finding fits Osgood's model perfectly since absence of meaning would cause serious convergent/divergent processing disruption.

Wolf (1980) in "Reading Reconsidered" says psychology had historically suffered great difficulty in analyzing the reading process until G. A. Miller (1956) wrote his famous paper on the concept of "the magic number 7 plus or minus 2." Miller showed that verbal materials tend to form classes/categories into which similar materials are stored. The entire class is activated as one retrieves even single items from the class.

The reader should note here the remarkable similarity of this to at least part of Osgood's conceptually more-incompassing "semantic generalization" model. As Miller clearly showed, we think of words in "chunks" rather than as separate words if we can in any conceivable manner create a class category. The class/category creation as well as "chunking" is nativisitic; we do not "learn" to do this in the conventional sense of learning via classical and/or operant conditioning. Wolf states that this "chunking" allows the reader to derive large quantities of meaning from a single focus (sampling) and, therefore, helps to account for the reading rates characteristic of adults. Wolf, as had Neisser (1967, pp. 105–137) and Dale (1976, p. 228), states that mature readers must use some technique far, far in advance of a grapheme/phoneme decoding process since the neurophysiological limits upon the reader could not possibly keep pace with the reading speed. It is interesting that all these researchers noted this. Wolf is apparently an S-O-R Behaviorist and a few steps removed from the "bottom-up" approach; Dale sits somewhere in the middle between "bottom-up" and "top-down"; Neisser was definitely headed toward a "top-down" conclusion even though his 1967 classic *Cognitive Psychology* started us from the "bottom-up." All three of these researchers would easily agree there is more to reading than a simple "bottom-up" approach as might have been proposed for reading by Mowrer and as was actually proposed by B. F. Skinner.

Illusion of "Top-Down" Membership

There are today about as many theorists and practitioners who are joining what they sincerely believe is a true "top-down" movement as there are those leaving the "bottom-up" approach. Yet, if you carefully review what has been proposed in this chapter, you will see we have spent considerable time somewhere in the middle of the debate. There is little company there. Carroll (1986, p. 140) says the most advanced trend today is actually toward a "mix" of the "word specific" (bottom-up) and "rule-governed" (top-down) approaches. We have seen the "bottom-up" and the "mix" (at least toward a few steps above "bottom-up"), but what should a true "top-down" approach include? And are those who are joining this movement truly "top-down" or more in the "mix" but cannot recognize it as such? Perhaps one's perception of the scientific method can cause the feeling of "advanced height" even when the model being proposed is far away from the levels our rationalist/mentalist peers routinely function at.

All through our discussions of Jean Piaget's cognitive model the emphasis was placed upon its "top-down" nature as so clearly seen in Piaget's insistence upon genetic/nativistic prerequisites before any cognition could develop. Vygotsky's model of semantic development is easily as "top-down" as Piaget's. One who is familiar with either model would logically assume that stages/phases in cognition must dominate how the child approaches reading. For example, how can a child in Piaget's Preconceptual Stage approach reading since reading's contents are conceptual in nature. The Preconceptual child cannot, according at least to Piaget, develop concepts. Indeed, not even the Intuitive Stage child has concepts. Not until Concrete Operations can concepts appear. This starts at around six to seven years of age. Vygotsky's model says there are no concepts until six or seven; this marks the child's entrance into "Ingrowth Speech." Both Piaget and Vygotsky believed the human learner's cognitive system was "heuristic," not "algorithmic." A heuristic system generates its own rules. An algorithmic system strives toward the goal of "self-generated rule development," but, as of date, not one algorithmic model (even with our most advanced computers) has generated its own rules. Since we do not even easily understand the complexities of algorithms, how is it that we propose to use heuristic models? We can describe Piaget and Vygotsky's stages and propose reading models to imitate them, but this leaves us far short of our goal unless our reading program is based upon an understanding/explanation of such heuristic systems. Who then has a current working model to teach reading heuristically? In this author's opinion, no one. It is also true that understanding the "genetic contribution" may, if ever, be far from us. So, what do we do in the interim? We entitle our approach to our reading program as "top-down" so as to join the trend and then we grab every tool, skill, and teaching method available to produce "a reader."

As Dale (1976, p. 223) puts it, we are engaged continually in Jeanne Chall's (1967) "great debate." Our answers regarding the definitions of syntax and semantics may lie in the study of reading, but it is more likely that the opposite is true.

Measurement

The measurement of anything depends upon how well defined that "anything" is. Language at the syntactic and semantic levels is, as we have abundantly seen above, far from well defined conceptually. Indeed, there is a storm of controversy over definition. Any test, therefore, will reflect the theoretical bias of its author. You are prepared now after having read the previous chapters of this book to understand how strong those biases may be and how vastly different the theoretical assumptions are. The S-R Behaviorists have an advantage of sorts in test construction since they have repeatedly stated that the "content" of language must be "observables." What the child says or writes or responds to upon command is easy to table, graph, and otherwise statistically analyze. Some of us who want to select a test may become so impressed by the statistics that we will forget to ask if we really accept the test's theoretical assumptions. The reverse is equally unfortunate. We cannot afford to select a test simply because its theoretical assumptions (and only its assumptions) support our biases.

Let us use the following questions' answers to guide our selection of any measuring device:

1. Foremost, what aspect of language are we specifically trying to measure? The measurement of speech is not the measurement of semantics or syntax, albeit some, but definitely not all, specific measures may correlate significantly to others. If, for example, the quality and frequency of babbling at age 11 months were significantly correlated to growth in semantics from ages two to four years, we could use the former measure to more or less accurately predict the latter. But, we will not know how the semantic growth appeared unless we wait until the child is two to four and specifically measure the semantic pattern.

2. Assuming we successfully answered the first question above, let us ask now: "Has anyone prepared a test which we may obtain and administrate?" We can easily answer this by reviewing the excellent materials provided in Buros' *Mental Measurement Yearbooks,* which are available in any major university's library. Buros has systematically reported reviews of tests from a variety of fields. Reliabilities, standard errors of measurement, and validities are presented in a very useful fashion. A very quick review of any introductory text in psychological measurement will enable the reader to learn the fundamentals which give meaning to reliability, error, and validity statements. The major statistic involved in these concepts is correlation, which can be easily mastered by even those of us who fear statistics.

Buros also states in his reviews whether a test is "restricted." If so, the publisher of the test will require proof of academic/professional competence before the test is mailed. Not all tests which are "not restricted" are truly suitable for the novice. Lawsuits abound today because of "unprofessional and/or unethical use/interpretation" of various tests.

Buros will usually briefly discuss the ease of administration of a measure as well as its ease of scoring the interpretation. Some paper and pencil tests require no more administrative skill than being able to use a stopwatch.

3. After the data is collected and scored, will the user be able to interpret its meaning at the present moment and possibly use it to predict future development? Many tests are selected because they are easy to administrate and are easily scored. Then the user finds that the scores have little meaning if no one has conducted systematic, large-scale studies to determine "norms" for various age levels. Also, tests that are easily administered/scored may tempt the user to employ the test beyond the definition of the concept upon which the test was based.

Dale (1976, p. 306) illustrates the preceding point when he said the *Peabody Picture Vocabulary Test* (PPVT) by Dunn (1965) has been used for measuring semantic growth (which is its purpose), for measuring syntactic growth (which is not its stated purpose), and for measuring intelligence (which certainly was never its expressed purpose)! If you have read Chapters 6 and 7 of this book, you may have found the "perfect Catch 22" in part of the preceding line. It was proposed in those chapters that semantics was the base of syntax. A good measure of semantics (as the PPVT is) would be a very likely candidate for correlational studies between semantics and syntax. But, as Dale puts it, no one to his knowledge has run the studies; users of the PPVT have "assumed" the correlation is significant and have then proceded to call it "factual." Recently, Dunn has developed a revised form of the PPVT; it is known as the PPVT-R and is easily reviewed in detail in Buros.

In the past, one of the most cherished tests of language functioning was the *Illinois Test of Psycholinguistic Abilities* (ITPA) by Kirk, McCarthy and Kirk (1968). The experimental test edition appeared in 1961 by McCarthy and Kirk. This test attempted, according to Dale (1976, p. 307), to divide language into (1) modality: auditory, visual, and motor, (2) process: expression, reception, and organization, and (3) organizational level: automatic or representational. As Dale notes, the ITPA has been suspect for some time. Some of its subtests correlate insignificantly to significant language parameters.

The current view seems to be that the ITPA has served its purpose insofar as we learned that the various parts of the language process are both difficult to define as separate entities and are, if defined separately, not easily remediated separately. A "holistic" approach has become the trend today. How long the ITPA survives in the face of this trend is yet to be seen.

The problems with the ITPA are significant to us beyond the specific use of that test. As measurement theory has gradually increased its accu-

216

racy throughout the past 100 years, there has been a growing alarm over how that accuracy was more and more requiring limits to be placed upon the mental construct being tested. This same type of alarm appeared in experimental psychology and is now appearing in experimental cognitive psychology as well. Reliability, validity, and lowered standard error of measurement require even greater movement away from holism. Yet, any mental construct is part of the whole. If the specific measures are abandoned, many today fear that "holism" may become "common sense" as that term was defined prior to the development of psychology as a field. It will be exciting to watch the dust settle on this issue! The holistic approach is "top-down"; the psychometric movement is, and always has been, "bottom-up." The issue is critical to our understanding of all aspects of language; reading is included as part of language as a whole. Literally hundreds of tests in reading and other aspects of language are going to be directly affected by the issue's resolution.

Animal Language

Contrary to popular belief, psychology has not historically relied upon the use of rats, pigeons, and other infrahumans to solve all its problems regarding theory building. The first use of animals dates back to the late 1800s with the work of Ivan Pavlov and the "Father of Educational Psychology," E. L. Thorndike. B. F. Skinner's work in his *Behavior of Organisms* (1938) and his *Schedules of Reinforcement* (Ferster & Skinner, 1957) did the most to create the public image of psychology as infrahuman oriented. The reader should recall that Skinner's *Verbal Behavior* (1957) was based upon learning patterns that were initially discovered using rats and pigeons. The reader should also recall Chomsky's (1959) reaction to the extension of animal research to human language learning. Skinner supposedly, according to MacCorquodale (1970), admitted that his position in *Verbal Behavior* was strictly hypothetical and had been presented more as a catalyst for research interests rather than as a "final answer."

There has, however, been one area of infrahuman research which has specifically addressed language development. The animals are chimpanzees; the language has been American Sign Language. Perhaps the most easily read of the numerous articles on this subject is a summary-type write-up by Premack and Premack (1972). Their chimpanzee was named

Sarah; her name gained fame as had that of another "language-learning" chimpanzee of the 1940s named Vicki. Both Vicki and Sarah approached language learning via the use of a "bottom-up" approach, which took the form of discrimination training via operant conditioning. The reader will recognize this as a simple S-R Behavioristic approach, and, unfortunately, we already know from having read materials throughout this book that the simple S-R approach will not be sufficient. But here we must grant the Premacks their due. They never claimed nor implied that they were looking for sufficiency in the first place. Their approach and writing did not leave the ambiguous impression Skinner's *Verbal Behavior* did, e.g., that "the answer" is there if the reader will but see it for what it (language) really is—just behavior.

In Premack and Premack's article, the position is taken that human language is but a subset of all the possible languages available to "animals" (including humans). Human language is perhaps the most abstractly defined, but the languages of other animals are not lacking in complexity. Certain types of sparrows found in South America show an incredibly complex communication pattern. The female begins the pattern and then produces every other note in a song which the male will complete by inserting the even-numbered notes! The listener hears only the completed song; it occurs at a remarkably swift pace. Questions instantly arise as to whether the birds are even listening to each other. If they are not, the question then arises as to how they pace their own segments so perfectly. Research by the U.S. Navy has for decades pursued the language patterns of dolphins and whales. As Premack and Premack point out, the chimpanzee was their choice of subject because they are closer than any other animal to us regarding evolution. Chimpanzees are also very active in their chattering and gesturing.

Sarah's task is like that of virtually all other chimpanzees in language studies. She is first to memorize a simple, pictoral "sight vocabulary" so she may respond appropriately when given each picture. The pictures are not "icons" (perfect duplicates) of objects or actions; the pictures are "images" that hold no particular shape or color resemblance to the real object or action each image represents. Once the memorization is completed, Sarah is commanded by giving her the images. The Premacks reported excellent success. But the second phase of the research is more difficult. Sarah is to use the images to communicate her own needs to her experimenters. This requires an "expressive" language function. During the first part of studies such as this, we may require the subject to distinguish among images standing for various people and actions. We may test to see if "Randy gives apple Mary" is reacted to appropriately as we actually see Mary giving an apple to Randy. We may rearrange syntax patterns in numerous ways and to various levels of complexity. A chimpanzee's gesturing/chattering provide easily observable responses. We control the sentence patterns in the first part of such a study; the chimpanzee must control them in the second part.

The second task was accomplished! "Mary give raisin Sarah" and "Raisin different apple" were produced by Sarah and apparently met her needs (Premack & Premack, 1972, p. 96). Premack and Premack referred to this behavior as a "linguistic leap" and noted that other parts of speech (other than nouns and verbs) were consistently evidenced in Sarah's behaviors. Careful study of this article by the Premacks (plus anything else David Premack has written on this type of research) shows the learner using a system very similar to M. D. S. Braine's "contextual generalization" (Braine, 1963). However, the chimpanzees seemed to generalize using closed class morphemes as their focal points rather than using closed class morphemes as Braine proposed for humans. Despite this, the research using Sarah draws our interests back toward the simple "bottom-up" S-R Behaviorist position. A chimpanzee's brain lacks (at least) the capacity to make as many S-R associative interneural connections that a human brain can. With the increased capacity of the human brain, is it possible a S-R approach may yet teach us something? But the research on Sarah and her peers has yet further value for us.

Most recently, that value has been expressed in research at the Yerkes Primate Research Center at Emory University in Atlanta, Georgia. The Center is dedicated to improving the health and well-being of humans through the use of primates as research subjects. One of the most recently famous subjects is Kanzi, a rare pygmy chimpanzee. Pygmy chimpanzees supposedly are as close to humans as any other animal. The research project with Kanzi is very similar to that used with Sarah. Kanzi's language is "Yerkish," which was designed by Dr. Duane Rumbaugh in the early 1970s. The results of Kanzi's performance are quite similar to those noted above using Sarah. Rumbaugh has, however, gone a step beyond basic research. He is applying his data to assist mentally retarded humans. In the Fall of 1985, over 20 mentally retarded students in Clayton County, Georgia, were scheduled to start learning Yerkish. The approach will hopefully allow for better transmission of information to the mentally retarded and vice versa. More information on this and related programs can be obtained by writing to the Developmental Learning Center of the Georgia Regional Hospital in Atlanta.

The research by the Premacks and at the Yerkes Primate Research Center are only a few of the projects dealing with animal language. It is interesting to note that the projects noted above have asked the chimpanzees to "read" the materials presented. No attempts, of course, have been made to ask the subjects to attempt the production of anything even remotely resembling human spoken language. Whether chimpanzee acquisition of written language symbols has any direct applicability to the understanding of reading processes in humans remains an unanswered question to date. The chimpanzee studies are admittedly "bottom-up," S-R Behavioristic in form. Those who are currently leaning toward the "top-down" approach in all aspects of language may simply overlook the chimpanzee studies; this would be unfortunate.

References

Braine, M. D. S. (1963). "On Learning the Grammatical Order of Words." *Psychological Review, 70*, 323–348.

Buros, O. K. (Ed.) (1972). *The Seventh Mental Measurement Yearbook*. Highland Park, NJ: The Gryphon Press.

Carroll, D. W. (1986). *Psychology of Reading*. Monterey, California: Brooks/Cole.

Chall, J. (1967). *Learning to Read: The Great Debate*. New York: McGraw-Hill.

Chomsky, N. (1959). "Review of Skinner's *Verbal Behavior*." *Language, 35*(1), 26–58.

Dale, P. S. (1976). *Language Development*. New York: Holt.

Dunn, L. (1965). *Peabody Picture Vocabulary Test*. Minneapolis, Minnesota: American Guidance Service

Ferster, C., and Skinner, B. F. (1957). *Schedules of Reinforcement*. New York: Appleton, Century, and Crofts.

Heilman, A., Blair, T., and Rupley, W., (1986). *Principles and Practices of Teaching Reading* (6th ed.). Columbus: Merrill.

Katz, J. J. (1964) "Mentalism in Linguistics." *Language, 40*(2), 124–137.

Kirk, S. A., McCarthy, J. J., and Kirk, W. D. (1968). *Examiner's Manual: Illinois Test of Psycholinguistic Abilities* (Rev. ed.). Urbana, Illinois: University of Illinois Press.

MacCorquodale, K. (1970). "On Chomsky's Review of Skinner's *Verbal Behavior*." *Journal of the Experimental Analysis of Behavior, 13*, 83–100.

McCarthy, J., and Kirk, S. (1961). *Examiner's Manual: Illinois Test of Psycholinguistic Abilities* (experimental edition). Champaign, IL: University of Illinois Press.

Miller, G. A. (1956). "The Magical Number Seven Plus or Minus Two: Some Limits on Our Capacity for Processing Information." *Psychological Review, 63*, 81–97.

Neisser, U. (1967). *Cognitive Psychology*. New York: Appleton, Century, and Crofts.

Noble, C. (1952). "The Analysis of Meaning." *Psychological Review, 59*, 421-430.

Osgood, C. E. (1963). "On Understanding and Creating Sentences." *American Psychologist, 18*, 735–751.

Pitman, J., and St. John, J. (1969). *Alphabets and Reading*. New York: Pitman.

Premack, A., and Premack, D. (October, 1972). "Teaching Language to an Ape." *Scientific American*, 92–99.

Skinner, B. F. (1938). *Behavior of Organisms*. New York: Appleton, Century, and Crofts.

Skinner, B. F. (1957). *Verbal Behavior*. New York: Appleton, Century, and Crofts.

Staats, A. (1964). *Human Learning.* New York: Holt.

Staats, A,. and Staats, C. (1959). "Meaning and m: Correlated but Separate." *Psychological Review,* 66(2), 136—144.

Staats, A., and Staats, C. (1962). "A Comparison of the Development of Speech and Reading Behavior with Implications for Research." *Child Development, 33,* 831-846.

Wolf, T. (1980). "Reading Reconsidered." In Wolf, M., McQuillan, M., and Radwin, E., (Eds.), *Thought and Language/Language and Reading. Harvard Educational Review, 14,* 109-127.

Author Index

SUBJECT INDEX

230